REVIEW COPY

The HUMANA Press Inc.

Crescent Manor • P.O. Box 2148 • Clifton, New Jersey 07015

Title: *Babelandia*

Author/Editor: *Demetrio Aguilera-Malta*

Publication Date: *March 29, 1985* No. of Pages: *384*

Price: *$17.50 US/19.50 export* No. of Illustrations: *26*

Special Notes: *Brilliant novel; extraordinary translation; many strong illustrations!*

Please send two copies of your published review to the Promotion Manager, Humana Press, at the address given above.

Babelandia

Contemporary Literature

Babelandia, DEMETRIO AGUILERA-MALTA, 1985
Don Goyo, DEMETRIO AGUILERA-MALTA, 1980

Babelandia

by

Demetrio Aguilera-Malta

Translated by
PETER EARLE

Illustrated by
GEORGE BARTKO

Humana Press • Clifton, New Jersey

Library of Congress Cataloging in Publication Data

Aguilera Malta, Demetrio, 1909-
Babelandia.

I. Title.
PG8219.A36B3 1984 863 84-9035
ISBN 0-89603-065-2

Crescent Manor
PO Box 2148
Clifton, NJ 07015

Printed in the United States of America

One

OUT of the whirlwind over the snowcapped volcano flew Captain Gleam, scanning the horizons of Babelandia. For several centuries he'd crossed swords with the Forces of Evil—or with whatever he thought represented them. Always on the border of "their" territory. First, against the native usurpers and imperialists of the Pre-Hispanic Era. Then, during the Conquest, pitting his primitive weapons against the iron-clad invader who had harnessed thunder and lightning, later trying to arouse the vanquished to work and vitality. And after that, in the glorious Age of Independence. Independence? Weren't the Masters of Our Era eclipsing that age? And right here, weren't the Verbophiles and the Pithecanthropi trampling on it? Did this mean he was condemned to fight the rest of his life? Would he expire one day with a sigh of relief? Or would he go on dying and returning to life, battle after battle? Or would true death await his ultimate victory? He disliked warfare. But it seemed simply the one way to stop violence. Fool! Only violence comes from violence. In the end the Law of Retribution propagates endlessly. Not just an eye-for-an-eye and a tooth-for-a-tooth, but armies-for-armies and nations-for-nations. The result: great pyramids of cadavers. Fighting and longing for a better world would always be futile. Every man's journey was an endless itinerary of battlefields. Whatever he might try, the final outcome would be the same.

But the powerful Babelandians had to be stopped. Peacefully if possible. By force if necessary. As if reasoning to himself, he said out loud:

—The trouble is, our resources are too limited.

Eneas Pioneer—who as usual was by his side—assented with an air of complicity.

—Now more than ever.

Seemed abstracted. Continued:

—And surely tomorrow less than today.

—In Babelandia all efforts are useless.

—Are you sure?

—Yes. It's not just a problem of communication. Here only money talks. No sooner does it appear than all the bigshots dance to its tune. Sacrificing their most venerable ideals and sentiments. Committing genocide without fear, without nausea, and without sadness. Yesterday's enemies are today's friends, or vice versa, as long as one can obtain the favors of Moloch. Nothing works against people like that. Any army we could recruit—if we were able—would be inadequate. We'll have to mobilize the living who're already on our side. Our enemies we'll have to persuade. And if there aren't enough still living, we'll start catechizing the dead. Of the latter, we know plenty who're just like us. They too love equity and justice. And they're ready to carry on the struggle for Mankind.

The Skeleton-disguised-as-a-man flew in through the window. On his winged ass. From his thorax he drew out a cassette of his customary speeches. He smiled throatily to himself. Dolts! Did they think he actually made the speeches himself? Bah! In the end, who really cared what the people believed? Pullulating bacteria. A microworld orbiting like a wheel around him. He could destroy them whenever he wanted. Satisfied with himself, he clapped his hands three times. His hands? Were they not his bones. Bacchus the Groveler entered. He lay down on his stomach. Extended his tongue. Carefully licked the upper bones of his master's feet.

—Stand up!

He stood. Reeling in his slick-strip anteater's tongue.

The Bony One's mandibles chattered again.

—Any news?

Mooing, dismal:

—Yes, Your Excellency.

—Tell me.

—It's horrible.

He pointed an authoritarian finger at him.

—Ipso facto!

His voice crumbled to a whisper:

—They've kidnapped a General.

The Skeleton—Holofernes Verbophile, Dictator of Babelandia—shrugged his shoulder blades. His bridgework did a tap dance.

—Bacchus, sometimes you make me laugh.

—Me, Your Excellency?

—You have the brain of a worm.

He turned. Took four steps. Stretched out his hands. Opened the curtains along the back wall of his office. Revealing an enormous closet. Inside they saw several colonels. One emerged from the shadows. He'd been suspended like the others from a plastic hanger. The Bony One contemplated him for a moment. He was fascinated by the uniform, the golden filigree of the embroidery, the multicolored medals, the bovine eyes. The Colonel saluted him, snapping to attention. The Dictator unhooked him. The Unhooked One commenced the hesitant march of a sick goose with murderous intentions. A gesture of the Chalky One stopped him. Radiantly—uniform, my uniform!—he came to attention again. His voice emerged acid and ghostly, as if from beyond the grave.

—At your orders, Dic!

The Skeleton—a Tutankhamonic mummy resurrected—smiled his special way, a phantasmal feast of fangs. Produced a fistful of money. The Colonel's mouth gaped. The bills floated toward it. The Officer straightened up. He gripped his sword. Now the weapon, like a hobby horse, was between his legs. Twice he slapped himself on the buttocks. And, charging forth on his impromptu steed of immaculate metal—yesterday it all came from Toledo! Today everything's US Steel!—he vanished through the window.

Holofernes, sphinx-faced, condescended to look at Bacchus.

—TV!

The Servile One complied, gelatin-like. He approached the set. Nervously adjusted the controls. Hoped. Not for long. The screen soon lit up. Congress appeared in solemn session. In the official seats were human chameleons. Polyphonic utterances gave way to peristaltic snoring. Then the Colonel-of-the-bills arrived. The human reptiles became animated. A rosy hue suffused their wrinkled skins. Their crests shook. Their claws—in a coordinated movement—reached for the visitor's mouth. The splendid dispenser was overflowing with green notes of several denominations. The Honorable Assembly—like a stampede of dinosaurs—converged on the Colonel. It looked as though the poor man would succumb to the live, spiraling avalanche. But someone detained the eerie deputies:

—Order, gentlemen, order!

It was their President. The most lizard-like of all the chameleons. They gaped at him. In his demeanor they sensed anger and admonishment.

He shouted clearly:

—There's enough for everyone!

His colleagues simmered down. Yawning and dragging their tails behind them, they returned to their places. Laid their accordion necks on their desks. Their eyelids began to close. And soon the snoring flowered again. The President ordered the Colonel to step forward. He extracted the money. As if goaded by an electric shock, the Honorable Ones half-raised their eyelids. The Caudillo was already undressing the Officer. First the decorations of rank disappeared. Then all his clothes. The Colonel was in his birthday suit. Then, in an instant, he was in a uniform of higher rank. The brand-new General did a right-face. He snapped to attention. Just as when he was a Colonel, he drew his sword. Again he mounted it. And he galloped away. The human reptiles returned to their peaceful ruminations.

Holofernes Verbophile turned triumphantly.

—See that? Another General!

—Yes, your Excellency.

—So who cares if one more is kidnapped?

Bacchus the Groveler dared to look back at him. He awaited the initial reaction of the Dictator, who had no idea who'd been kidnapped. How would he react when he found out? Would he nibble his fingernails? Would he run kicking through the palace? Stupid dung-eater! Why would he have to take it out on him? Just because Bacchus was conveniently nearby? Suppose he—Bacchus the Groveler—had been misinformed? Suppose he decided to say nothing? It would be still worse! When the Bony One discovered his cover-up, what would he do? So? It was time to talk. There was no other way out.

—With Congress' help we'll get as many as we need. But . . . this time the kidnap victim . . .

He let his silence hang for a moment. The Chalky One leaned toward him swiftly. Drew near with his big eyes. Big eyes? Or rather his lack of eyes? He held out his hands. Ivory petals of phalanges, phalangines, phalangettes. Shoot him. His voice became thunder.

—Who, goddamit?

Groveler flung his words like fire-ants:

—General Jonas Pithecanthropus.

Stuttering, confused:

—Jo-nas Pithe-can-thro-pus . . . ? How do you know?

—Some crazy parrots gave the news.

He released him. Curled around his own vertebrae. Simmered down. Uncurled.

—How, when, where, and by whom was he kidnapped?

—Nobody knows.

He gulped a quick cocktail of bile and scorn.

—Idiots!

Now he came apart. Grew limp, dilapidated. His jawbone dropped. He picked it up with his right hand. Let it go. It dropped again. Once more he raised it. It tired him. He loosened his grip. It fell. He lost composure. He groped for speech. Roared:

—Hold it up for me!

The Genuflector stepped forth. Raised his arms. With them raised, he took the angular mandible into his hands. Meanwhile, the Skeleton machine-gunned conjectures and schemes.

From the roof came a feminine lament.

—Ay! Sinbad! Ay!

The Dictator shook himself. He took his jaw in his own hands. Ran out. A huge skylight covered the patio. Above, hills crossing in x's and z's; below, green-helmeted, green-monkey, green-faced guards, trigger-fingers poised. Above, stars blinking in an obsidian sky; below, fountains rolling out streamers of water.

—Harpie! Harpie!

No answer. He shouted louder.

—Harpitune! At it again?

—Ah yes, Holofernes!

—Stop complaining.

—I can't, husband.

The ghostly visage was in the skylight. The dictator tried to read her expression.

—You're wearing out my Government.

—I know, Holie. But it's Sinbad, our child. Where could he have gone? How he must be suffering! When will we see him again? Who knows? Who knows? Who knows?

She disappeared. Her sorrow echoed more softly among the arcades:

—Ay! Sinbad! Aaaayyy.

Her accompaniment, the hoarse noises of scraggly skin slithering along. The Dictator sighed:

—How much longer with that stuffed boa?

In spite of his self-control, Bacchus the Groveler remarked:

—Well, in the absence of a live boa . . .

—What?

—No, nothing.

Over the mountains yawned the moon. The city glowed like amethysts. Church towers muffled their clocks. Suddenly, the opening strains of *Cavalleria Rusticana.* The Bony One seemed to float in the air. He extended his arms imploringly. He also noticed his jaw was no longer falling off.

—Don't anybody touch it now!

His enemies enjoyed exasperating him. Bacchus knew it. No use trying to stop it. He waited for the worst.

—I won't listen. It's driving me mad. No! Stop playing it!

The music soared. Flooding the air with its bursts of notes. "Tell them to stop!" Only then did he remember his rank of General Generalissimo. He took off his cap. "I'm afraid." He took off his uniform. "An injection of trumpets!" He tore off his belt and sword. "I'm drumbeats and cymbal clashes!" He was in his underwear. "No!" Tell them to stop playing!" He was quivering to the beat of the music. "Please! No, no, no!" He grabbed an ocarina. "No! No!" He raised it to his lips. "No, no, no!" Ancestral sounds emerged from the clay. Then, the voluptuous cadences of Mascagni. Unexpectedly, his fingers relaxed. His senses beat a retreat. His chalky arms became a windmill. He moved to the center of the room. With great leaps, he began dancing. Luminous bones, white acrobatics. But an explosion of glass broke the contagious melody. A rock wrapped in paper. The Groveler seized it. He showed it to Chalky. Weakly insinuated:

—There's news.

The weird dancer went on. He paid no heed. Could he have heard? If he had, could he ignore *Cavalleria Rusticana*?

—News of the kidnapping!

The same indifference. Bacchus then tried following his commander's steps. His leaps accompanying the incessant music as well as they could. He shouted:

—The kidnapping of Pithecanthropus!

This time the Dictator saw him, but did not stop. A tall waltzing giraffe beside a micrometric rat. He let the ocarina fall. Still dancing in accompaniment, the Groveler watched him. Mechanically, from sheer inertia, he too surrendered to the galloping rhythm.

On the roof Harpitune still dragged the Stuffed One. From time to time she stopped. The Boa showed signs of life. A green light shimmered in her pupils. Madame Dictator observed her peristaltic movement.

—Melopea, why aren't you the way you used to be?

—What do you mean?

—You know. I adore your encircling narcotic loops. The jungle-nest of your scales . . .

—You know I can't now. Besides, what good would it do?

—At least I'd forget about my son for a while. It would be a brief consolation.

—There are so many serpents in the world . . .

—Don't you see? I need you.

The green glow dimmed in the serpent's eyes. She uncurled the ten yards of herself. Like ocean riplets expiring on the beach. Madame Dictator dragged her scaly skin—now only skin—stuffed with cotton. Ceaselessly. Tirelessly. Intermittently, her bitter cry pierced the darkness:

—Ay, Sinbad! Aaaayyy!

Two

HOURS before, Jonas Pithecanthropus had arrived at the Embassy of Great Entanglements. In a gold sedan chair. Borne by Members of the Cabinet. At the door, the host Ambassador and his wife—he, wiry beard and old-style moustache; she, a mother-of-pearl meringue of foamy breasts—applauded. The High Commander half inclined his minihead. The illustrious bearers knelt without releasing their burden. Only the Secretary of State let go. He went on all fours. Offered his back as a step. Pithecanthropus descended. His beady eyes took in the multicolored sea of uniforms, dinner jackets, and decorations of the men; and the provocative dresses—silken springboards of sex—of the women. Then he stood still, reddened, stonelike, tattooing a glare in a certain direction. On his lips, a sneer blending into a smile. He bared his eye teeth.

—Are you all right, General?

—What would you like?

—Your wish is our command.

He remained a statue. Staring across the room. The cause of his hypnosis was quickly evident. Everyone understood. Of course the General was excited. A suit of armor was in view. Time had eaten away its sheen. Its helmet had been damaged by several soldering irons. Its breast plate was split. In spite of this, both the glare of great lamps reflected from the mirror-like finish of the furniture and the lustrous baldness of many guests lent it a deathly glow. And the armor's lance conjured the Middle Ages. Pithecanthropus came to life. He gave four leaps. Not from two of his extremeties, but all four. Four in each leap. Feverishly, he commandeered the ancient object. He embraced it. He smothered it with kisses. He caressed it with trembling hands. The ambassador stepped forth solicitously.

—Can I help, General?

He nodded acceptance. Showing all his ancestral teeth for the first time. He changed costumes. That is, the archaic armor replaced his uniform. He grasped a lance. Two more leaps—his only way of moving now—and he was in the center of the room. He studied the panorama. The red and gold decor; the convoluted furniture; the tight clothing; the stylish gestures and manners of the guests; it was all from the late 15th century. Or was it earlier, or later? He could feel seven phantoms prancing on his belly, clawing at him. He smiled to himself. Fireworks began to sizzle in his eyes. Then glimmered playfully in his pupils. Suppose he killed everybody there? What if he ran them through, one by one, until the immaculate gray stone floor was carpeted with their cadavers? Or if he just forced the gentlemen to kneel in impotent anguish while he made biological love to the ladies? The second idea pleased him more. For an instant, he fancied himself defiling them. Tearing open their delicate garments. Shredding their lingerie. Forcing them to display the honeyed flower between their legs. Mounting them. And his power, his renewed power crushing all resistance. For a moment he suspended the violent imagery. Suppose one of them welcomed his assault? Poor dreamer! All would receive you with rage, with resentment, with revulsion. Love will never be a dish on your menu. Rape is your only recourse. Domination only through acts of terror. Women for you will always be the last spoils of war. Like enemies on a battlefield: lying at your feet with the light gone from their eyes. His musings ceased. After all, what did it matter? In the end wasn't it the same? Getting up courage, he shouted:

—Wiley Warhorse!

The Secretary of Defense rushed in. Snapped to:

—At your orders, General.

—On all fours!

—He tried to rebel. The eloquence of protest was in him. But it died on his lips. All considered, I should refuse. I'm tired of him riding me. Why not free myself? I am who I am. Babelandia is in my hands. Or is it? Has it ever been? As long as Jonas Pithecanthropus is alive, it won't be. I ought to kill him. It's my only way out. I'll try it while we're still living in this 400-year-old world. I'll find a mace covered with spikes and barbs. I'll whirl it around and increase its momentum a hundredfold, and smash his head. I'll watch him explode. He'll be pulverized. Am I up to it? Do I have the courage? Maybe I'd better use my army. To blow him into 1000 pieces. With my soldiers, tanks, machine guns, and cannons. Or will it be catapults, slings, and crossbows? In this century, or some other? What's the difference? I'll make him drink his own blood. Consume his own flesh. Gnaw his own bones. Can I persuade my men to stand up to him? And the Dictator, what will he think? He's sure to be against it. He'll finish me off with rest. Pithecanthropus is his government's backbone. His skeleton's prop. Everybody depends on him. Even I, wretch that I am. But if this isn't my day, some other day will be. And will give me a feast. With him. On him. All over him. I'll devour him in imperceptible slivers. Just to prolong my pleasure. The command resounded again:

—On all fours!

Warhorse slumped. What a disgrace! Helpless. His jawbone was already elongating. Hard as he tried, it was useless. His feet and hands were being transformed into horseshoes. Slavery—miserable horse slavery—tightened its chains around him. An undulating tail began to grow. Futile! Everything was futile! I can feel myself bending. An invincible force crushes me like tissue paper. My ears grow straight and pointed. In my humiliation, short hair sprouts from my skin. I'm turning a dull reddish brown. I'm on all fours. My back, saddled. Belly straps, tightened. The crazy swing of his stirrups degrades me. The trappings—especially the reins and the bit—hold me at the ape's mercy. I feel his weight. The savage horseman has mounted—spurs me on. I hear the fearsome howl from his angry snout:

—Uaaa! Uuaaa! Uuuuuuaaaaa!

Two

Pithecanthropus spurred him twice. The human horse galloped. Then—leveling his lance—the jungle knight charged the astonished assembly. Terror was engraved on their eyes. A sudden paralysis commenced to immobilize them. Before the impression sank in, they tried to back against the wall. Then seeing it was useless, they unsheathed their swords, daggers, and other arms. The aggressor ignored them. He went for the first one, intending to liquidate him. But an unexpected shout stopped him.

—Looking for a fight, General?

The tone of voice froze him for a second. He turned to see where it came from. Right away he found out. Just below the ceiling, seated on a chandelier with his arms crossed, was Captain Gleam. Possibly from the force of his leap, the antique was still swinging. An ironic smile was on his lips. His gray eyes were piercing. At the sight of him, green froth dropped from the jowels of the anthropoid. His eyes reddened. His rage vibrated like an electric current.

—You!

The onlookers got hold of themselves. Their fear took wing. Their eyes widened in order to absorb every detail. The Captain persisted:

—A fight, General?

Instantly the interrogated one's hide flushed brown. A gutteral voice of murderous overtones sprung up from who knows where.

—A duel! A duel to the death! First with you. Then with the rest.

The silence seemed to stiffen the listeners. Against their will and against the atmosphere. They were glued in place. One and all. Nothing but eyes and ears.

—I'm not enough for you?

—Bastard!

And he crouched. He stretched. On a sudden impulse, he hurled his lance. A collective Ah! was heard, especially among the ladies. They watched the weapon's lightning-swift trajectory. On target? They breathed again. Also like lightning, Gleam had parried the mortal thrust. Raising his right hand, he caught the long spear in full flight. For a brief moment, he displayed it—still smiling—while scrutinizing his opponent. The latter was stupified. His right arm still up. His jowels gaping. Outsmarted. Gleam broke the silence.

—Now what?

Jonas restrained himself. Lowered his arm. Tried to calm down.

—You name it!

The Captain looked at him. Then looked at the others. Looked at the weapon in his hand. Looked at Warhorse, who was trembling. Looked at the others. Looked at himself. Looked at the others. Looked at the frustrated assassin—but frustrated only for the moment—consumed by rage. Looked at the others. Up came his steady right hand. His ironic smile vanished. His breathing was heavy. "I'll kill you!" The echo of his words reverberated within—I'll kill you, I'll kill you . . . "—and restored him to reality. This killing, what good would it do him or the others. Why kill, after all? Bah! It really wasn't worth it. Besides, he had better plans. Better plans? Suddenly he felt as if he had escaped from a page of Dumas. Isn't this absurd? Am I just an imitation musketeer? Should I again play my solemn role of Defender of Mankind? His ironic smile returned. He feigned retaliation with the lance. Jonas did not budge. Not a single muscle twitched. A statue again. A mere semblance of a man. Gleam returned the weapon to him. With the handle extended toward his enemy. Gave it up gently. The other brandished it violently. The Captain leapt down from the lamp. Drew his sword. Amid the echoing murmur of the castle, he faced the anthropoid.

Oh, the interminable *Cavalleria Rusticana.* The Dictator was exhausted. His epileptic–acrobatic ballet had almost undone his bones. They were out of kilter. A tibia was drumming on his cranium. A fibula took refuge in his left armpit. Over and over, and while still dancing, he had to retrieve with one hand the finger bones of the other, which had scattered like loose rosary beads in the air. His movements grew lethargic. Almost death throes. Groveler was trying, for his part, to follow the steps. Vain persistence. He grew increasingly dizzy with vertigo. He could hardly move. His breathing became more labored. His legs dragged more and more. Tongues of fire licked his toes. He seemed to be riding a lunatic carousel. On it, the seats were contemporary, but the animals were antediluvian: triceratops, plesiosaurs, pterodactyls . . . And worse yet: they were all bare skeletons. It was as if the merry-go-round had been turning and turning in a prehistoric necropolis. In the realm of a dream that had solidified. He could bear no more. He fell. The futility of his efforts returned him to passive expectancy.

Soon the last of the music was gone in the wind. Holofernes, in turn, collapsed. He became an arbitrary geometrical figure. His Jack-of-all-trades stepped forth solicitously. Finding his master in such a forlorn state, he began rearranging as well as he could—which wasn't much—the rebellious ivories.

—Your Excellency: can I fix up your skeleton?

He looked at him as if through binoculars of bone.

—Leave it alone!

Bacchus was itching to tell him about the kidnapping. If he didn't he'd pay—who knows how much—for his failure of courage at this moment. The Bony One would never in this life forgive him for disobeying an order—the Dictator's own order—in an attempt to inform him. So it was. But he had to. Would he dare? He dared.

—Please, your Excellency. Do you want to know about the General?

He nodded. Snatched the paper from him. Raised it to his eyes. Rubbing it against them. But he saw nothing. He'd forgotten that he was only permitted to use his sense of vision in the sunlight. At hours such as this—impotent from day blindness—he was enveloped by darkness. He ordered:

—Light my candles!

Groveler complied. With a match he lit the wicks that were set deep in each of Holofernes' sockets. Minute flames emerged. By their light he could finally read:

—Soon you'll know the ransom we demand for General Jonas Pithecanthropus.

*The Amautas**

—Amautas?

—Yes. They're guerillas.

—Why wasn't I told before?

—What good would it have done, your Excellency?

Unexpectedly changing, the Skeleton's tone grew plaintive.

**Translator's Note*: The Amautas were ancient Incan sages who possessed great moral authority in their villages.

—And now what can we do, Bacchy?

—Yes. What can we do?

Deftly, he pulled part of his osseous self together. He fell on his knees. Grasped a corner of the desk with his arms. Distributed his skeleton on top of it. The candles flickering in his eyepits lent a macabre glow to the surroundings. Shadows and lights trembled from the force of his screamings.

—We must find Pithy! Right now! Afterwards, will be too late. Tomorrow's celebration—his birthday—marks an epoch! Anyone can miss it, except him!

T
w
o

Three

JONAS dismounted from Warhorse. Already he had become an encumbrance. Everything was an encumbrance. Warhorse quickly regained his human features. Like the others, he backed against the wall, ready to enjoy the spectacle. And what a spectacle. The combatants studied each other intensely. Both smiling: Gleam again with his ironic smile. Pithecanthropus with a crocodile-jaws-of-fire smile. Lance and sword sought each other out. Muscles were taut, living strings of a crossbow. Suddenly Gleam feinted with one arm. Jonas leapt clumsily. The Ironic One's smile grew. It was too much. His opponent at the breaking point. Exasperated. Out of control. He squatted. All arms and legs, he charged his enemy, trying to run him through. The defender simply ducked. So great was the General's momentum—that without making contact—he continued his blind dash. Far beyond his adversary. He turned quickly on the weird lancer. Propelled by a good kick in the rectum, Pithecanthropus was flung toward the wall. Into which he involuntarily embedded his lance. For an instant he was bewildered. Did not know which way to move or what to do. Gleam closed in. He proceeded to swat the armored skeleton with the flat of his sword. The Humiliated One faced him. Red-eyed, foaming with saliva. The other again feinted at him. He parried the thrusts with his gauntlet. He noticed clearly that the Captain was striking only with the flat of his sword. Obviously playing. Weaving a pattern of steel strokes with his right hand, he pried the lance loose with his left. When it was free he bowed. Handed it to the anthropoid. Just as before, Jonas snatched it away angrily. Then he was motionless. Sepia. Stone-still. Slowly turning in a half-circle, he observed all the guests. On their faces there began to appear a strange calm, with traces of scorn. He stopped. Riveted his eyes on the agile enemy. He had not seen him since Military College days. He was tall. More or less. He was thin. More or less. Breathed intelligent vitality. How old could he be? Thirty? Forty? Fifty? Who could know? Sometimes he seemed centuries old. Or millennia? And he? He—General Jonas Pithecanthropus, Commander-in-Chief of the Armed Forces of Babelandia—of what era was he? Before or after the cavemen? Like a broken machine his brain began grinding out the onomatopoeic words: "Who who was he was he was he who who who who who . . . '' Again the disdainful voice shook him: ''Wake up!''

—Wake up!

He lifted the lance as if it were a club. Brought it down on the other man's back. On his back? On the floor. Captain Gleam seemed to have turned into mercury. Slippery. Out of reach. The general, out of control, blinded, raving, flailed at him repeatedly. His movements were so rapid they seemed like a whirlwind of muscles and steel. But the human Mercury—like a reverse magnet—continued repeatedly to repel him, dodging his multiple blows. Finally the Ape—realizing the uselessness of his effort—gave up. Desolately, he fell to the floor. Bit the lance. Reduced it to splinters. First the handle. Then the spear. Finally banged his helmet on the greystone floor. Was he trying to destroy his head? Or preparing a cocktail of his brains? People could no longer contain themselves. They exploded in laughter. At first Jonas didn't hear them. Or he paid no attention. A small awakening. Could they be laughing at him? Would he stand for it? Never! Not even Captain Gleam would be permitted that. He simply continued watching. At the slightest sign of carelessness he'd jump him. His past and present humiliation would be avenged. Unarmed, he'd depend on teeth and fingernails. At that very moment, they began to grow as in better times, when they were still adequate for attack and defense. No sooner had he thought this than he gave a jungle leap. No one could stop him. Before they knew it, he was swinging on the chandelier, as had his adversary before him. From there he looked below. Chose his prey. The very daughter of the Ambasssador of Great Entanglements! Again there was no time. He dropped on the girl. Grabbed her from behind. Opened his mouth. Disclosed between his mandibles a double row of yellow teeth. Sank them into the nape of the girl's neck. Horrified, she scarcely uttered a cry. And lost consciousness like a cut flower. When it looked as though he was going to slay her, the Simian stopped. He turned to his enemy. His grin was a poster of death.

—The sword!

A hypnotic moment. No one moved. Not even the one spoken to. Then the points of his fangs half-penetrated the alabaster neck. The Captain dropped the sword at his feet. Without releasing the girl, he picked it up. He raised it to his jowels. Then he chewed it to pieces, spitting the bits of steel at everyone around him. Expectation grew. What would be next? Would he devour his prey? Would he only break her neck? Would he tear off her clothes right there? Rape her in front of everybody? Or would he drag her to the next room and do it? His trapped-beast behavior—a starved beast, an animal in heat—made anything seem possible.

After that would he attack the rest? Was it just a matter of time? Again Gleam had doubts. Was he reenacting an episode of *The Three Musketeers*?

—The most urgent thing—declared Holofernes—is to notify the entire country. The kidnapping affects us all.

—Especially the Government, and most of all, you.

He stared him down. Assumed a bombastic, declamatory tone.

—All of us. Our sword is the guarantee of order and progress. The salvation of the Republic!

The Bootlicker would like to have replied: "It isn't *re,* but *res.* And not *public,* but *private.* Belonging to the few families who have been devouring it for so long." . . . How and why would he reply? Especially at that moment. The Skeleton would bombard him with his bones. He bowed.

—Yes, your Excellency.

The Dictator put on his military uniform again.

—Call the Secretary of Defense.

Groveler obeyed, moving to the private line. Holofernes, meanwhile, went to his library of cassettes. He shuffled them, nervously, as if searching for a particular one. Finally, a rage saturated with melancholy overcame him.

—*Mea culpa.* I'm lost.

—Can I help at all?

—No one can. There's no tape for kidnappings!

He rummaged through the writing desk. Rested his lower maxilla on his right radius and ulna. Reacted. Got hold of himself. Rose up.

—Did you call Wiley Warhorse?

Bacchus nodded. At that moment, the telephone call from the eminent Secretary of Defense came through.

—Have you heard the news?

—What news?

—I see you haven't. It's something horrible, frightful. It'll convulse the nation.

Warhorse was worried.

—Did they find out that all the armaments we recently purchased were junk?

—Cold, cold.

—Was the peso devaluated because the One Hundred Admirals burned out their flagship, *Every Man for Himself*?

—Still cold.

—I know. All the jet planes crashed. It was hopeless. Your Excellency. In this day and age, they were only good for camouflage. They were World War II carcasses. That's what the rich countries sell us.

He raised his arms. His skeleton swayed between its metacarpals.

—No, no, no! Worse than that.

—I'm on pins and needles.

—Well, they've kidnapped . . . General Pithecanthropus.

—I don't believe it.

He handed him the message.

—Read for yourself.

Warhorse obeyed.

—It's a joke.

—I doubt it.

The Secretary of Defense thought for a moment.

—Just a while ago we were together at the Embassay of Great Entanglements. Nothing seemed to indicate . . .

He was interrupted by the arrival of the Commander of the Palace Guard.

—With your Excellency's permission.

Holofernes answered his greeting.

—Speak.

—General Jonas Pithecanthropus, Commander-in-Chief of the Armed Forces of Babelandia, has disappeared!

Three

Captain Gleam—whether in a serial novel or in real life—couldn't decide what to do. Was convinced that the first move he made would cause the Anthropoid to tear his unconscious victim to pieces. Nevertheless, he couldn't stand by passively. He'd never live it down. Notwithstanding, he could find no solution to his predicament. He thought feverishly. A few possibilities came to mind. He rejected them immediately. They were unsatisfactory and, worse, might produce terrible consequences. Agitated as he was, the monster might do anything. It would be like playing with dynamite near a fire. Even so, we can't let him have a free hand. Not just because of the victim between his jaws. After satisfying himself with her, he'll want to continue his rampage. He'll be more ravenous than ever. He must be stopped. There's no alternative. I have to destroy this weed of evil at its roots. But how? Involuntarily he shouted:

—General!

He didn't seem to hear. He was indifferent, made no movement, spoke not a word. Suddenly he came to a decision. Commenced to walk slowly toward the door of the huge ballroom. All were struck by a vision. The armor-clad beast—a giant metallic beetle—slowly advancing, dragging along his distinguished hosts' daughter. Gleam stepped forward, trying to get his attention.

—Listen to me!

Jonas stopped, finally. Without looking at him, he half-turned. Tightened his grip on his prey. The Captain went on:

—If you free the girl, leave everybody alone, and let the party continue . . . , I'll do anything you say!

Now he turned completely. He fixed his little eyes on them with scorn. A remote, wild, ancestral scorn.

—Even if you don't want to, now you'll have to obey me. Everyone will obey me!

He turned to the rest. Ordered:

—On your knees!

For a moment they hesitated. They looked at each other, not knowing what to do. He persisted:

—On your knees . . . or I'll cut her throat!

That said, he again sank his fangs in the girl's neck. The Ambassador's wife sobbed.

—For God's sake . . . please do what he says!

They complied. He who had given the orders turned triumphantly to Captain Gleam. He too was on his knees.

—Understand?

Disarmed, helpless, he murmured in spite of himself:

—I understand.

The Victor felt like a giant. As if he were walking on stilts and touching the roof of the castle with his head. Actually, I'm almost a pigmy. Especially compared to my father. My father! How tall was he? Two hundred centimeters? Three hundred? Five hundred? Maybe more. *Uuuua! Uuuua!* We were different. Will we always be so? I have short bowlegs, squat-like, perfect for spurring Warhorse's belly. My father's were just as short but curved like a drawn bow an instant before release. My father! *Uuuua! Uuuua! Uuuuua!* He remembered him outlined against the brownish-green jungle like a great jet-black acorn. I'm hairy, like all men. But I only show the primitive hair on my chest when I'm in a rage. An all-gray, dry, thick fur. My father, on the other hand, had gray hair only on his back. The rest was black, like a well-aged shadow. Gleaming, bluish black. Even his dirty fangs were black. When he walked he seemed to be swinging in a green hammock. He looms like a monarch in my memory. Even his dark crest was like the tassels of a crown. *Uuua! Uuuua! Uuuuua!* A retinue of females followed him. Many happy fat females with quivering breasts and long nipples. My first recollection of myself is a nest on a high branch. Me in that nest, hanging onto one of those nipples. Me—a dangling hairless spider—swinging from my mother to and fro. Then traveling on her back, from tree-top to tree-top, and on the swim across rivers. Always under her care and protection. But to continue—back to my tale—the long itinerary of my adventures. More and more remote from my father. His black fur even more diffuse in the misty distances. *Uuuua! Uuuuua! Uuua! Uua! Ua* . . . One fine day, food acquired on my own: a tender bamboo shoot. Peeling it, as if it were a plucked flower. Sucking the sweet nectar. Later on, standing up to beasts and men. Hiding from them. Trying to attack them at the opportune moment. Capturing one of them. Giving him no chance to complain or defend himself. Climbing to the highest branches. Choking him until his eyes bulge and his tongue hangs out. Then throwing him to his followers. Because we don't kill for hunger. Meat disgusts us. We kill only for the pleasure of killing . . . Eventually the final apprenticeship in jumping. The jumps, each time greater, with a few friends. From one branch to another. From one tree to another. From one mountain to another. Suddenly, he discovered a banana. The miracle of the banana. The banana miracle. The fever of the banana. Banana fever. Feverish bananas. And longer jumps ever closer to men. From one camp to another. From one city to another. From one shore of the ocean to another . . . Then one fine day, waking up in Babelandia. And another fine day having the Babelandians in the palm of one's hand. And now if he were to jump back? And if he took with him at least these people he had before him? If he exiled them to the jungle where his father remained king? That would be a master stroke. Who could prevent it? He moved toward them. A strange odor—noticeable only to him—held him back. His nostrils flared, trying to breathe more deeply. He released the girl, who fell to the floor, unconscious. He forgot everybody. Looking at no one and nowhere, he advanced toward the inner rooms. The astonished gathering watched him. What diabolic idea was germinating in his mind now? Right away they found out. Running in short steps, the Unpredictable One returned. Like another person. To be sure, he wasn't the same as earlier. He was peeling a banana. He began to devour it. He was no longer in armor. And the people all looked different. Their clothes were of this century. Of this century were the furniture, the interior decoration, and the magnificent ballroom. The Ambassador's daughter was standing, with a smile. The servants were passing out sandwiches and drinks. Gleam pondered—with increasing anxiety—on the power of that fruit. The banana. A banana. A single banana.

A desperate cry stopped all conversation. It came from above, a howling, discordant siren.

—Ay, Sinbad! Aaaayyy!

And then, changing her tone a bit:

—Holo! Holofernes! Holo! Holo!

The Dictator girded his bones. He rushed into the hallway that led to the skylight. For there, overhead, sphinxified, pallid, ectoplasmic, appeared his spouse. The sight of her filled his thorax with tenderness.

Another *coup d'état*? Or some disaster, fire or earthquake?

—No, Harpie.

—Then what? Why so many people? Why such an uproar?

—Pithy's been kidnapped.

—That's great. Now he's paying for the evil he's done us. If it weren't for him, Sinbad would still be with us.

—Please! Seal your lips, Harpie.

—If they ask for ransom, ignore them.

—Quiet, Harpie! You're jeopardizing my position!

—Let them keep him for good. We don't want to see him again.

—You're endangering the Government.

And he came away from the skylight, conjugating:

—If he's rescued . . . I lose, you lose, he loses, we lose, you lose, they lose!

Four

THE Dictator could no longer stand. His skeleton slumped—to its full length—on top of the desk. The high officials surrounded him like vultures awaiting their meager carrion. They approached in diverse ways. Some with a muzzle. Others on all fours. Several on their knees. Very few erect and calm on their two feet. The Cabinet was in full session. The cream and elite of the Army, the Air Force, and the Navy. The puffed-up bureaucracy that was preparing, as usual, the sumptuous banquet of the Budget. For his part, Bacchus the Groveler—busy little squirrel—skittered here and there, attending to this and that. Suddenly he stopped. Announced:

—The press is outside, gnashing its teeth.

Verbophile shrugged his shoulder blades.

—Let them continue gnashing.

Inside himself he wove a web of anger. Why hadn't he recorded a cassette for kidnappings in time? Abducting people, the whole world over, was fashionable. And it was good business besides. He understood. If I weren't wrapped up in the dictatorship business—transforming the country into my own hacienda and its inhabitants into chained peons—I'd be competing with the kidnappers. But what are you saying, Verbophile?—*Cassette, cassette, cassette,* that other self of mine, why have you forsaken me?—Maybe I should have picked out another place on the planet. Richer and more developed, of course, where ransoms would be higher amounts. For example, I'd kidnap the Pope, some President, or a Rockefeller, or Onassis. Never would it occur to me to kidnap a diplomat, a Secretary of State, or a high military officer. That's all right for idealists and thinkers who still believe in Thermopylae, Leonidas, and his three hundred Spartans . . . Bah! Enough empty speculation, let's get to the heart of the matter. It is terrible that I have not made a cassette for kidnappings. It is a tribulation that distresses me more than the distressing convolutions of Broca's brain. Without a cassette, how could I speak? What could I say? He searched for self-confidence, began to come to life. Reacted. Behave yourself! But who am I? Who am I, really? Temptation got the better of him. No less than the Dictator of Babelandia, the polyglot country. Where every Babelandian, using the same tongue, speaks a different language. Where communication is a perennial taboo: nobody understands anybody . . . He peered fixedly—still straining to see by the flickering candlelight in his sockets—at everyone around him. What a fine zoo! A sight to behold! What could he do? *Cassette, cassette, cassette!* Where are you hiding? He gave up on it. Then commanded:

—To start, I'll have to padlock the universities. Classes and admissions will be canceled. Faculty and students will be kept out. The living as well as the dead.

Piggy Rigoletto, the young Secretary of the Interior—a meatball with a head of meringue—obsequiously reminded him:

—All the universities are closed already.

—How absurd!

He thought for a moment. Decreed:

—In the future we'll only close them one by one. That way, we'll always have a few left for special occasions. Opportunities for publicity pyrotechnics can't be wasted!

—You're right, Excellency!

He paused. A brilliant idea was being born.

—If you like, sir, we'll open them all up. Then we can start closing them again, little by little.

Holofernes evaluated the contents of that cranial cavity. Smiled paternally.

—I advise you to stop making such noises with your mouth. Talking amounts to more than that. And, to change the subject, at least we still have political adversaries to track down, right?

—Not one remains, Generalissimo.

—Come now, Mr. Secretary! Don't tell me that I, that my government, that our party . . . have run out of enemies!

—Practically. There are a few—very few!—stored away in jail. The others—most of them—have been dying off inexplicably.

He stopped. Looked like a cow with hoof-and-mouth disease. Half closed his eyes.

—Providence is on our side.

Holofernes paid no attention to those words. He was furious.

—You mean there are no more troublesome, dissolute, provocative, agitators of the extreme right or left—no hairy, tattered, emaciated poets, artists, professors, students, intellectuals, and others of that stripe? They're all my enemies! Capturing them would help us out of this fix.

—They also are extinct, your Excellency. Some, filling our ranks. Others, disappearing.

—Then use your imagination! Invent new ones. Make them grow, from the underground if necessary. We must catch great numbers of them in our nets, combing the country inch by inch! No effort can be spared to find General Pithecanthropus! We'll begin by asking Congress for Emergency Powers.

—No need to, your Excellency. Your word is the Law!

He smiled. His jawbones cracked like nutcrackers splitting.

—I had forgotten.

He was filled with the contentment of a milk-fed calf. He smiled. Was he able to smile? With the phalanges of his thumb and index fingers, he snuffed out the candles in his eye sockets. Suddenly he sank—before everyone—into the welcoming arms of Morpheus.

Before his visit to the Embassy of Great Entanglements, Pithecanthropus had received a copy of *The University Voice*. His caricature—a uniformed gorilla—was on page one. His adjutant, full of anxiety, observed:

—Do you see, General? They're still printing it.

—Didn't you assure me the editors were imprisoned?

His reply showed the simplicity of a moron. He said ambiguously:

—That's the rub.

—Besides, it has the seal of the National University. They're publishing it there.

—Impossible. The university is deserted. Nobody goes in or out. It's surrounded by tanks and artillery. It's watched by guards day and night.

Jonas stared at him with a rage seasoned with dashes of scorn.

—Then they've turned invisible! Or have they hired a ghost service?

The Assistant scratched his head.

—Ah, I forgot . . . Nobody wants to do guard duty anymore.

—Why?

—They say there are souls in torment there.

Pithecanthropus broke out laughing. The other didn't join in.

—That's the story that I heard, my General. They hear steps at night. Shrieks. Running. And sometimes the typewriters and printing presses begin to sound. As if they were working.

—That's all we need! A terrorized army! Believing those sounds are from the hereafter! Don't you understand? Obviously, some people are still getting into the shops and offices. Impossible by day, but not by night! Maybe they dug a tunnel, and can get in or out anytime they want.

A fierce smile broke out on the countenance of the Simian.

—It's gone far enough. Let's go! Right now!

—Where?

—Where do you suppose, idiot? To the University!

He ordered a substantial military escort, armed to the teeth. The jackanapes would soon see. He would bathe them with bullets. He would convert their bodies to sieves. No! That might not be appropriate. He'd rather capture them. Put them in cages. Keep them alive. Care for them as if they were made of gold. Then, after the reception at the Embassy of Great Entanglements, go back to see them. To hold a productive conversation with them. First I'll try to persuade them verbally. He knew it was useless. He'd have to try it anyway. After the conversational phase, he'd change his methods. He'd subject them to persuasive violence until they revealed the identity of their accomplices. Then they'd have to give him the frosting on the cake: the essential details about the new editions of the *Voice* . . . its procedures and collaborators. And if that wasn't enough to loosen the knots in their tongues, he'd administer sadistic refinements. Those that were reserved for "special" cases. He was almost always inventing new tricks. He had a paranoid's imagination. And a laboratory scientist's patience. He smiled to himself optimistically. It was going to be a perfect night: University, embassy, taking prisoners, and maybe later, an offering from Venus . . . The jeep pulled up to the University Campus. The guards saluted. He responded sourly. The officer on duty came forth. Pithecanthropus got right to the point.

—Are there really souls in torment here, Captain?

—That's what they say, General.

—And you?

—This is my first shift, sir.

—I see. Well I'll find out for myself. No one is to leave or enter. No one!

He smiled like a fox slipping into a chicken coop.

—Not even the ghosts.

Stretched out there. Snoring there. Dreaming there. There, the Skelton-disguised-as-a-Man. There, the Dictator of Babelandia. There, the imponderable Holofernes Verbophile. The Vital Force of the Nation there. His every breath like the wheezings of a perforated bladder. There. There. There. Had he been sleeping for minutes or hours? did they dare to wake him? How would he react?

Would he understand the emergency? Or, on the contrary, would he rather take out his anger on them? It was unlimited sleep that he needed. But General Pithecanthropus? And the measures to be taken against the kidnappers? Or to have a clue at least? Or a plan of action to argue about? Anguished looks were exchanged. Time was precious. Should they waste it foolishly? No one spoke. No one moved. They feared awakening the ivoried sleeper. Bacchus the Groveler assessed the situation. He neared the desk stealthily. Opened the drawer containing the ocarina. Took it out. The others seemed ready to grab him. How dared he perpetrate such disrespect? It would cost him dearly. They had to stop him. To prevent him from emitting the slightest toot. To honor that noble slumber. They thought quickly. The Dictator *had* to wake up. To confront the situation. To help find solutions. If the ocarina was needed for that, blessed was the instrument! And blessed Bacchus the Groveler for using it. But on the other hand, who would pay for the broken dishes afterwards? Still they didn't interfere. They waited off-stage—temporarily. All eyes and ears. A melody sounded. Its rhythm swelled. The Skeleton curled. A white snake gathering its bony spirals. Unwinding, it struck with a leap. Landed erect. In time with the music, he took a few measured steps. The music stopped. So did he. Smiling a bare-jawed smile.

—Dreamt I was dancing.

He stopped smiling. His voice was funereal and dark-toned.

—To what do I owe the honor of this visit?

Piggy Rigoletto replied:

—To the kidnapping of General Jonas Pithecanthropus.

—Of course, of course. But I have no cassettes for kidnappings.

—What did you say, your Excellency?

He came to his full senses.

—No. Nothing. I store all information on tapes. But there's none on this subject.

—That figures, your Excellency. We've had no kidnapping for a long time. By the way, let's increase the budget for extraordinary expenses. There'll never be enough. Maybe five million to start with. You know: We'll have to investigate. To jail thousands. Mobilize the secret service. Torture every figurehead. Bribe who knows how many. Etc. Etc. Etc.

—Your move, Mr. Secretary.

Wiley Warhorse stepped forward.

—Well, whatever I need I'll take from the reserve fund. We're in a national emergency. The helicopters have to be repaired. The last time they were used, two out of three crashed. Since we got them with the loans-in-kind that they granted us, we had to accept whatever they gave us. Also we should import a few tanks. Munitions for the artillery and machine guns. Those that we have won't even shoot blanks.

Admiral Neptuno Río del Río* spoke up.

**Translator's Note:* The Admiral's last name, *Río del Río* constitutes a pun ("I laugh at the river").

—And if they're carrying him off by sea? If they already have him on a ship that's sailed?

—You're not asking me to mobilize the *Every Man for Himself*, are you?

—Dispel your fears, Excellency. Not that. but we'd do well to import a few torpedo boats.

And now Pánfilo Wincewing, Commander of the Air Force.

—Jet fighters! Let's fill the sky with them. We'll pursue the kidnappers from the air.

The Skeleton trembled.

—Use whatever is necessary. We've got to find the Amautas, even if we have to follow them to the North Pole. We'll mangle them, we'll pulverize them, we'll liquidate them, we'll make them vanish!

Placido Hotwheels, Secretary of Public Works, raised his mellifluous voice.

—To catch kidnappers, highways! Many highways. A country stitched every which-way with highways. One billion! Highways! Give me a billion and tomorrow I'll deliver the kidnappers bound hand-and-foot!

Verbophile had a roller-coaster hiccup.

—But Mr. Hotwheels

—Highways! A billion!

Warhorse intervened impatiently:

—I think . . .

—One billion!

—Enough! roared the Dic.

—One . . .

—Enough, I said! You'll all get the maximum, within the limits of our meager treasury. Warhorse persisted:

—I think . . .

—If you're going to ask for more money . . .

—I'll take it from the reserve funds. As I already mentioned. And there's something else.

—What do you mean?

—We're losing time. I think we ought to give a substantial reward to whoever gives us information about Pithecanthropus or his captors. Or any related data. We can promise absolute secrecy.

—How much?

—Half a million pesos.

—Fine.

He turned to Bacchus.

—Light my sockets!

The order was obeyed. With his own light he tried to analyze these men of government. He attempted a frown. Impossible. With what forehead? He tipped his skeleton until his lower jaw touched his breastbone. Then he straightened up.

—Couldn't we close down a radio or television station? Or at least, at least a newspaper? That always helps. Then all the country would know immediately that we're on a campaign.

Piggy clarified:

—The most closeable ones—the forlorn low-circulation press, that is—we've already taken care of.

—And the others?

—The others are our allies. They share our interests. And when they change—or give the appearance of changing—their politics, the answer is easy: it's only a matter of more or fewer pesos.

The Bony One looked at the Meatball's meringuey head. Smiled like a decayed domino. Who had yet suspected the existence of ideas in that vacuum? Had he underrated young Rigoletto?

—All right. Bring in the reporters!

F
o
u
r

Five

PITHECANTHROPUS and his assistant advanced onto the University campus. The mounting pandemonium of the printshop and offices: Drumming typewriters. Shrieking linotypes. The coming and going of sheets in the printing presses. The intermittent suction of paper feeders. The roaring of the small rotary press. Infinitesimal noises mingling like the din of a gigantic apiary. Something attracted the General's attention. There were no voices. No echoes of footsteps. Nothing that revealed a human presence. Moreover, it was completely dark. Who can work without light? Bah! They must have been practicing a long time. Like woodsmen in a forest. Or fisherman on the sea. People who can see and do everything in the dark. When he crossed the threshhold into the printshop, his astonishment swelled. Not a machine stopped. As if his presence hadn't been noticed. He, Jonas Pithecanthropus. How could they have missed him? Or were they ignoring him? So much the better. Such indifference was one more motive for his vengeance. Now he'd teach them some respect. To greet him. To drop everything they were doing to listen to his orders. He roared:

—Lights! On with the lights!

His Assistant complied. An absurd spectacle. The machines kept running. As if operated by invisible beings. Iron pinions and flywheels. Steel axles and levers. Synchronous gears and belts. Mountains of paper: everything needed for the fulfillment of their dynamic task was in endless movement. His subordinate babbled:

—It's true. Souls in torment!

—Shut up, idiot!

He absorbed in detail all that was occurring. The linotype keys jumped swiftly with no fingers pressing them. Matrixes sped to the small rotary smelter. Ingots lined themselves up. Automatic printing plates seemed to dance with their sheets of paper. Stacks of it flipped their white greetings from one side to the other. Rollers squeezed out their endless cellulose snake. Desperately he shrieked:

—Stop!

The deafening roar swallowed up his words. His rage grew. He climbed the steps to the press. Insisted:

—Stop! Stop, you sons of whores!

His assistant—carrying a branch of papaya—followed him. Took him by the arm. Tried to restrain him.

—Come now, General!

He was floored with one punch.

—Out of my way, coward! I'll kick the shit out of these fools.

His fury blinded him. He turned a darkish brown. Gorilla. Gorilla growls. Livid rage. Uncontrolled temper. He rushed to a switch. Turned it off. The press kept running. Preposterous! What to do? What could he do? Didn't they realize he owned Babelandia? Anytime he wanted, he could overthrow the Government. Kick the bones of the Dictator himself into the street. Well? Didn't they see they were risking their lives and those of others? He would liquidate prisoners and any others who dared confront him. Fools! Opposing him was like trying to contain volcanic lava. Or the flow of some great Amazonic river. Peripetatic bile, he accosted a linotype machine. Tried to sink his eyeteeth into it. To no avail. He grappled with it. Same result. The machine continued running. Distraught, black flowers in his thoughts, he rushed to a workbench. Seized an enormous monkey wrench. He began flailing at everything in sight. No results. Not a scratch, not a crack, not a dent. The print shop kept up its own pace. But he didn't give up. He went on, crazy madman, with wild, blind swings. The whirlwind of madness choked his nose, his ears, his eyes. The Assistant made a fresh attempt, this time keeping his distance.

—Calm down, and let's get out of here, General!

What was going on? He sank deeper and deeper into his frustration. Then another surprising thing began to occur to him. It was unimaginable. The machines were no longer machines. They were Dragons. Gigantic three-headed Dragons, with mineral bodies and entrails of fire. Blinding, kaleidoscopic armor. Jets of green flame in their eyes. Leaping red flames on their tongues. Dancing on the walls and ceiling. Their claws stretched like sickles gorging themselves. The fantastic creatures never ceased their great, menacing dance of war.

Five

Holofernes stepped under the skylight. Shouted anxiously:

—Harpie! Harpie!

The Nostalgic One looked down.

—Did they find him?

—Not a trace.

—I hope they never do! And the ransom?

—None yet.

—Don't let anybody pay it. When Sinbad hears about it, he may come back.

—Don't say that.

A momentary silence. The Lady of the Desiccated Boa seemed full of scorpions.

—Then leave me alone.

—Some other time. Not today. It's a bad situation. You must come down!

—And leave Melopea on a bitter cold night?

—The Press, Radio, and Television have arrived. Come with me.

She changed tactics. Used the sweetest voice she had:

—Well I won't meddle with them, Holie. Please give them my apologies.

The Dictator's tone hardened:

—Harpie! Don't make me lose my temper. Your absence would be conspicuous; they know what you think about Jonas. You've got to be there!

—All right, then. All right. All right . . .

Soon the tender voice was echoing softly in the distance.

—Melopea, I have to leave you now, poor thing!

The press conference began a while later. The technicians from remote control were restless and alert. Some of the announcers—glib, though not always clear in thought and expression—were happy. It was a chance to talk. Talk talk talk talk . . . To speak to an audience chained to the radio and television chain that chained all Babelandia. Needless to say, the announcers for the various brands of wine, liquor, beer, cigarets, etc., that sponsored the program were especially pleased. And much, much happier, of course, were the owners of the media: the event attracted a great number of listeners, viewers, and readers on the one hand; and on the other, a hand-over-fist influx of money: the myriad commercials financed by several government agencies and by advertising for the businesses just mentioned. They didn't say it—

how could they say it? And to whom could they say it?—But they were secretly thankful to the Amautas for the kidnapping. They hoped that it would take several days, or weeks, or months to find the anthropoid. There were wonderful instances in other parts of the planet in which kidnappings lasted nearly a year. Why couldn't that happen in Babelandia? They would light candles to their favorite saint in order to help the kidnappers hide from the military. How could he permit—he so miraculous, so full of benevolence—that unexpected source of income to exhaust itself so quickly? Of course, they didn't so much as insinuate it. Rather, they attempted to conceal their feelings: put on a face pained with toothache or acid indigestion . . . In every sense, Golden Ace—honey, dean, and jewel of announcers—would be in command. Depending on how "erudite" the sponsors were, Golden Ace was such an ace of aces that he would "elocute" only at fixed rates and times. To take advantage of his quarter hour, he had had a coin slot installed in his cranium to swallow up their money. The producer on duty would drop in a fistful. When the calibrated announcer stopped functioning, they had to pay him once again. Then right away—overcome by euphoria—he would return to announcing with words, harmonious movements, and automatic gestures. That's why it was Golden Ace—who else?—who began the show as soon as the required coins had been deposited. He greeted the viewers. He explained the program's content and purpose: to acquaint Babelandia with the awful news about the kidnapping of its imperishable general. He explained the broadcast was sponsored by Light Beer and Ditto cigarets, both of which he praised extravagantly. Continuing, he handed the portable microphone to the Dictator. He seized it violently. His bones wanted to unweave themselves. He controlled them with great difficulty. They were moving in concentric circles. As if he had no power over them. Rage rattled his teeth like a dice-box. A line from Darío flashed through his mind: "When I want to weep, I cannot." He finished it: "And sometimes I weep without wanting to." He was about to bleat. He restrained himself. He was losing the great chance of his lifetime! He controlled himself. He felt deep in a shower of sawdust. "Rip and cut, hither and yon, the freshed lumber of St. John." Behave yourself, Statesman! He parodied Napoleon at the Pyramids of Egypt: "Through the lenses of these cameras, millions of Babelandians are watching you!" Then his ego deflated. It wasn't possible. He was unable to continue for lack of a cassette! In short, there was no other remedy. He had to say at least a few words. He said them. He stressed that there was little time to act. Later on he would discuss at length the problem that had filled Babelandia with fear. For now they should have faith in him their beacon, their mentor, their guide and, at the same time, the first and last of their most humble servants. There was also a brief speech by Wiley Warhorse, who announced the reward being offered. Several times he emphasized the amount: Five hundred thousand pesos. Half a million pesos. Two-quarters of a million pesos. Each time the heavenly sum was mentioned, Piggy Rigoletto's belly trembled. As for the latter, when it was his turn to intercede, he swore to give no respite to the abductors. He would install microphones in the armpits of his countrymen. He would search house by house, room by room, bed by bed, every city of the nation. Further, he would order every citizen inspected down to the smallest wrinkle of his soul, to say nothing of his body. Fifty thousand serpents would be hired for this project. Thus, no one should worry about inopportune harassments or detentions. The serpents would carry out their mission by slipping under doors, bothering no one. Finally, he declared he had commissioned a pair of eyelid props for his personal use. And he would continue using them until the culprits were found and his friend Jonas Pithecanthropus—symbol, treasure, glory, and blessing of the Fatherland—was safe. He was the last of the authorities to speak. As a sidelight, it seemed that several idiots said and did identical things for identical cigaret and beer commercials. More involved in the problem, the Secretaries of State took advantage of these breaks to figure how much the kidnapping caper would leave for them. For them it would be—it had to be!—a lucrative deal. Not a blade of grass moved in Babelandia unless the sweetest and most succulent nectar sprinkled from heaven: one-thousand peso bills. Ah, if they could only collaborate with the Amautas in carrying out other important kidnappings! Might it pay off to get in contact with such guerillas? Maybe they'd accept a substantial commission for a long-range large-scale project. These edifying lucubrations were interrupted by the deep-throated voice of Golden Ace:

—And now, good televiewers, something sensational! We have with us Inocente Quasimodo, the General's chauffeur. His is the honor of having been the last witness. The last to enjoy the privilege of his company. To hear his words. To accompany him on tonight's late adventures. The last to . . .

Suddenly his head dropped. He was motionless, speechless, expressionless. The producer hurried over. Just as before, with a handful of coins. He began slipping them into the slot in his cranium. With the first clink Golden Ace came to. He straightened up. Moved his arms. Speech again jingled on his lips.

—Come here, Quasimodo!

Inocente stiffened to attention. His myopic lamb's eyes squinted under the floodlights.

—Tell us what happened to the General.

Inocente wasn't up to it. He lapsed into involuntary gestures.

—Since I first met him?

—No! since he left the Embassy of Great Entanglements just a while ago.

—We went out the door. That is, he went out. Out the door. In the gold sedan chair, as usual. He went on until he got down from the chair. then he got in the car.

—Alone?

—Alone.

—Then did you drive him home?

—No, to the University. And from there . . .

—Where?

—The usual place.

—What place?

—I can't say. The General has forbidden it.

—But now you have to tell us everything.

—Everything, yes. Except what the General doesn't want me to.

—Well, he's not here now to give you orders.

—That's why.

—You're the only one who can give us a lead to find him.

—The chauffeur's eyes widened. Me?

—You! The whole country hangs on your words!

—You're kidding!

Inocente was swept away by the floodlights and by Golden Ace's verbosity.

—Speak up, Quasimodo! The last place you saw him was . . .

He blurted it out:

— . . . The House of the Odalisques.

—The Odalisques?

Quasimodo loosened up.

—Right. The Odalisques. It's very well known. Haven't you heard of it?

—Yes. Of course. Of course I've heard of it. But what was the General doing there?

—Well, he was . . . Do I have to say it?

—No. Better that you don't say . . .Did he, er, take a long time?

—The usual. He's very fast. He doesn't fool around.

—When he came out, what?

—I opened the car door. He was about to get in. He stopped. Seemed to hear, or see, or smell something. But I didn't. He said to me: "Wait! I'll be right back." Turned around. then he took off.

—Was anyone else around?

—I didn't notice anybody. Who knows?

—Did he return to the house of The Odalisques?

—No. He kept on down the street. It was so dark I couldn't see him anymore.

—And then?

—I waited a few minutes. It seemed he wasn't coming back and I began to look around for him. Nothing. Not a trace. As if he had been swallowed by a tidal wave.

Five

Captain Gleam turned off the television set. He said to Eneas Pioneer:

—Idiots!

His friend's dark eyes glinted like steel.

—More than idiots! Bastards!

—Probably both. They're schizophrenic and now a murderous greed is guiding their steps. Nobody's safe. Nobody can live tranquilly. Babelandia could become a cemetery growing at a geometric pace.

—Then they must be stopped!

—Yes. They must be stopped.

With a wry smile he added:

—That's where we come in.

Six

EVER since they came to Babelandia—the capital of Babelandia and also part of the world—attempts were made to arrest them. A praiseworthy purpose that only sputtered into failure. The city was walled in by infamy and silence. Little by little they became aware of it. Although they could communicate, Babelandians were deaf-mutes in the realm of beauty and truth. The humble, because they lacked the interest, the spirit, and the time to speak. And the powerful, because they spoke a language that was exclusively theirs. Honor, love, work, and happiness, for example, all meant something else. In some cases, the exact opposite of the usual definition. Nevertheless, Gleam, Eneas, and their followers were not frightened away. Day by day they won the modest secondary battles. The great epicentric one—just as remote as the glories that filled Gleam's unreal world—was still to be won. It wasn't the young Captain's fault. He was up to the struggle, valiant in every test. And the transformation that was taking place inside him gave him sufficient stature for these arduous undertakings. But I don't have the means to do it. Neither inside nor outside the country am I able to obtain the arms needed to fight. For now, all I can do is to continue preparing and, at the same time, contribute to the preparation of my old and new comrades, who keep joining our ranks even now. My ancestral roots of several centuries have given me exceptional strength. My military career, as a result, always leads along the crusader's path. I have firsthand knowledge of the instruments and tactics of war; constant experience has made military history, so to speak, my own history. Theory and practice converge in me and give me meaning. If I were interested, like others, in hollow prestige and compensations in position, or in cash, the die would be cast: promotion to the top, an unending cascade of honors and sinecures. But that would be to whittle me down. I'd be reduced to midgetism. Converted unredeemably to a miserable microbe. A shameless betrayal of myself and those who have joined my life and destiny. So I can't compromise or divide my cause. Still less should I forsake my immaculate mission. I know where I'm going and what I want. Some day my side will prevail. Each obstacle has only strengthened our forces. Clarified our ideals. We'll make up for our lack of material resources with other assets. In the end we will win. It will be neither a personal nor a group triumph: rather, a total victory for equality and justice among men.

Still, at times he was overcome by a premonition of impotence and premature defeat. It seemed he was longing to build a metropolis in the sea. There was conflict after conflict: those in the past that he'd participated in had usually replaced one despot with another. The same relationships endured. Those who had everything were traditionally succeeded by others who also had everything. By contrast, those who gave blood, effort, and sacrifice were in the same fix—or worse—*before* and *after* Columbus discovered the New World. For the same reasons this struggle in which he aspired to improve his people's lot would be the most difficult to win. But it was the definitive one. One of such value that even the stones intervene. Upon reaching this conviction, he made a decision. With all his strength he would fight to the end. Would die and be resurrected—over and over, if necessary—for this noble cause.

—Yes, they must be arrested. To keep Pithecanthropus' abduction from working to the culprits' advantage, we'll move heaven and earth!

—The hour has come in which Babelandia will fulfill its destiny.

—And this way we will keep the promise we made on leaving Labyrinthia. Remember?

—Who could forget it!

Eneas Pioneer ascended on a spiral of dreams and longings. Long—how long? How many years ago? Long ago. They imagined themselves living in that distant land of infinite space and time, so hard to reach or escape from, either psychically or physically. He already played the organ then: religious and classical music, and aboriginal tunes. From the start, Polygamo the Parish Priest had given him complete freedom. On occasion—when some anxiety was burning in his breast—his own melodies flowed from the instrument, spontaneously composed as his fingers flew over the keyboard. He had the impression that the metallic throats lifted him on soaring wings beyond the horizon's boundaries. He loved the gray shimmer of the distances. To set out was to arrive. And to live in Labyrinthia. He yearned for light to other worlds. And the labyrinth was not only in streets and squares, but also in interior pathways. He inscribed his name on the unknown. Occasionally he went up the spiral stone staircase of the church tower to chat with the bell ringer, Agapito. The latter translated for him the language of the resonant bells whose phrases returned echoing from the mountains. Many times—drunk from alcohol, height, and distance—he regaled him with kaleidoscopic landscapes: cities suspended from clouds; antediluvian or fantastic monsters; worlds from dimensions beyond. When Eneas descended from that high stone tower to the tangible reality of this world, he observed the weaving of the Labyrinthians in their comings and goings like enslaved ants with a truncated itinerary. The spindly shacks like rows of cages along the streets. And, above all, Father Polygamo on his stroll after saying mass. Middle-aged and long-legged, he seemed to be walking on stilts. His cassock stretched out on the wind billowing like great bat wings. His customary stops along the way: the pharmacy, the barber shop, the general store. In short, the seedbeds of gossip. And gossip enveloped him like a wild vine. "He's changing," they said. "He's no longer the severe and circumspect priest we all respected." The wave of gossip followed him to the home of his godchild Ludivina, who in those days was depriving Eneas of peace and sleep.

Six

For his part, Gleam was crazy for Maria. Unqualified love—love at first sight, from the first time he saw her at church. He had gone with Hermogenes, his progenitor, to help him carry his newest piece of sculpture. To look at the girl was a revelation. Faces like that were only for the saints carved by his father. She dressed simply. Her eyes evoked twilight lagoons, and the undulations of her body were a synthesis of honey and music. He was a mere butterfly pinned to the wall. Hermogenes had to call him. They were supposed to carry the sculpture to its proper altar. He obeyed mechanically, without taking his eyes from her for a moment. Noticing his tattoo-like stare, Maria awarded him a scarcely perceptible smile. He and his Old Man carried out their assignment. Then he approached the girl. He tried to talk to her. She put her finger on her lips, imposing silence. Gleam immediately realized she would be engraved on his mind and heart as long as he lived. Back at the studio on the mountainside, he riddled the sculptor with questions. The latter, taken by surprise, told all he knew about the girl—which wasn't much. She'd been a student in the capital. Had returned two years ago. Since her arrival, she'd scarcely been seen in town. Reportedly her parents—in Labyrinthia it was rumored she was only their foster child—intended to marry her to a widowed carpenter. Owner of a carpentry shop, that is. Maybe that's why they'd had her so long in safekeeping. That afternoon's encounter was, accordingly, most unusual. She almost never went to church. And when she did, the purported authoress of her days was always with her. Little by little, Gleam confirmed everything that his father had said. He didn't meet her again. Not in church, nor on sunday retreat. Not even shopping or on visits. He hovered near her house all the time, hoping in vain to see her. But his hope was dashed. Their paths were not again to cross. At times, he was overcome by doubt. Had he really met her that afternoon? Wasn't it a figment of his imagination or some dream? He soon had evidence that it wasn't: Her wedding day. Even though he had heard rumors of her imminent marriage, he hadn't believed them. Even though he saw the decorated church, he remained skeptical. Maybe it was for some other wedding. He was convinced only when he saw her amidst a group of people unknown to him. She advanced slowly toward the church door. Was someone accompanying her? Her eyes were lowered and she seemed desolate. He wanted to shout. To force his way through the crowd, take her in his arms, and escape with her. But he held back. It was useless. The whole town would be against him. They would be separated. She would be snatched from him. He would be torn apart. For another thing, what if she actually agreed to the wedding? If—for better or worse—she really wanted to be that man's wife? After all, he'd never been able to learn what she thought. He was trying only to accept the facts. Resigned. So deciding, he felt like a top. Spinning around irrepressibly, in circles, on his two feet. Or was it that the others—the church, the streets, the people—were whirling around him, vertigo, vertigo? How long did the absurd whirlwind last? Who knows? People were crowded around the main door. Maria appeared. A growing murmur enveloped her. Finally, their eyes met. Or did they? She seemed to want to speak to him. Perhaps to explain what was happening. But she said nothing. How could she? Or was she going to anyway? Something—if she had any such inclination—restrained her impulses. The brand new husband stumbled. He fell. The news spread as fast as a sharp pain. He was dead. Sour gossip was seething. Had he died of remorse? For fear of impotence before his bride? In anticipation of conjugal pleasure? The town physician diagnosed heart failure. Possibly because of the feeling of anxiety that dominated him at the moment. Malicious tongues were telling another tale: his death resulted from a raucous bachelor's farewell celebration, generously showered with liquor. So Maria was already exchanging her virginal bridal trappings for a widow's weeds. Gleam saw her at the cemetery. She appeared absent. As if nothing existed, or as if everything were infinitely remote to her. Several gaunt hags—their candles burning rancid with over-aged beef fat—whispered in unison: "A miracle! A miracle!" At first no one seemed to hear. Actually many people had heard. Soon the word had pierced their ears and minds. "Miracle!" "Miracle!" "Miracle!" this, as one might have expected, "nettled innocent Labyrinthian hearts." They reached the conclusion that it was a sign of God. All Labyrinthia had to defend that virginity by fire and blood. Like Jesus' mother, Maria must live without being touched by any man. For his part. Gleam disagreed. "It's not right, it's not right." He began to think. Even assuming she wasn't allowed to love or be loved, who could prevent his looking for her, or at least *at* her? Now she went to church frequently. He kept watching her from a distance. Meanwhile, adolescence throbbed its arpeggios of light over her body and soul, and opened new horizons before him. Once in a while, Maria looked at him too. Smiled at him. And that was all. Until one day—when they were the only ones in the immense nave of the church—he approached her.

The Dragons. Pithecanthropus was beside himself. the Dragons. He drew his pistol. He squeezed the trigger. Emptied the chamber into the Dragons. The bullets were striking them. It was as if he'd scarcely grazed them. The Dragons. They continued advancing. Threateningly, they extended their claws and polymorphic tongues. The General threw down his automatic weapon. He turned to his assistant:

—Get them!

His subordinate continued serenely. As if he'd neither seen nor heard him. Jonas moved closer to him. shouted very loudly:

—Get them, goddamit!

He was still paralyzed with fear. He wanted to talk. Or to move. Or to show in some way how he felt at that moment. But it proved impossible. The Dragons. In view of all this, General Pithecanthropus launched into him. He gave him a tremendous jolt. He snatched away his submachine gun. And more and more a growling gorilla, he faced the incredible Three-Headed Monsters. He began firing fan-shaped volleys at them. The Dragons. His weapon leapt in his hands. The Dragons. The Dragons kept advancing. The broadsides continued to burst against them. He was blind. The floor was spinning beneath his feet. The walls were stretching upward uncontainably. They went higher. Still higher. The Dragons were advancing. Waves of bullets seemed to fly with oceanic force. they undulated. They burst, cracked, and sizzled from his hands. The Dragons advancing. A slow advance, millimeter by millimeter. If he wanted to, he could touch them. They raised their tongues of flaming spume. Or torture them with the talons of his claws. The Dragons. The Dragons advancing. Always advancing. He flung himself at them. He beat them with his fists. He bit them. Steel. Steel scales. No longer dragons but Machines. Still advancing. And he, backing off. Machines. Defeat. Humiliation. Scowls. On all fours. Machines. Backing off. Toward the door. Pushing at it. Getting out. Machines. Dragging his assistant along with him. Retreating. And the machines not stopping their work. Not stopping a single moment. Amplifying the song of their gears, wheels, and levers. Advancing. A song embellished by the whiplash of laughter. Still advancing. Machines. Outside, Pithecanthropus was even wilder. He turned to the officer in charge.

—Prepare for attack!

As if bugling signals for the first charge, he went on:

—With tanks, cannon, everything!

—Our objective?

—The presses!

—There are only two machines there.

—Destroy them!

The officer gave the orders. The men and their fighting gear were readied for the attack. The weapons' murderous mouths were about to speak. At last the General began to calm down. Now the wretches would find out. Dragons against me? I'll make them eat dirt. Crawl on their knees. Drag along like legless crocodiles, only trunk and tail. They'll see! All the jungle instincts that pulsed through his veins were gathering force. Now those sons of whores would see how he'd reduce them to dust and smoke. The first cannon volley would mix their metallic guts with the winds. That would be something magnificent, and give him deep satisfaction. They would be talking about it across all borders. On radio and TV, and in the newspapers. He imagined the headlines that would appear in the early editions: "PITHECANTHROPUS PULVERIZES SUBVERSIVE UNIVERSITY PRESS," "PITHECANTHROPUS SILENCES AGITATORS' ORGAN," "UNIVERSITY PRESS NOW A PERMANENT TOMB." His assistant showed signs of life. Looked at his watch. Addressed his chief:

—General, it's seven o'clock.

—So?

—You have to go to the Embassy of Great Entanglements.

—That's right.

He clenched his teeth, looked at the officer.

—We'll leave the show for later.

—As you wish General.

—After all, there's plenty of time. All the time we need.

For nothing in the world would I miss this spectacle.

Everybody had left. Even Bacchus the Groveler himself. In Babelandia, capital of Babelandia, a great silence reigned. It seemed that even automobiles feared circulating through the city. Only now and again was the hoarse rumble of a bus to be heard. Or the whistle of some heedless night watchman. At the Palace, in the muffled regularity of its atmosphere, the monotonous footsteps of the guards and the whisper of the fountains grew louder. Rising above it all were the swelling, undulating snores of Holofernes. Harpitune looked at him. The Bony One on a bed. Asleep, inert, helpless. His skeleton stood out in clear contrast to the covers. A pitiful sight. So calcareous, fragile, and vulnerable! She thought of finishing him off simply by scattering his bones. But no. How could she do that? Poor little Dictator! And poor little Babelandia without its calcium compass. Intermittently, he quivered. He groaned. Sweetly she would ask:

—What's the matter, Holito? Does something hurt?

His reply was a rumbling snore that, it seemed, might jiggle him into a thousand pieces. What ailed him? Was it the extremes of the recent calamities? Or was it just the cold? His bones seemed to emit waves of frost. His bared mandibles were clicking. His gumless teeth chattered. Cold. Suddenly she remembered Melopea. Fortunately, she was downstairs. Something to protect herself from the nocturnal cold's bite. She looked toward the corner of the room. The Constrictor was curled up there. And if the cold persisted? Why not, rather, give warmth to such beloved ones? Why not lay the Embalmed Entity in the bed between them? Out of the question! The Dictator might notice. And he'd never forgive her for depositing that scaly-skinned barrier there. The best solution—for Melopea, Holofernes, and herself—was the usual one. She got out of bed. Found the chest appropriate for those occasions. She placed it on the table. Opened it. It had a red velvet lining. She approached the skeleton. She carefully folded him into sections. Converting him into a compact pile. Delicately she fitted him into the chest. Lifted it. Put it on another table. Then she went to Melopea's corner. Took her up. Placed her on the bed. Stretched her out lengthwise. Covered her with her blanket. Finally—with slow, quiet movements—she snuggled up to her. But she couldn't sleep. A persistent idea afflicted her. Suppose she set out with the box of bones to look for Sinbad? Her son would be hard to find. Where? Where could he be? What did it matter? With that skeleton on her back she'd roam the world over until she found him. Crying, "Ay, Sinbad! Ayyy!" Her voice would echo over deserts, seas, and mountains. One fine day she would find him. If not, she'd convoke poets from all over the world. She'd tell them: "I'm looking for Sinbad, he's one of you. He preferred his poetry to inheriting a lifetime dictatorship. He broke all his links to an antipatriotic and antihuman dynasty." The poets would help her. She was certain. Yes. I must leave. But how? How can I leave Babelandia? Sinbad did. Of course, Sinbad is Sinbad. Defiant, like a proud ship with seven sails of mother-of-pearl. I, poor Harpa—Harpitune—dragged down by seven leaden anchors. He, in eternal pilgrimage. I'm here. Shackled in Babelandia's main square.

Seven

GLEAM and Maria grew more and more friendly. He told her about his life in the clouds suspended from the belt of mountain peaks encircling Labyrinthia. And about Hermogenes' toil—from dawn to sunset—infusing new life into the tree trunks that he carved. He, Gleam, worked with him every day. He also helped him with all the household chores, where the lack of a woman was ever more noticeable—since losing his wife, his father had not remarried—And he told her about the mockery of the condors. Swooping down to watch him. Peeping through doors and windows. Laughing at his solitude and abandonment. Despite everything, two of the youngest ones took a liking to him. Sometimes they took him for rides. Perhaps out of pity. Or because they had tired of the others' mockery. They had grabbed him by the shoulders with their claws and flown him over the mountains. He saw the snow-covered slopes close-up. The fiery circus of the volcanic craters. The ghostly lakes in mists of silence. Then later on they carried him over teeming cities. Strangely enough, he began to hear those cities' voices as an open invitation to live in them for good. From that time on he knew that one day he would live in such a city. Preferably in Babelandia, the national capital. There he'd study until starting his military career. And there he would prepare for the fulfillment of his goal: to be a guardian of the peace, well-being, and rights of others. He'd cultivate his work and leisure in such a way that he could realize his great purposes. She listened in silence. Maybe she sensed that they had crossed the threshhold of friendship. She looked at him intensely. She smiled at him. And she waited. And he, as he spoke, continued to feel that his love for her was impossible. Strong as his attraction to the virgin-widow was, it would always be just a one-way love. Only he could give his whole self. She, no more than her looks and smiles. Nevertheless, in spite of that strong conviction, he couldn't leave her. To be sure, their relationship never went beyond those minimal encounters. That's why, even after a long time, he never dared utter a phrase of love or longing. Why should he? He was sure she knew and understood. And so days and nights passed as if he had been bound to a tireless pendulum. Then one evening, unconsciously, unconsciously, they held hands. And silently they began to decipher the complex lessons of the landscape.

With a net of a thousand eyes, the Labyrinthians tried to catch their least perceptible movements. Tracked their steps. Converted their ears to wings in the winds. Some people readied their shotguns and pistols. For others, knives and sickles would do. They were expectant. Determined. On the pretext of his slightest indiscretion, they'd punish Gleam. Didn't he realize that so prized a hymen belonged to all of them? It was communal property, and as such, it could be no one's exclusively. Furthermore, it was a miracle. And if that miracle were not protected, the seven millennial plagues would ravage the community. The most impatient could scarcely restrain themselves. They argued:

—The early bird gets the worm.

—So what?

—Right now we could put an end to his misguided illusions.

—But they're not doing anything bad.

—Are we going to wait for them to start? What remedy will there be then?

—We'll keep our vigil day and night.

—What we really ought to do is castrate him. Then, much as it's against her will, she'll always be safe.

—In the end, it's God who giveth and taken away. How could we ever live down such a sin?

—And if they're sinning already? Isn't that a worse crime? That virgin belongs to the community. She must live and die in an immaculate state. For the salvation of us all.

—We must go on watching them. If they try to transgress, we'll limit them to intentions alone.

We'll tolerate not even a caress. Not a kiss. Much less anything else.

—Remember: an ounce of prevention. . .

—Here they come, holding hands as usual.

And that was it. Friends—just friends still, in spite of themselves—drifting as if they were sliding over waves. They walked among the Labyrinthians, almost touching them. Not noticing them. And how could they? They were in another world.

Meanwhile, Eneas Pioneer went on playing the organ and climbing the tower. Organ and bells. Bells and organ. The two voices began to merge. He was transported on his journey to the infinite, Ulysses riding a musical score. He felt his wings growing. The stones of the steeple uplifted him. Transformed him to an almost aerial being. On moonlit nights he gazed at the horizon, a blend of sapphire and silver. And far up, near the stars, Ludivina. When the bell tower lost its attraction as a watchpost, Ludivina became everything. He would visit her at home. Often he crossed paths with the priest. They wouldn't stop. And they scarcely greeted each other.

—Good evening to you, Father.

—Good evening, Eneas.

The Cleric made a quick gesture. A genuflection? Moved on without altering his pace even a moment. The musician, again disturbed over the village gossip about Polygamo, continued on his way. On the short trek to his beloved's house, that is. It was she who absorbed all his thoughts. Down the stairs drifted the pungent aroma of chocolate. He scaled the steps two at a time. Upstairs doña Prudencia—gazing like a vulture lacking nearby prey—watched over them. They couldn't be alone. On the least pretext she'd sit down across from them, evaluating the tiniest of their words and gestures. Sometimes sleep overcame her. Her head nodded, raising high her topknot. She'd breathe heavily. Occasionally she'd even snore. They'd take advantage as much as they could. Not much to be sure. Holding hands. Moving closer. Maybe a furtive kiss. Almost immediately the old woman would come to. Again straightening up her imposing head. Her eyes open. Trying to guess what could have happened during her short snooze. And then she spoke the customary phrase:

—It's getting late, Ludivina.

The girl acceded:

—Yes, mother.

Then firmly to her beau:

—You should go, Eneas.

His old doubts returned. Could it be that her godfather was influencing her? Or was it just the antipathy of his future mother-in-law? He uttered a timid protest.

—It's scarcely ten.

—You call that early?

Doña Prudencia had the last word:

—No need to expose ourselves to gossip.

Perplexed, he would leave. In the sickly light of the lonely streets he still saw Ludivina. She was so lovely and appealing! Each day he loved and wanted her more. As in a double exposure, he saw her naked against the trembling buildings and the quivering trees. With her dark, piercing, ardent eyes. Her hair, an undulating, ebony flame. Her delicate nose. Her provocative lips. Her breasts, an offering. Her tense thighs from which her sex rose like a challenge. Sometimes he felt a crazy urge to go back. To climb the stairs. To throw himself on the girl. He made an effort to master himself. Gained control. Accumulated reasons in his eagerness to persuade himself. There would be time for everything. Why be careless, when circumstances called for order and formality? Why resort to violence, riding roughshod over everything, when one day she would be united with him, wholly and without obstacle. Besides, she was his symphony of love. Many of her instruments waited to be played. The slowest and the deepest. The highest and most spritely. The serene and the allegro. But he was worried even so. No one listened to his troubles; his only confidant was his organ. Pedalling. Pressing the keys desperately, he transmitted to the brass tubes his hope and anguish, which waned in the gray distance. Still, as the days came and went, his uneasiness grew. Ludivina too seemed to be changing. As if she loved him less. Or as if some secret affliction had taken hold of her. Often she was out when he called. Or she frequently left him alone. When he spoke to her, she'd answer in monosyllables. And she tried to steer their conversation away from their love and even themselves. Instead, they'd discuss the problems of Labyrinthia and its people. Or just general, remote topics. Now she allowed hardly any caresses. And only innocent caresses that stopped short of a kiss. Her expression was distant. Sometimes she didn't hear him. He'd have to repeat his words. Or reiterate everything when he talked to her. If he reproached her for her attitude, she justified it by referring pointedly to the matriarch.

—We have to be careful.

—Why?

—She's watching us. She's on guard night and day.

—I don't understand. We never go out alone. Not even to the corner. Much less far from the house.

She grasped at an explanation:

—You know her. Always distrustful.

—Aren't we getting married?

—That's just what makes her angry. She doesn't think you'll be able to support me on your organ playing.

He insinuated an objection.

—That's our problem, isn't it?

—All mothers worry about their daughters' future. Besides, she's really right. You ought to get another job.

—I'm going to give classes. Play at parties and dances. Or with the village band. I can play several instruments.

—To her, that amounts to nothing. She wants you to look for a job. You know how to read, write, and keep accounts. And "La Providencia," the corner department store, needs somebody like you. Why don't you take that job?

—Music is my life.

When the General left the Embassy of Great Entanglements he was euphoric. He didn't wait for them to lower his sedan chair. He jumped down from it. Boarded the car immediately. Ordered:

—To the National University!

Now the bastards'll find out. They'll see who I am. Why they'll crap from fright and then I'll make them eat their own shit. When I'm finished with them, I'll visit the Odalisques. I'll open the legs of the first one I find. I'll give her a good reaming. And then to sleep. Ah, what a day! A day befitting my character and rank. Besides, you have to be ready for tomorrow. Tomorrow there's a festival in your honor. So precaution is called for, God's Chosen One! Enjoy what you can today. Tomorrow you'll have to behave as you should. It will be an international assembly. Hundreds of guests coming from all over! How does that grab you Jonas, Big Jo, Jo Jo Boy? You're deserving of envy. Holofernes Verbophile himself would like to be in your place. Of course he doesn't say so. He knows he can stay in power only with your consent. If one day you were to blow on him, his bones would collapse like a house of playing cards. You are the real Dictator of Bab. No. A dictator's nothing. You're the King. The Emperor. Lord of all lives, haciendas, and assholes in the nation! You are wonderful, General of Generals! Who would have thought it when you began with only the look of the jungle in your eyes! You have risen so high! So far above all other men. To places you had never dreamed about. And now? How far can you go? Will Babelandia be enough? How about starting a war against one of the border countries? That way you can broaden the sphere of your command. Why don't you do it? Why not?

—We've arrived, General.

That's where the neighboring dictators outdo us. They know how to kindle the fire of patriotism when their regimes falter. To make everybody believe that on the northern, southern, eastern, or western border there are territorial violations. Attempts at massive invasion. And that their respective towns are ready to leap into the struggle and the defense of the fatherland.

—General! General!

—What, damn it?

—We've arrived.

The University. The officer on duty. The necessary orders. The artillery ready to fire. The tanks with their engines running. The troops—with their fingers on the triggers of their automatic weapons—and ready to charge.

—Ready! Aim! Fire!

A thundering cannonade. An endless rumble. Greyhound flames leaping from the long mouths of steel. The walls buckling. Crumbling. And curiously—amidst the disorder, the destruction, the terrible dance of the projectiles, the plaster, the rocks, and dust—dominating them, swelling again, was the whirr of the printing presses in high gear. As soon as he heard it, Pithecanthropus erupted in bellowing:

—Knock everything to pieces! Leave no stone unturned! Destroy the buildings! Pulverize the machinery, especially the typewriters! Don't miss a single screw! Mangle and disintegrate them! Have no mercy! I hate them! How could anyone invent such a dangerous and perverse contraption!

The spectacle continued. Artillery fire. Walls caving in. Pillars, beams, rooftops—losing support or equilibrium—trembling and plummeting. Rubble. A deluge of rubble. Like an earthquake. Or better, a volcanic eruption. Building materials mixed with earth and water from the broken pipelines. A kind of unstoppable lava. Advancing slowly. Inundating everything. Nevertheless, the noise of the printshop persisted over everything. Again, the machines. The soldiers stopped. Stupified. Now they were convinced. Ghosts! Certainly from another world. Why not give it all up and escape? They held back. Behind them, the General. He did not play around. To retreat or step to one side was to die. He wouldn't think twice about liquidating them. As they hesitated, his voice thundered:

—What's the trouble, bastards? Waiting to have your balls shot off? Like sleepwalkers they renewed the attack. New firing, explosions, and rumblings. Corpselike with fear, they zeroed in on the machines. In spite of the blasting, they continued working. Amidst the rubble. Floating. They seemed impervious to the tremendous attack. The linotypes, the presses, the paper cutters, the typewriters—all continued with their incessant clatter. As if it were a peaceful day. At their labor without a single adversity. Convulsive. Blind. Beside himself, Pithecanthropus expelled a fresh shout. Was it a roar or a mere bleat?

—Tanks!

The armored vehicles advanced. Over everything. Their rotating steel cleats crawled on, trampling all obstacles. They neared the printing presses. Which continued their labors. Pithecanthropus's heart leapt expectantly. Today he would have his triumph. Total victory. The damned students would find out now. He'd eliminate their presses, which was the same as cutting out their tongues and extracting their vocal chords. Nearer the machines. Almost touching them. They'd be dragged. Then run over. Transformed into sheet metal. Into absurd metallic strips blended with inks and papers. Already they were touching. This arm first. They were disintegrating, being crushed. He could feel the vibrations under the bellies of the monstrous war machines. He was riding in one. Right inside. Unable to resist the temptation. He'd jumped in like an acrobat. They drew near a table. Typewriters lined up along its top. What joy! They hit the table. The table fell. The table crumbled. The typewriters were massacred. Oh to have eyes to see beneath the tanks! To be able to assist in the shredding of typewriter keys! To watch the P's, the I's, the T's, the H's, the E's, the C's, the A's. . . , and all the other letters of his name reduced to dust. In short, he could imagine it. And enjoy it, just imagining. What a night! What a night of nights he would have, that night! What a night awaited him between the legs of one of the Odalisques! Night? No, not the whole night. Not with them. Only a moment. Women, after the act, get on my nerves. They're only good for "that." And to enhance my macho fame. Macho. Machine. Super macho. Machete.

—General! General!

—What?

—Look back there!

Damnation!

The printing presses—unscathed—were still running. Even as the tanks continued their advance, they emerged anew with all their vigor. As if no attempt had been made to stop them. As if they'd never been struck by so much as a canary feather. He shouted:

—Cease fire!

Think you've beaten me? Numbskulls! They're crazy! It's a good thing all the university ringleaders are in jail. I'll soon have them singing. Use every kind of torture imaginable. And maybe invent a few new ones. They'll sing all right. Until their melodies sing me to sleep.

Ever since the day they went out to the fields, Maria warned him repeatedly:

—Watch out. They'll stop at nothing.

He tried to reassure her.

—It's just your imagination. They're not even thinking about us.

—You're wrong. They're watching us. They haven't let up a single day.

—I haven't seen or heard anyone.

—Neither have I. But I sense them. I feel as if they were constantly handling me with their eyes. Perhaps they're hiding. Maybe they are keeping their distance. They're waiting for us to make the move that would justify their pouncing on us like wild beasts.

Hand in hand they devoured the distances. They never stopped. Maybe sensing how dangerous it would be. They'd lose control. They would embrace. They'd devour each other with a myriad of caresses. And would culminate with the victorious song of their inflamed sexuality. Virginity sacrificed to love would light the torch of their flight to exile. To him that didn't seem so crucial. He was prepared to give his life as the price of this maximum biological hymn. Clearly he wouldn't surrender easily. He'd fight tooth and nail against the Labyrinthians. Especially to protect her. Before touching Maria they'd have to destroy him, reduce him to a luminous hallucinatory dust. Hallucinatory! Because even turned to dust he'd overwhelm them. Attacking their eyes and ears, their noses and mouths: at every point that proved vulnerable. But to her it would be crucial. To be possessed by him would be to lose him. To begin by taking him into her deepest recesses would result in his departure. Perhaps they would never achieve intercourse. Nothing could follow their beginning. On the brink of supreme delight, they'd be forced apart. They'd get no further than the present indicative of "to kiss": I kiss you; you kiss me . . . Then the wolfpack—absurd defenders of what had been granted to them—would leap to violent action. Especially against Gleam. Most likely they would kill him. Or they'd strip him of his manhood. And she didn't want to lose him. She still wanted, even with all the present frustrations, to have him close by. Perhaps one day the sewage-laden minds of the Labyrinthians would be filtered to rid them of their infections and outlandish ideas. Or he and she might solve their dispute with the town. The town that had made her maidenhead their battle cry. Sometimes he wondered feebly:

—And if we ran away?

—Where?

—Anywhere. Any place far from the Labyrinthians. Maybe to Bab, our capital.

—Could we?

—We could try.

—They'd follow us. They'd catch us. And you'd get the worst of it.

—I'd risk that. We'd get married in the nearest village. So even if they found us, it would be too late!

—Not for their kind. It would never be too late!

—Think about it. There's no other way.

—Who knows? For now, we must have patience. It's the only way to beat them!

—I hope you're right.

The Bell Ringer, when descending from his tower, was transformed. He was a different person: Agapetus. Vagrants always trailed behind him, shouting "Cagapito, Cagapito!"* He didn't care. He wouldn't see them any more. Old as the bells, he seemed to be from another world. The alcohol rocked him from side to side, like a living hammock. He had been drunk just once in his life. The first time. The first and the last. That one time. Ever since he had tasted the juice of fermented cane, he had been an addict. Never regained his full lucidity. He drank himself to sleep. And when he woke up, he began to drink, until sleep again called him to its cradle of shadows. He walked, resonating with the contagious bronze reverberations, along the sinuous and dusty streets. Especially those that led to the taverns. There he spent the endless hours adrift on spiritous rivers. His feelings aroused. No longer was he the bell ringer in weird conversations with Eneas. Instead he gathered and circulated gossip. He had retained nearly all the town talk since days no longer remembered. Had stuck his nose—on attentive coral antenna—into every corner and body and soul of the Labyrinthians. They fed on his words. They unfurled his tongue by buying him drinks.

—And is it true that Clench—Maria's father or whatever he is—really is protecting "that"?

—Of course!

—What do you mean, "of course"?

—Just what I say.

—Then why did he marry her off to the widower?

—Ask him.

—Maybe he knew he was dying?

**Translator's Note:* A vulgar pun on the name Agapito; *caga* is from the verb *cagar* ("to shit").

—Could be.

—Or he thought he was too old to . . .

—What do you think?

At those moments he put on a look fit for purgatory. He finished off the bottle in one gulp. Then he looked down at them, as if they were a swarm of insects. Or had scarcely heard them? How curious! They sounded as if they were bells of flesh producing strange vibrations. Labyrin, labyrin, labyrin! Bzz, bzz, bzz! Labyrin, labyrin, labyrin! Bzz, bzz, bzz! Images and sounds surrounded them. They wanted the complete story. The first gossip was only a prelude.

—And what do you think, don Aga?

—About what?

—About don Clench always guarding what he's guarding. Remember?

—Only He-Who-Is-Above knows that. And maybe the Reverend Father.

—Father Polygamo?

—Who else? He knows everything.

—And you, don Aga? Come on, now!

—I'm nobody's confessor. And even if I knew, I wouldn't tell you. Besides, I like the girl.

—Who doesn't, don Aga?

—And if she wants to give it to somebody, that's her business, isn't it?

—But she's the village virgin. Even though she wasn't born here—it's as if she'd come down from heaven. She's ours!

—Ours! We had wanted that: what was ours as a gift. For that we will defend everything!

—Good old Agape!

—But you'll never see yourselves in that mirror.

Tumbling, a vibrating bell himself, liquor himself, drunkenness himself, hounded by a swarm of street urchins—Cagapito! Cagapito!—he returned to his tower. Climbing toward the clouds like a vertical snail, he became once more the living antenna of distant events.

Piggy Rigoletto had recruited only 10,000 serpents. Of course it didn't matter. Because in my accounts I'll put down 50,000. After all, who could count them? Even if they wanted to, how? To get as many as he did was a feat. Still more to persuade them to limit their work to investigating and spying. However, the reptiles wanted to take advantage under the protection of the law. Perhaps they could try their poison on some useless person. Or scare as many as possible. Or drink the milk of a newborn's mother. The Secretary of the Interior was adamant. They had to obey orders. Grudgingly the wrigglers began their work. The invasion was at dawn. Since it had been announced on TV, nobody was surprised that they were circulating in the streets. Climbing up walls. Getting into houses. Rummaging through everything, seeking some clue, some reference, any lead at all that would put them on the track of Pithecanthropus or his abductors. Most people tried to avoid them. When they heard the least rustling. Or noticed little phosphorescent eyes at a distance. Or heard a hiss—maybe communicating some information or news—they would move away. In the streets, sheltered by cold solitude, silence, and distance, the thick scaly creatures moved in groups. And since they couldn't offer one another a helping hand, or arm, their bodies undulated in unison. With grand camaraderie they formed intersecting rings. And in circular harmony they set out to complete their mission. Only an occasional evasive night-walker—asleep, or in pain, or in his cups—obstructed their way. Believing it was some kind of hallucination, he would continue on his way, seeking the right place to exchange these visions for more agreeable or edifying ones. For his part, Piggy Rigoletto, as he had promised, put on his eyelid openers to stay awake. This made him smile again. Eyelid openers! Instead of having them made, he had found them in his pocket: two one-peso coins. What a view he'd have! But with or without them he'd stay awake, anticipating his profits. Not forgetting that at home two others were already calculating them: his father, whom he had imprisoned on the top floor and who did it simply to keep his mind working; and his wife, who controlled every penny he earned.

Eight

HARPITUNE woke up very early. Coiled up Melopea. Took her to the roof. Stretched her out, full length, in the sun. The huge boa stirred. Yawned.

—Thanks, Harpie. Thanks a lot.

Her confidante sighed.

—Thank you, for accompanying me again.

The Constrictor stretched. Shook herself. Tried to raise her head. Couldn't. Fell asleep again. Then the Dictator's wife left her , descended. Back in her bedroom she lifted the chest that protected her husband. Put it on the bed. Opened it. Carefully unfolded him.

—You have to get up, Holie.

—It's still very early.

—It's time for the news.

—Ah, so it is!

He got up. Turned on the radio. The Announcer said: "So far there is not a trace of General Jonas Pithecanthropus. As if he'd been swallowed by the earth. The citizenry is alarmed, and does not know what to believe. In spite of the half-million-peso reward offered by the Secretary of Defense, not a single lead has come in. Remember, there's no better companion than a Golden Brew. To ease the shock this abduction has caused, keep a cool one at hand! Sensational news is expected any moment. Keep tuned in. We're a chain of stations and will remain chained until we're unchained, when the Commander-in-Chief of the Armed Forces reappears. All we know is that he continues to be held by the Amautas. Until they free him, hold on to your Golden. The premium brand. Enjoy it. Enjoy it 'round the clock. Miss not an instant of its sweet company. Early this morning we interviewed the Secretary of the Interior. He hasn't slept. Nor will he until he finds the Missing Person. He has told us about the snakes' survey—50,000 snakes!—the many leads they've discovered. These cannot be made public without compromising the cause of justice. Speaking of justice, do *yourself* justice! Get loose with a Golden Brew. A comfort any time. Holofernes turned off the radio. He said to his spouse:

—Pass me a Golden!

She looked surprised.

—What's that!

—Give me a Golden.

—A beer? So early?

Then he realized that the collective hypnosis had stupefied him. He composed a neat skeleton's grin.

—These commercials make everybody stupid. What I need is a towel.

—Why?

—Why do you think? For a bath.

—And if you dissolve?

He looked at her disapprovingly.

—You too, Harpie?

She was uneasy.

—Said without malice. Just a precaution.

—All right, then.

—Wouldn't you prefer—just to be safe—that I rub you down with cologne?

A bit later they went down to the Palace dining room. Narcissus Vaselino, Chief of Protocol (evil tongues called him "Vaselino Prostatocolo") was melting with rage. How could a breakfast be improvised? People had to be seated according to their rank and background. How could he plan it if he didn't even know who was coming? Or how many? He scurried into the kitchen for a moment. Nibbled the ear of Disgusteaux, the fat cook recently imported from Paris. The Import, in response, kissed the back of his neck.

—Calm down Vaselino!

The latter rested his cheek on the shoulder of his friend and protector. He was on the verge of shedding a couple of mini-tears. Contained himself. His nostrils sensed the simmering dishes, spices, and sweat that held him back. He looked at him with a deer's quivering in his pupils.

—You know my sorrows. You understand me. Without you I wouldn't know what to do in this world.

—Come now, Narcissus. You're letting those vandals play with your cares.

His companion withdrew. To himself, he quietly cursed the moment that Pithy—that's what he called Jonas—had been kidnapped. Cursed the Amautas as culprits. Cursed Holie—Holofernes—for fretting about it. Cursed the cabinet memebers for meddling in this affair. Cursed his countrymen for following him in everything. Cursed himself for living in Bab. For not having free will, and for not telling them all to grind up some glass with the lips of their anuses. Now they had ruined his plans for breakfast. Who knows what they'd ruin for him in the future? Forcing his bitterness into a smile, he began to accommodate the recent arrivals. Rhythmically, unctuously, he bowed his head and stretched his arms and legs, as if they were slippery chutes, for the quick placement of his guests. When all—almost a hundred—were seated, he vanished into thin air. Verbophile asked:

—Mr. Secretary of the Interior, is there any news?

Piggy Rigoletto pulled himself up.

—Marvelous news, Excellency.

Expectant. Phosphorescent eye sockets. His skeleton braced. Skeleton, skelebones, skele-cadaver.

—Has Jonas appeared?

—Not yet.

—Have they found the Amautas?

—Not them either.

—Ah! Then they have some clues.

—No, Excellency.

—Then what?

—Your people. The people are here, down there, outside the Palace!

Two tears—well, two dehydrated tears—slid from the eye sockets of the Dicdic—tatatatortor.

—Ah Rigoletto, Rigoletti, Rigolettito, what inspiring news you give me!

He lowered his eyes in modesty.

—They've come spontaneously, in a demonstration of nearly one hundred thousand souls.

Wiley Warhorse chimed in:

—Almost two hundred thousand.

Rigoletto thought quickly: "That booboo of my colleague's will cost me plenty. Then, in a high voice:

—Your people want to express their solidarity in this difficult hour, Excellency. To offer you their support, their lives, and everything they own—for the salvation of the fatherland. Can you hear them?

Then there was silence. All jaws stopped moving. Listening expectantly, while grasping their knives, forks, or spoons. To be sure, the crowd's rear rose from the plaza. Cheers were clearly interspersed among them.

—Long live Holofernes Verbophile!

—Viva!

Long live the Savior of the Fatherland!

—Viva!

—Long live our Guardian Angel!

—Viva, viva, viva!

The roar subsided. As if on signal to start a 100-yard dash, mouths, tongues, teeth, and tableware sprang into action. But the pleasure was short-lived. The Bony One was on his feet.

—Let's go!

Dejectedly they ceased their gastronomic movements. They also got up. Piggy sensed the collective fear.

—Where, your Excellency?

—To the balcony. To witness the demonstration at its peak.

The Secretary of the Interior looked at the breakfasters. Anguish and hunger were painted on his face. He looked at his own hands. In his left, a roll; in his right, a cup of coffee. He half-smiled.

—It's too soon, your Excellency. The crowd is just beginning to gather in the plaza. Others have not yet arrived.

—Right. Absolutely right.

He sat down again. So did the others. And right away, as if possessed by irrespressible dynamism, as if they were about to miss a train, they resumed gobbling the morning vittles. For a while only the unmusical rhythm of grinding teeth and tinkling tableware was heard in the room. Holofernes couldn't eat anything. Inside he bubbled with pleasure. It was great that the demonstration had been organized! Certainly there were many Verbophilists. And even if there were anti-Verbophilists, they would constitute a small minority. Piggy Rigoletto knew how to get things done. Things like that. That's why he had made him Secretary of the Interior. Most probably he had let loose a few reptiles among the people. They would perform at the slightest indication of disturbance or aggression. Moreover, for those situations he had made appropriate cassettes. In the last few hours he had recorded some sensational tapes. He checked his authoritarian index finger. Flexed it several times. It was functioning marvelously. The technical devices were at this command: balcony, cassette, and finger. All he had to do was wait. One minute. Two minutes. Three minutes. Five. Ten minutes. What a joy! Unconsciously he started a cassette. More precisely, he pushed a button on the recorder. It began working. He heard its declamatory voice:

—Babelandians!

He jumped to his feet. The guests looked at one another in confusion. Was he going to unleash an after-dinner speech? Oh no! Not that! The Skeleton furtively pressed another button. He looked at them sheepishly. Smiled. Skeleton, Skeleskinny, Skelecranium. Timidly he mused:

—My impatience is killing me.

He had terminated breakfast. Again the cheers from below swelled:

—Long live the most Babelandian of the Babelandians!

—Viva!

—Long live the greatest great of the great!

—Viva! Viva! Viva!

A shuddering jolted the elegant residence of the Odalisques. Jonas' limousine drew up. As usual, this made the renowned and skillful professional ladies nervous. They calmed down when Madame picked out the name of the chosen one for that evening.

—It's your turn.

—What can I do?

The Old Girl didn't seem to catch the tone of resigned protest. She said:

—The usual thing. Even though the man is a beast, we have to accept him. If he weren't who he is, he wouldn't set foot in my establishment.

—If there's no way out, I'll get ready. That guy hasn't got time for anything. With the pretext that he's in a hurry . . .

She went to her room. Quick as a wink her clothes were off. She lay down on the bed. Waiting. Pithecanthropus burst in like a tornado. Gates had been opened—a mini-bullring to run the horned one into his designated area. He began disrobing on the stairs, tossing his clothes to one side or the other. When he reached the bedroom of she-who-was-waiting, he was already naked. No pause, no greeting. Not even a pleasant expression, much less a smile. He flung himself on top of her, as one takes a running leap into a swimming pool from a diving board. The victim groaned:

—Barbarian!

No apologies. No change in attitude. Not a word was said. Rudely he pried open her legs with his knees. He closed his beady eyes so as not to see her. He nailed his sexual instrument into her sexual instrument, as one gives a hard blow with a hammer. The girl could bear no more. With clenched fists she struck him in the face. And he smiled, as if she had caressed him. He uttered a stupid commonplace:

—Bear it, as the recently deceased one did!

Then he mechanically completed his biological offering to Venus. For the Odalisque on duty it was as if a locomotive had run over her, backward and forward, several times. Despite knowing "who he was," despite his monthly payments "for using them," despite the difficulty and danger of contradicting or resisting him, if she'd had some way of doing it right there, she'd have stood up to him without hesitation. If she'd had a pistol, she'd have blown his brains out. With a sword she'd have cut him into small pieces. The experience was more nauseating than painful. And more humiliating than nauseating. A horrid nightmare transformed into a wakeful torture. The only good part—was any good possible?—was the rapidity of his violence. The Apocalyptic Beast was up with a leap. With neither a word nor a minimal expression of satisfaction. He half turned and entered the bathroom. From the little window an odor attracted him with magnetic force. He came back quickly. Began to pick up his clothes to dress. She persevered, as if mortified by hundreds of iron barbs. She lamented having been born. For this profession that had befallen her. For having to withstand the physical onslaught of that human gorilla. Now he descended the stairs still dressing. He approached the automobile. Opened the door. The odor again tickled his nostrils. He breathed deeply. He was guided by the invisible tentacles of that delicious fragrance. He turned to Quasimodo.

—Wait for me. I'll be back.

As if the shadows had beckoned him, he gravitated toward the odor. It got stronger and stronger. He hesitated momentarily. Should he get back to the car? With his gifted nose as his guide he could direct his chauffeur. But if he got off track? If the smell of the gasoline spoiled his perfect orientation? But on the other hand, the object of his longing seemed so near. His doubts vanished. With short, quick steps he set out. Walked a little. The odor was stronger. He searched for the place from which it was coming. Quickly discovered it. Something yellow was hanging from a balcony. Hastened his steps still more. And now there it was before his eyes, his nose, and his mouth. A banana! He extended his right hand. Grasped it. Trembling, he removed its skin, as if opening the petals of a flower. He ate it with great gulps. He half turned, to go back. The car's burning headlights looked far away. Once more the aromatic tentacle teased his nose. Once more he turned. And again he ran. Without a thought. The image of the fruit was swelling in his mind, neutralizing all other sensations. Everything was fruit. Fruity fruity fruit fruit. Then he discovered, hanging over the edge of a cornice, winking at him, another banana. He ate it still faster than the first. A third banana began to summon him. He pursued it, running until it was his. Ate it. And then there was another. And another. Another and another. And still another. As if he were dealing with a long olfactory chain of bananas. Until he arrived at one suspended from an iron bar. He approached it. Took it. Just as with the others, he peeled it like a flower. Was doing this, when he heard the metal gate fall. The banana that had filled his cranium disappeared. He looked around. It was dark. Squinting hard, he was able to distinguish what enclosed him. They were very thick iron bars evenly spaced. He approached them. Grasped two of them. Tried to force them apart. Impossible. To shake them loose. Also impossible. They were very strong. He kicked them, punched them, banged his head against them. Useless. His injured limbs ached. He came, then, to a quick and horrible conclusion. He was in a cage. The bananas had been placed, one by one, so he would encounter them: a trap! With hands and feet he made his way up the bars. The top was also enclosed, with a radial shaped-iron grill. They've screwed me, those sons of whores. He pranced on the floor, trying to make noise. He hadn't noticed until now. The floor was iron too. And now? What would happen to him now? They'd torture and humiliate him for sure. They'd take it out on him any way they could. But he wouldn't give them the satisfaction of seeing him defeated and destroyed. I'm a real man.—A real man, or a real gorilla?—Too much of a man to keel over. I can take it. I'll withstand everything, baring my teeth. What they do to me, they do to me. As long as I'm breathing. The only bad part was to know that there were a lot of things he couldn't accomplish. Everything was left pending. For example that night's party at the prison, when the university students were to "sing" to him. And the party the next day. He was the main attraction; how could they celebrate without him? Suddenly, before he realized, he heard himself shouting:

—Get me out of here!

Not even an echo answered his words. He shouted again:

—Get me out of here, Goddammit!

Not a sound did he hear, nothing moved. As if he were enclosed in a static world. His voice grew hoarse. Sounded so strange that it surprised him.

—You'll pay for this, you bastards!

Two human shadows of different sizes approached. The taller one spoke:

—No point in screaming, General. Here, nobody can hear you. Besides you might lose your beautiful voice.

His pent-up anger left him quaking.

—You'll regret this, you degenerates.

The other shadow had the same mocking tone.

—We're shaking, General.

Pithecanthropus threw himself at the owners of those shadows. They stepped back. The aggressor banged against the bars. He was blind with rage. His jowls were covered with foam. He roared:

—Laugh, sons of bitches. You'll see who laughs last.

The one who had just spoken asked:

—So! He knows how to laugh too?

And the other:

—If he laughs the way he talks, we'll be frighened for sure.

Jonas clenched his fists.

—We'll see, when you're in my hands.

—That's if we ever fall into them, General. Meanwhile, you're the one in our hands. And now we'll find out if you bite the way you bark.

He turned to his partner.

—Did you bring the rat cages?

—Yes.

—Are the rats hungry?

—They haven't eaten for three days.

—Good. Let's begin then. We'll chain the General to the bars.

The latter was defiant:

—Let's see if you can.

Scarcely had he said it when a mysterious self-propelled chain moved toward him. Before he could defend himself—as if it were an iron python—it wrapped around him, imprisoning him against the bars.

The one who'd been talking went on casually:

—Now we'll pull his pants down. We'll give him the rat treatment. We'll open the little doors. So that the rats can make him feel everything those who fall into his hands have felt.

Jonas' eyes burned into them:

—Sons of whores, sons of sluts, sons of bitches.

There was a pause. The taller one said:

—Maybe the rats can wait a while.

—Why?

—There's something better we can do.

—Really?

—Much better. Something appropriate.

—Like what?

—We'll hang bananas just outside his cage. So the General will enjoy gazing at them round the clock. But he won't be able to reach them. He'll have to be satisfied with smelling and looking at them.

Pithecanthropus shivered. Just thinking about it started the banana in his head growing again. He was speechless. That was excessive cruelty. Surprisingly, he no longer felt his chains. Had they been removed? Had they existed to begin with?

Nine

AS he entered the church one day, Captain Gleam had a surprise. Seated right on the steps of the atrium was Peter. Not that that was especially noteworthy. In those days it was rumored that the famed fisherman was in the area. Or rather in the nearby lakes. To be sure, each time he could, he took a vacation, spreading his nets. He had recently converted his ancient profession into a favorite pastime. And these places appealed to him because of their solitude and isolation. He seemed worried. Stopped him.

—Sit down. I want to talk to you.

He obeyed.

—Yes sir.

—Is it true you're seeing Maria?

—It is.

—And what do you think of her?

He was disconcerted.

—Me?

—Yes, you.

—In what way?

—What do you mean what way? Every way.

He responded. Blurted with emotion:

—She's supreme. The most beautiful. The most virtuous. The most intelligent. She's unique.

The severe Saint muttered:

—All right, all right. How could it be otherwise? My question missed the mark. I should have asked how you feel about her.

—I love her. She is—I'm sure she'll always be—my first love.

—Have you forgotten she was the widowed carpenter's wife?

—So? Now he's dead. And even if he were alive . . .

—You'd best be quiet.

— . . . How could I be jealous of him?

—Jealous? You? Of him? I never heard such a thing. No, it's not that. It's just . . . to leave her like that . . . seems quite strange.

—Why?

—She still must be a virgin, right?

—Why?

—Because it was written.

—Where?

—We could find out . . . Well, who knows? I suppose it was, somewhere.

Gleam was becoming worried.

—Well, I didn't know that. From what I can see, this is getting too complicated.

—It's your own fault. Your eyes got you into trouble.

—I'm understanding less and less.

—That doesn't matter.

He seemed absent-minded. Went on:

—Even I can't understand some things. Every time I go fishing, the same thing happens. Is the water affecting me? Or is it the sight or the smell of the fish?

Gleam stuck to his own theme.

—Anyway, it's not fair. Why shouldn't I love her?

Peter came back to the young man's world.

—Well. There are many kinds of love. Loves that want to give everything and to receive everything. But other loves demand very little. For example, that of the wives of Christ. That is purely spiritual.

He seemed to be drifting off again.

—At least that's what they say, isn't it?

—Who?

—That's right. Who?

In spite of everything, the Fisherman treated him affectionately. Without doubt, he'd had good fishing. His good humor showed it, as did the silvery scales and fins in his basket, which he picked up before leaving. He smiled.

—All right. Why should I bite off more than I can chew. It's really your problem. Farewell, Innocent One. Try to get over your absurd infatuation, if you can.

—Impossible

—You'll only be hurt.

—Why?

—Well, because . . . Oh, why! I'm sick of so many whys.

He turned his back. Walked away slowly.. The basket looked heavy. The young man followed him.

—Can I help?

The Fisherman shook his head, adding cryptically:

—It's not time for it, yet.

And just then, as on previous occasions, Gleam had a vague sensation of space and time. But he returned directly to his own problem. It was evident that his interlocutor was in another world. Possibly transported by the product of his fishing, he had confused one virgin with another. But what other? For an instant, he thought that he must clarify everything. Perhaps in order to have more tranquility. It was too late. The Fisherman was gone.

Many tourists had arrived for the celebration of Pithecanthropus' fiftieth birthday. They were not the usual tourists. It seemed that they all had the same appearance: tall, pink-cheeked, burly, bespectacled, blond, big-footed, in many-colored clothing. On the other hand they bought no souvenirs or curios. Carried no cameras. Weren't seen in the typical places. They were interested, rather, in other things: the numbers, the statistics, the attitudes and opinions of the people. Their eyes and ears seemed to be super-sensitive antennae that lost not a sound or image. Even though they spoke different languages, their purpose was one: to function like living electronic computers accumulating information. They were accompanied by domestic and foreign zombies. They drove speedy automobiles. They took up positions on the streets near the main plaza of Babelandia. Or they peered from windows of hotels and other buildings that face it. They all were scrambling to witness the spectacle, which seemed of crucial importance. In front of the Palace, the impassioned throng cheered Verbophilia. Of course, the demonstrators amounted to fewer than 100,000. No more than a third of that number. And no one was there by choice. Or more exactly, from loyalty and in disinterested support of the Dictator. The whole show had been planned by Rigoletto. He had contracted them all at five pesos per cranium. Setting aside, of course, a tidy profit for himself. Moreover, he had intelligently chosen the occasion, the site, and the mercenary herd. Their identity was easily discerned. Few were humans. The majority were various animals, among which lizards predominated. There were also some ruminants. They rambled from one place to another. They swirled together. Every moment more arrived, giving the impression of an interminable mass. They carried large, provocative posters: "WE'LL FIGHT TILL GENERAL PITHECANTHROPUS IS FREE"; "LONG LIVE HOLOFERNES VERBOPHILE, OUR REDEEMER"; "DEATH TO THE ABDUCTORS OF THE COMMANDER OF THE ARMED FORCES"; "ONE RESOLVE: TO FIND GENERAL PITHE-

CANTHROPUS"; "PITHECANTHROPUS OR DEATH"; "VERBOPHILE AND PITHECANTHROPUS: THE PEOPLE ARE WITH YOU." The serpents wriggled among them, trying to catch suspicious conversations. Or some men and animals. The roar subsided.

—Long Live Our Savior!

—Bravo, bravo, bravo!

—Long live Number One in the Republic!

—Bravo, bravo, bravo!

Suddenly there was a great silence. All eyes were turned toward the Palace's central balcony. It was a huge balcony. Just the place for the Dictator of Babelandia, paradise of the confused and the imprisoned. The *crème de la crème* of the nation's big shots surrounded him. Bacchus the Groveler hovered behind him. When the first hypnotic spell inundating the plaza had passed, there was a great burst of applause. The Bony One raised his arms, gesticulating. It lasted several seconds. An ox moved up to do his thing. He neared the microphone. Again, complete silence reigned. The bovine stood up on his hind legs. Inserted his tongue in each of his nasal pits. Paused. Commenced solemnly:

—Your Excellency . . .

Then a strange calm came over him. His eyelids grew heavy. And he began to chew his cud rhythmically. At such a distance the crowd found that it couldn't see him clearly. If they had been closer, they would have recognized the easy oscillation of his jaws—minute, indefatigable rocking chairs—and of the total ecstasy of his chewing. Holofernes stepped over. Tapped the nape of his neck. The ox opened his eyes. Smiled. Bowed:

—That's all.

The crowd applauded. Holofernes gave him a tight hug. The crowd went on cheering. Several photographers and cameramen approached. They captured, in still shots and on movie film, the imponderable tenderness of the occasion. The Ruminant returned to his place, wholly satisfied with his performance. The crowd stopped applauding. The Bony One grasped the microphone in his left hand, as he raised his right hand, index finger extended, high in the air. The applause began again, this time resonantly. In addition to the thunderous sound, the spectacle of clapping hands was fascinating. It was like a field of ripe wheat waving in the wind. The applause dwindled, until once again silence reigned. The Skeleton gave the impression of a mast made of elephant tusks.

—Babelandians!

Renewed applause muffled his words. Again he raised his hands in greetings. Then asked for silence. There was silence.

—Babelandians: My heartfelt thanks to you for coming here. As always, it means you're on our side. That's the way it had to be. The Nation is at peace. Its problems are being solved. Everyone collaborates with us: our friends, sharing love, glory, and good fortune at our side; our enemies, beneath the earth, transformed into fertilizer. And at this moment, the Amautas, a little group of gangsters, want to sow panic and disorder! Can we permit that?. Never!

A new salvo of applause. New bravos. The Celebrated One went on:

—We have set a new rate of exchange. From this day forth, 10,000 Babelandian pesos to the dollar! Thus, for each piece of fruit, for each pound of raw material, for each liter of petroleum—that is, for everything we export—we'll receive mountains of pesos. And this at the very moment when these unprincipled and heartless fools have deprived us of the most heroic of our heroes, the redoubtable Jonas Pithecanthropus! Shall we stand by with folded arms? Never!

—Never!

The Dictator's elongated index finger increased its energy. It became a baton. A baton that had a life of its own.

—Because the overdeveloped countries disapprove of 200-mile limits, we're building an ocean within our own borders. An interior sea. We'll relocate all our natural marine resources there. So, whoever would dance, let him pay the piper. In other words, those who expect to exploit our underwater resources will be required to have their vessels transported into our country, to pay our tariffs, and to obey our laws. That way there'll be no reprisals, and we can continue importing more planes, ships, tanks, guns, missiles, technicians, etc. But in these wondrous times a little band of reprobates, of unpatriotic ones, corrupt politicians, are out to destroy our efforts. Can we tolerate their impunity? Never, but never!

—Never, but never!

More applause. More cheers. Two lights began to glimmer in Bony's eye sockets. His excitement had acted as an automatic pilot light, igniting his wicks. Each moment, he grew more euphoric. Now his index finger gave the impression of cramping itself into a tiny fencing foil.

—We have studied the digestive system of the boa constrictor. It feeds, as you know, just a few times a year. Well, then. I assure you that we are at the point of being able to apply this process in Babelandia. Thus, we Babelandians can put an end to the revolting, monotonous, and costly custom of eating three meals a day. We'll ingest food only from time to time. And, after each meal, we'll last a long, long time with our bellies full—full stomach, happy heart—without major problems. And now this terrible thing has happened! Those venemous enemies who hate progress and abhor the highest values of the nation . . . have kidnapped the Commander-in-Chief of our Armed Forces! They know that today—a day of glory for Bab—is this man's fiftieth birthday, one of the country's greatest assets. A half-century . . .

Did his voice fail him? The skeleton skittered to the left. Perhaps a heart attack? Would he fall? Was he falling? He bared his teeth. A smile? A galloping shiver spread through the plaza. Did those on the balcony also feel it? Couldn't they have moved closer to find out what was going on? The Orator realized his eye sockets were darkening. Would he fall asleep? Was he already asleep? Fortunately, he turned off the cassette in time. And then? Then. From deep within him surged something like music. It swelled, tingling his spine. Now it was tickling his cranium. No. It wasn't from within him. He was beginning to function like an antenna. Because of this, he was the first to hear that melody. The melody traveled on the winds. Broke out from the rooftops. From the crowns of the trees. From the church steeples. From the nearby hills. It grew and grew. Now all could hear. It filled their ears. It caressed their bodies. Overwhelmed them. Slowly the rhythm and the tune became clear. It was, of course, *Cavalleria Rusticana*. But where was it coming from? And why? For what purpose? Undoubtedly to drive Babelandia mad. Babelandia? No. Just him. And he—as the volume of the music swelled—was changing his posture. As if awakening from a brief slumber. Then he stared, terrified, in all directions. Raised his arms imploringly.

—Don't let them play it. Don't let them play it.

And who was playing it? His enemies? The souls of those he had sent prematurely to heaven or hell? God knows. Just as before in his office, he began a frenzied acrobatic dance. And disconcertedly, sheeplike, almost unconsciously—first on the balcony, then in the plaza—Holofernes' audience started imitating his movements, gestures, contortions, and steps. They reached a moment when—absolutely everyone—was dancing to the rhythm of Mascagni's score. Nevertheless, the music didn't last long. When it stopped, many sat down. Or lay down. Only a few remained standing. They felt dizzy. Couldn't figure out what had happened. Even though they had only done their duty, they were told they'd receive extra pay. They were delighted, body and soul. The only one who didn't seem fatigued—for him it had been a short dance—was Verbophile. He took the microphone to continue his harangue. Just to make sure, he tested his cassette. It worked perfectly. but something was wrong. The microphone was moving away. The Orator looked at it fixedly. Perplexed, he cocked his head. Made a short leap toward it, as if to take the apparatus by surprise. But it jumped the same distance. Then, with a longer leap and arms outstretched, Holofernes got closer. The microphone jumped symmetrically. The Dictator paused, with his finger on his forehead bone. Suddenly, as if to surprise the apparatus, he made a series of leaps. The pursued instrument did the same. Not content with that—like a deer in an open field—it began to run. The other was close behind. The chase moved first in one direction, then in another. Finally, it moved upward. It seemed that at any moment the Rosary of Bones—held erect by who knows what kind of magic—might spill out over the plaza. The onlookers were astonished, with their eyes frozen on this circus act. They were breathless. They were motionless. As if they had been transformed into a colossal group sculpture. Something made them even more tense. Eluding all his moves and calculations, the microphone was again free of Verbophile's grasp. Began to bounce off the heads of the demonstrators. Many of them tried, in vain, to seize it. But their timing was always off. The length and direction of the leaps was unpredictable. Soon it was no longer touching anyone's head. It bounded up onto the Palace roof. Stopped itself. And then four parrots flew down. Four absurd, ungainly parrots. Their deliberate, harmonized voices drilled the air:

—As ransom for Pithecanthropus, we demand the release of all political prisoners. Two hundred first-class funerals designated by us. And one pound of Holofernes' bones.

Ten

LUDIVINA now refused to see Eneas. Doña Prudencia was his only connection. Finally she told him:

—Don't you get the point? My daughter no longer wants to see you.

—Let me hear it from her.

She seemed to swell, like an irate toad. Could she tolerate such insults and humiliation? Would she allow such impertinence? Was this what she'd been preparing for so carefully and during so many years? Was this why she had struggled to seal the pact—green, sulfurous green, or sickish green—that had enmeshed her in a hypnotic spider's web? Ah no! I'll fight with all my cunning and strength. This poor devil—No, Devil, no! Not even in thought can I use that word!—That poor musical horsefly won't have his way with her, and least of all harm my daughter's future and my own. She fixed her beady eyes on him.

—Why don't you go away and leave us in peace?

—Not without seeing Ludi. Without her repeating everything you've said.

From inside the house came the girl's voice:

—My mother speaks the truth. It'll be the best for all.

—Give me a reason. A single reason.

—The reason is this. I don't want, don't wish to see you anymore.

Desperate, without hope of appeal—stupid automaton—one afternoon he presented himself at the vestry. Since there was no sexton—he had fled sometime ago, shrieking like a madman: "The Priest is not a priest; the Priest is Satan! Get another priest to say Mass! Give Polygamo a scrubbing with holy water!"—and the parish priest came to the door in person.

—Who is it?

—It's me, Eneas.

—Just a moment.

He received him coldly. Avoided his eyes. Didn't invite him in. Much less to sit down.

—What can I do for you?

—I wish you might, as Ludivina's godfather . . .

—What?

—Intercede with her and her mother.

The Cleric—with a monastic air, and completely poised—appeared to soften. A sarcastic thought tickled his mind: "Idiot. You're inviting the rat to guard the cheese." He bowed his head. Made a sign. Not the Sign of the Cross, to be sure. He smiled affably:

—Calm down! Be seated! And tell me more!

The organist in a few words told him all that had happened. The priest—despite an urge to dance a high step—advised:

—For the time being, do what they say. Stay away for a while. Who knows what reasons or troubles they have! For I myself, contrary to what I would hope, have heard nothing.

—But . . .

—I'll try to find out. As soon as I hear something, I'll let you know.

He arose. It was another sign. Was it an evil one? Maybe it was. Self-absorbed, Eneas thought nothing of it. Extended his right hand. Took that of the Priest. Drew it to his lips to kiss. But the priest—who knows why?—quickly withdrew it. The Organist thanked him. Or did he just think he thanked him? Outside he had a strange sensation, in flashback. The hand. The hand he was going to kiss. Burning. And it was green. It was a burning green hand. He had left in a daze. Meanwhile, the Priest, for his part, was writhing in laughter. Was transformed into laughter that climbed the walls. As far as the ceiling. On which it strolled. Guffaws. Soon the bed: laughter. On which it strolled. The chair: laughter. The Table: laughter. Everything was convulsive interminable laughter. As if the air had been inoculated with this strident, uncontrollable mirth. But in town it was business as usual. The silly wave of gossip had scarcely begun to ripple.

—Polygamo still visits his goddaughter.

—Can the bird already be singing in that cage?

—Maybe. As the saying goes,

Happy is the monk
With his woman,
His chocolate
And his bunk.

—Do you think so?

—Don't you?

—The girl is naive.

—The mother, an opportunist.

—Would she deliver her own daughter?

—Only she can answer that.

—And the Organist?

—That's it. And the Organist?

At this point Eneas scarcely spoke to the bell ringer. On certain days he was unable to play the organ. He walked around aimlessly, bumping into people and things. Sometimes he set out for the countryside. In the lap of the wild landscape, he felt better than with people. Disenchanted with everything, he longed to be a ship adrift on an unknown course. To live at the margins of all shores. To keep moving. Never to arrive. On occasion, something in the far distance seemed to hold out a hand: he would watch Gleam and Maria, hand in hand, endlessly walking. Since they were moving constantly away from the world of everyday things, they were unaware of his tribulations. One fine day they greeted him. He responded as if they were old friends. And weren't they? He had often seen them at church or in town. On another occasion, looking up, he saw two condors flying. At first, he noticed nothing unusual. Then, yes. He could see that one of them was carrying Maria in its claws, and the other, Gleam. He felt a sudden anxiety. Was it a kidnapping? Were they being exiled to the mountain tops above the clouds? Would they be devoured? How had it happened? Should he cry out? Or go look for a shotgun? The word and image "shotgun" vibrated in his mind. "Shotgun-shotgun-shotgun . . . " But there was no time. He should have seen them taking off, in the clutches of those giant, majestic birds. His fear calmed when the condors landed near him and he could hear Gleam's and Maria's voices. Voices that merged. Musical. Intimate.

—Goodbye, Eneas!

—Goodbye, Eneas!

They were smiling and waved affectionately.

—Goodbye, Maria! Goodbye, Gleam!

The following day there were three condors. When Eneas least expected it, one flew down. It clutched his shoulders and carried him off—together with the impossible lovers—to lofty heights. Soon, far below, where the church with its steeples, bell ringer, and cleric. Far below: Labyrinthia, Ludivinia, Prudencia, the little houses, the winding streets, life entwined from beginning to end with digestions and possessions rather than with being. Meanwhile, Labyrinthians lost sight of them for not an instant. There was a tacit agreement among them: flying itself was of no importance. But if they landed in any out-of-reach place, immediate action would be taken against Gleam.

Ten

The Bell Ringer's drunkenness was intensifying. He no longer needed to imbibe much liquor. Just to see the bottles, to smell them at a distance, sufficed to kindle his "sacred inner fire." He seldom climbed the belltower. He hardly ever rang the bells. When he did, it was counterproductive. His alcoholic daze seemed to infect them. They tolled anarchic, capricious, dissonant sounds. Since all the townspeople lived haphazardly, they failed to notice—or did not wish to notice, or simply didn't care—whether the great bells were silent or going like the devil. Moreover, the confirmed drunkard talked less often with Eneas. And when he did, it wasn't a dialog, but two disparate monologs. Each lost himself in his own itinerary of phrases. And the talks were shorter. Agapetus wandered whole days and nights through the streets and plazas. He stopped at the taverns. Sometimes accepted a drink. But he wouldn't rest. Seemed obsessed with renewing his dusty pilgrimage. Urchins no longer followed him in little groups but in swarms. They circled like relentless horseflies: "Cagapito! Cagapito!" He seemed indifferent to them. Didn't even try to wave them away. Absorbed in himself—in an absurd nirvana of the alcohol he had drunk—he tumbled on, a living wave of fermenting rum. When they saw him coming, women crossed themselves and scurried off. For their part, however, the men tried to listen from a distance. Because this was so—he kept his internal earthquake within—he went on talking, talking, talking. His discourse was a strange mixture of dream and reality. Speaking in any other town, he never would have been understood. On the other hand, in Labyrinthia everyone's life and miracles were known from A to Z. Accordingly, his pronouncements were quite informative. In the snarled network of his thought he knew that the truth was always partly visible. This began to cause them fear and concern. The bell ringer left them "stark naked." Even if they already knew almost everything he revealed, they reacted to their neighbors' behavior with a hypocritical combination of tolerance and collusion. Strangely, these sentiments, expressions, and ideas were jumbled in Agapetus' mind like a kind of Easter-week *potpourri*. His deficient reading, the priest's sermons, his conversations with Eneas, church life, the Labyrinthians . . . everything was complicated and confused. He had exchanged the name of the town for another: Sodom. In total disregard for the implications of the word, he called the inhabitants Sodomites. "Sodomites!"—he would bellow—"It will rain fire and shit on your evildoing." Few would escape that *sui-generis* inundation. Their Sodom would be punished like Gomorrah, Zeboim, and Admah. No stone would remain on a stone, nor any bone joined to a bone. All were condemned to disappear, to drown in a boiling lava of excrement. Then he'd identify them all, one by one. Only then, it seemed, would the townfolk begin to show their natural individualities. How would it be possible—he thundered—to keep anything from Epifanio San Toro. One of this hippopotamus' schemes for getting rich had been to stick his huge thumb in the liter measuring jar, thereby preserving for himself part of the milk he sold. And now he had other people's cows killed, so as to eliminate all his milking competition. This way he could charge whatever price he wanted. As owner of all properties for several kilometers around, he could obtain a lifetime rent from whoever built a house . . . How could the political boss Domitilo Mercenario avoid becoming an ignorant flaming turd? The business he ran was good for nothing. Nevertheless, he took advantage of everything. He spontaneously created new laws. For braying at midnight, for example, he was able to jail the donkey's owner. Then the victim had to pay a bribe or do forced labor on the most perilous mountain heights. But this wasn't all: Single-testicled and impotent, he would often retire at dawn with some of the local vagrants. Who knows what he did with them or he had done to them. The truth is that they would wake up lying in the streets, drugged, and their clothing torn to pieces . . . How could the Highest One let the syphilitic Lindorio Necrópolo, owner of the only funeral parlor around, continue to circulate? In connivance with the doctor—and the officials of Sodom, of course—he exhumed instead of interring. Or at best he did both. Burying by day and digging up by night. Then the following day he'd give a thousand excuses to the relatives and heirs of the deceased. Especially to the more ignorant. He told them, among other things, that souls in purgatory, vampires, thieves, devils, and any others so inclined, would open the graves and leave the dead—unprotected by shroud or casket—lying on the ground. Consequently a new burial had to be paid for and silence maintained in order to prevent gossip. But that wasn't enough for Necrópolo. As a partner of San Toro—and what influential Sodomite was not?—he shared ownership of a fertilizer factory that produced bone meal from cows. If there were many deaths, "in order to find a place for a newly deceased," he removed older corpses from their graves. And ground them into a mixture of cow bonemeal . . . How was the Lord going to let Quíndolo Sheepbang, whose origins were unknown because so many could have been his father, circulate freely? Unprotected by any of his possible progenitors, he drifted about playing a rustic flute, splattering slaver and disconnected melodies to the four winds. Then, almost naked, he took pleasure from his notorious masturbations in public places, or from slicing off the paws of stray dogs, leaving them to hobble away spurting blood from their mangled stumps . . . How could the Almighty possibly allow the survival of Pepita San Toro, the most widowish of all widows in Sodom? To be sure, this did not constitute a sin; rather, it was cause for pity. But Pepita was a prize pip. Despite being Epifanio's only child and sole heir, she was not sought by suitors. Ostensibly, out of fear of her father, someone should have submitted to the marital yoke. But fear of the daughter surpassed fear of the father. Besides, the latter didn't concern himself with the problems of Pepita's pip. At first, however, he did try to place his heifer in good hands. The first time he was euphoric. He wasn't very rich yet. And Pepita was a delectable dish. The chosen one was Cantharidos, a young apprentice in the albescent cheese business. As expected, he got along famously with the rotund cattleman. The young girl, for her part, was wild about her fiancé. Soon there were nuptials, and supernuptials as malicious tongues would have it, which overexcited the female partner. So much so that she was determined to repeat what had happened at the Wedding of Cana. Except that, in place of the bread and wine, she kept trying to multiply "that." Cantharidos did what he could, burning up in a few days all his lifetime quota of energy. Result: the first widowhood of the insatiable one, followed over a few years by many widowings. That is, in the period that her uterine fever grew and grew. But then it diminished, as one by one the adventurers dropped off . . . How could the Great Lawmaker prevent the flames from consuming Polygamo? By day he anathematized lewd women, the temptresses who had made from their bodies a bridge across Lake Avernus. But by night he closed the temple and turned out the lights. He drank the sacred wine. Lowered the images from the altars. And danced like a madman with them. That was just the beginning. Then with a few leaps he left the church. Fleshly entertainment was what he really craved. With the same females he had condemned in his sermons. That might explain why his phallus was growing longer and longer. Otherwise he might have walked less awkwardly. The phallus interfered with his legs. Made a pup tent of his cassock. Struggled to get out in whatever way it could. Weaving through the narrow streets—wrapped in his cloak of alcohol, fever, and fantasy, Agapetus kept on talking. Most of the Labyrinthians turned down their radios and cocked their ears to hear him better, crouched behind their windows, spying at him through the curtains. Those who came off worst stewed in their indignation, rage, and fear. When people met—in nocturnal retreats or in bars—the talk would come out. They carried on dialogs that might have begun years before. It wasn't necessary to mention the subject matter. In one way or another they were involved in his game.

—Who could have believed he'd get into that?

—That's the way it is. That's his pretext for saying what he says. But drunkenness is not an excuse. No drunk eats fire.

—But he's right about some things.

—Might always makes right. And around here he has the might.

—But he's right about the priest. Have you seen how fast the thing that's growing is really growing?

—Who hasn't seen it?

—Only the organist.

—Well. He who won't look can't see.

—A lot of people are changing. Going to Mass less. Not speaking to the priest. Sometimes they even turn their backs on him.

—Shouldn't we do something about it?

—About the Priest? God help us! Anyway, he's one of us.

—That's so.

—And the only problem is his virility.

—Virility? It's not just that. But who cares? Anyway, he knows very well how to ask. Or how to get it without asking. As long as he doesn't interfere with us and with what concerns us . . .

—You're right.

There was a pause. They looked at each other knowingly. Evil intentions toward the bell ringer phosphoresced in all their minds. They imagined numerous possibilities: They would tie him to the bell clapper by his feet. That way, in his desperate swinging to and fro the bell would go on tolling and no one would hear his words. Or they could carry him off to the sugar mill, grind him up with the cane, and convert him to rum. Or maybe coax him up into the tower, and there give him a shove to scatter him—words and bones—over the churchyard below . . . Finally somebody who was more realistic said:

—Somehow we'll have to fix his pecker.

—You mean his kisser.

—What's the difference, so long as he doesn't stir up the waters he's muddied.

—And if we threaten him?

—He'd just laugh at us. Would shout it to the four winds.

—And already he's taken Clench Tremolo, Maria's father, under his wing.

—Father?

—We have to call him something.

—Certainly. And—if he's telling the truth—we won't stand for it. Nobody's going to take our miracle away.

They lowered their voices.

—Nobody? How about Gleam?

—We'll have to put him to rest.

—Meanwhile it looks as though neither he nor Maria is resting. We'd better not be late.

—Let's hope not. Right now the bell ringer is the biggest danger to our good consciences.

—Right. The Bell Ringer!

The Bell Ringer. One fine day—or horrible day—he woke up sober. Sober and mute. The Bell Ringer. All Labyrinthia was startled to encounter him. They were paralyzed with fear. The poor man was in the Plaza, hair disheveled, eyes agog, legs trembling. He was clutching his throat. He was surrounded as soon as he was recognized. The Bell Ringer. Panic. Then silence. Even the street beggars suspended their cat calls. The Bell Ringer. All eyes were fixed on him. Blood spurted from his mouth. In a torrent. The Bell Ringer. His lips moved, trying to speak. But only a weak gurgle was heard. He pointed his right hand. With his index finger he pointed accusingly at everyone. Then he opened his mouth. Showed it as evidence. His tongue was missing. Did this only for a few seconds. Broke into a run. An absurd trance kept the crowd from following. Or maybe they didn't want to. The Bell Ringer. He ran down the main street. He was becoming smaller and smaller and smaller until he disappeared over the horizon. Minutes passed. Hours. The whole day. The night. The following day. Only then did they begin to realize: the Bell Ringer had been silenced. Of course. And the bells had been silenced along with him. That meant that all Labyrinthia had been silenced.

Harpitune was up on the Palace roof. She appeared neither at breakfast, nor on the balcony. She preferred to watch the spectacle from where she was. Besides her, Melopea—all phosphorescent green eyes—began to poke out her head. They didn't want to miss a trick. But, faced with the ransom talks, their tenseness gave in to their emotions. The anticipated upheaval rocked all four cardinal points. Still, over it all, came Warhorse's voice:

—For one of them, alive, 100,000 pesos!

Automatic weapons blazed. Bullets whistled. Sticks, rocks, and tree branches flew. The snakes and apes clung to the Palace columns, trying to catch the impromptu orators' phrases, but to no avail. Four emerald flashes flew, becoming four green points. Four gray dots. Then nothing. Harpitune felt the heat of infuriated voices rising. She clasped the Constrictor's cold neck.

—Poor Holito. How he'll suffer!

—We all will suffer.

—He's willing to pay.

—It'll be difficult now.

—Very difficult, dear. Even accepting the other conditions, how could he sacrifice his bones? He needs them so much. They're all he has.

—Don't worry. That ransom's impossible. It must be a joke. Besides, who can obligate your husband?

—Oh, you don't know him, Melo. He thinks he's Christ. Nothing's too much for the Fatherland. That's why he let Sinbad go. Now I'll bet he's already deciding which bones he'll give up.

And so he was. The Dictator dismissed his Cabinet. They understood. Maybe they were glad. He needed peace to make plans. They would reconvene later. When they could make a rational assessment—rational?—of these unprecedented occurrences. Only the faithful Groveler remained at Holofernes' side. When they were alone, the two of them examined each other silently, without moving. Finally, the Chief stretched out on his desk. His index finger on his frontal bone, pensively.

Later, the half-skeleton arose. He looked—could he see in the semidarkness?—at his docile companion.

—What are you thinking, Bacchy?

The latter scratched his head. As if digging for some idea. It was in vain. Only a plateful of food danced in his mind. He stammered:

—Me? Nothing, your Excellency.

—Can the message be true?

—Who knows, Excellency?

Another silence. Verbophile broke it:

—Let's suppose it is. The first two conditions are negotiable. But the pound of bones is up to me. Which bones should I offer?

—It's a hard choice, your Excellency.

—Think about it.

The homunculus sat on the ground. A pocket edition of Rodin's Thinker. He grew weary. He slumped. Sleep was overcoming him when Bony got down from the desk. He came over. Shook him.

—Have you thought of something?

—No, your Excellency.

—Think!

Harpitune entered. Without her boa. Right away she blurted:

—Not an ounce of your bones, right?

—The nation's honor is in peril.

—And only you can save it. If you can scarcely manage now, with all your bones, what would you do with a pound less? Besides, if you lose any of what little you have, what will be left?

He looked into her eyes firmly, affectionately. But he was adamant.

—All you say is useless.

—She didn't give up.

—Free the political prisoners. Concede the two hundred first-class funerals. Maybe that's best for your country and for you. But none of your bones. I won't allow it, now or ever.

The Dictator moved closer. Extended his long humeri, radii, and metacarpals. He fondled her hair with all his metacarpals.

—Why prolong this painful and useless argument? Instead why don't you help me choose the bones I need the least.

Surprisingly, his spouse then remembered Melopea. Just for a moment. And right away, she began to cry.

—It was enough punishment to lose my son Sinbad and to be left with a pile of bones for a husband. Now I'll be losing these as well.

The Skeleton was confused. But he soon transcended, in spite of himself, his "insignificant domestic problems."

—Weep if it does you good, Harpie. But if I mean anything to you, tell me what bones I can give up.

Babelandia's First Lady got hold of herself. Dried her tears as well as she could. Let her head fall back. She shook the luxuriant wig covering her own meager sprigs. Breathed deeply. As if inhaling optimism.

—All right, Holie. Even though he deserves

nothing, especially after what he did to us, if there's no other way, let it be as you wish. But . . .

—What?

She took one more spoonful of poise. She half-smiled.

—I have a proposition for you.

—Well?

—Why does it have to be your bones? Couldn't we send them somebody else's?

Index finger on forehead.

—Not a bad idea.

The finger came down.

—And if the trick were discovered?

A candid vanity transformed his maxillae.

—I don't believe it. My bones are unique.

—While they were investigating, we'd gain time, Holie. The Kidnapped One would be freed. It would be simple. We'd confiscate the remains of someone who happened to die at the time we needed them.

—Or an enemy of ours could die.

—Right. But remember. Your worst enemy is Jonas Pithecanthropus. This would be an opportunity to do away with him.

—Are you at it again, Harpie?

—All right then. Forget Pithy. Will you take my advice?

—As you wish. You could be right. That way we'd all be satisfied.

—And whole.

The hot-line telephone rang. Bacchus the Groveler answered. He turned to the Dictator:

—Are you here, Excellency?

—No, not for anyone.

The other repeated into the phone:

—He's not here for anyone.

Then he turned pale and faced the Dictator:

—It's . . . The Amautas!

—Ah! I'll take it.

He turned to his wife with an air of triumph.

—Now they'll get an earful!

He gripped the phone. He'd make a speech. But there wasn't time. A severe voice came from the other end of the line:

—We're listening. You'd never guess where we have microphones. Even on your own body. Wake up! *Your* bones are the ones we want. Listen to us! We'll remove them ourselves. From the choicest places. You have until tomorrow to fix up your affairs. Twenty-four hours.

Ten

If that day they had wrung out the newspapers, Babelandia would have been flooded with their tears. As people picked them up to read, the printed surfaces quickly wrinkled. They became desolate, weeping countenances. There was mourning crepe on every page. Radio and TV joined in. In place of words and images, they released soothing, melancholy intonations. The City also joined their chorus. The bells gargled metallic, sobbing sighs. The steeples of the churches curved beneath the weight of the collective bereavement. The crowns of the trees swept the earth like colossal brooms of sorrow. Babelandians—in black clothing, black mourning, black speech—walked on tiptoe over their bitterness. Some fasted—irony of ironies—and many abstained from such biological pleasures as shellfish consumed with alcohol and extramarital sex. The news—a mongrelization of scorpions and bats—besieged all receptive ears. The news multiplied. Besides appearing in the usual places, it sprang up in the bars, drugstores, barber shops, clubs, WCs, etc. Its pestilential wings began to intrude beneath ladies' skirts. Its glittering eyes in dark corners of houses and automobiles. Its poison oozed from the churchyards and from the tongues of vipers. Sometimes its hairy legs tickled the noses of the commentators themselves. News grew out of the streets, squares, and buildings. News.

—Guess what? The Kidnapped General has been converted to a toy top.

—What do you mean?

—They have him spinning on his ass. They give him a kick in the head or on his feet to make him twirl.

—It's a lie. Nobody knows anything.

—It's what they say. Also, they're using him as a bridge.

—Explain that one.

—Over a crack opened up by the last volcanic eruption. He grips one edge with his hands; the other with his feet. Anybody who wants to cross walks over him. If he bends or folds, everybody ends up in hell.

—That's not true.

—No?

—He's a candlestick.

—Candlestick?

—A candle holder or candelabra—whatever you call it. They undress him. Ass-end up. Stick an Easter candle in it. Then sit there and talk by its light.

—Who?

—Who? The Amautas!

—And will their conditions be met?

—Could be. To release the prisoners is easy. Just as easy as putting them behind bars again.

—And the two hundred cadavers?

—That's a hairy one. The dead remain dead. There's no way to revive them.

—Who are the candidates?

—I suppose the parasites of Bab.

—Hurrah!

—Are you tired of living? Shut up!

—You're right. There are plenty of reptiles among us . . .

—But the one who suffers most may be the Dic.

—Of course, he has to give what they're asking for.

—If not, the government will crumble.

—More? Everything around here is crumbling already.

Eleven

SPONGY Sumptuoso had spent the night on a stormy sea of anxiety. He was a farcical pygmy. About as wide as he was tall, he gave the impression of a small, pregnant elephant. He moved slowly, dragging his feet, wiggling his buttocks. He had seen fifty autumns, but he looked thirty. Pink-cheeked, puffy, virtually hermaphroditic, with a baby's smile and pudgy, milk-white hands, he seemed bread for the eating. But his manner was deceptive. The midget was never flustered. His smile was permanent. As were the timid nun's emanations from his larynx. On the other hand, he never gave way in his decisions. And they were always important. Downright crucial to the high life of the city. Spongy Sumptuoso was no more and no less than the owner of the Boll Weevil Club. The

Boll Weevil Club was the snootiest, snottiest, sneeriest in Babelandia. He had ordered Narcissus Vaselino to report to him extra-early. This puny youth, excited by that ambivalent person's presence, had been carried away and had given Spongy Sumptuoso two big kisses—one on each cheek. The Caressed One, in an innocent sugary voice with dark overtones, replied:

—Behave yourself, don Sissy.

He stepped unsyncopatedly to a sort of St. Vitus' dance. Restrained himself. Then all his movements and gestures became crisp and precise, as befitted his severe manner. He drew closer:

—Excuse me, don Spongy. I couldn't control myself.

A smile interrupted—in the middle of his words—the Fat One's mouth:

—I understand, don Sissy.

Still smiling, he changed the subject.

—Now let's get down to business. Is the priority list ready?

—Here it is.

He handed over a little paper scroll. Took it without reading it. Then he looked it over, with its candy smudges. He moved his head from side to side with the rhythm of a fan.

—You'll have to make a new one.

—Vaselino's gaze dimmed.

—It just can't be, don Spongy. The party's tomorrow. It took me a week to prepare that list. There's no time left. Ten thousand people.

The smile of the club-man-woman* was accentuated.

—Ten thousand five hundred.

He breathed heavily.

—Ten thousand five hundred?

—Yes, five hundred signed up at the last moment.

Vaselino quivered. He had dampened the southwest corner of his fly. With a leap, he embraced the tiny one. Nestled his chin on his cottony shoulder.

—Oh, no, Spongy Sumptuoso, no! . . . Let this chalice pass from me.

Spongy fondled the hair as greasy as his companion's name.

—Oh yes, Narcissus Vaselino, yes!

The Chief of Protocol broke away from the owner of the Boll Weevil Club. His professional demeanor returned. He tilted his head. Maintained his imperturbability.

—Then tell me.

Spongy's smile was like a honeycomb. With dimples in his appled cheeks. His baby brown eyes were narrowed to a squint. His minivoice had something of a pig's caress.

—It's not really the crowd that matters. There's food for all. Besides, two can eat as well as one. Imagine! Here it's a matter of making do with just a little more. As for drink, there'll be plenty.

**Translator's Note*: "Club-man-woman" in the original.

And if we run short, we'll repeat the miracle—naturally without a miracle—of the Biblical Wedding! Our real problem is something else: the size of this place.

—Absolutely. If magic was needed to fit them all in the Garden Terrace before, how can we handle five hundred more now?

—Come and see.

Vaselino suppressed the fury building within him. Cradling his elbows and standing erect, he had placed himself on the left side. Tilted his shining head far back.

—After you.

Soon they arrived at the place. Vaselino couldn't believe his eyes. Wasn't he pulling the leg of Mini-Pudge? Tables and chairs covered the floor. Of course, even though they seemed crowded together, one on top of the other, this was understandable because of the size of the festival crowd. Less understandable was what hung from the trees. Suspended from one tree to another by what looked like thick steel cables were platforms with still more tables and chairs. Dominating it all from the highest treetop was the biggest of them, loaded with furniture. Spongy's smile, meanwhile, had changed strangely. he displayed vanity and self-assurance.

—What do you think?

—I don't think I get it.

—It's a very simple matter. Since there isn't room for all the guests on the ground, we'll place some of them at aerial tables over the branches, or hanging from them. And General Pithecanthropus will have a chance to show off his acrobatic accomplishments.

—Not a bad idea. But there's something I don't get.

—What?

—How will the guests get up there?

—The Fire Department will lend us extension ladders.

—And the waiters? How will they be able to serve?

—We've hired stilt men.

—Stilt men?

—They walk on stilts.

—I see everything's been attended to.

—Everything.

—And the highest table of all. Is it for the the presidential party?

—Right. General Pithecanthropus will be there. His Excellency, Verbophile; Rigoletto; Warhorse; Wincewing; Neptuno Río del Río; Hotwheels, etc., etc. In a word, the Babelandian Government in plenary session.

There was a pause. Narcissus broke it:

—And when do you need the precedence list?

—By dawn.

—Impossible!

Spongy got out a thousand peso bill. Vaselino of the Prostatocolo extended his left hand, palm upturned. Received the money. Pocketed it.

—Difficult.

He was looking now at two thousand-peso bills. He did the same as before. Then, more sweetly:

—Perhaps!

Three bills of a thousand appeared. This time he practically snatched them from the pudgy hands.

—It's a deal!

Eleven

As the sun rose, Jonas Pithecanthropus began to recognize his surroundings. Was he, as he deduced, inside or on the edge of a volcanic crater? The night before it had seemed the cage was floating in space. Maybe over an abyss. Wrong. It was on the ledge of a huge amphitheater of rock. How did he get there? Walking was impossible. He had a clear recollection that when following the banana trail he had ended back on a street. Or had it just seemed that way? Was it an open tunnel in the city? Was it one of those underground passages built by clerics in colonial times from one convent to another? But how could they have covered such great distances to reach this place? Well? Had they carried him, cage and all, for several hours? Who? In what way? Why hadn't he noticed? Or had they just dragged him? He looked up. The big opening was far above. But then the cage undoubtedly was very heavy. Could they have lowered it on pulleys? Had it been flown from the city to the inside of this mountain? Or had the same thing happened as with the printing press? Were the University students—who else could it have been—also controlling all objects? Or had these assumed a life of their own and begun to operate in his behalf? In that case, the cage with him inside had been moving on its own. Afflicted by a sudden superstitious panic, he looked quickly around. At the moment he was alone. All around him rose hostile walls like the ghostly circles of some macrocosmic amphitheater. And in the middle there was emptiness. An awesome emptiness showing through shrouds of mist. His hair bristled. He had never been near a volcano. Much less climbed its heights. Not even a little one. Much less had he thought of looking down into a crater. All to the contrary, in his memory the presence of these monsters of the earth had always evoked terror. He returned in memory to other epochs nearly vanished from his past. When he was still a resident of snarled, dark green regions. When the specter of a volcano conjured up feelings of desolation, defeat, and catastrophe. Colossal tremors in the jungle. Subterranean thunder striving to transmit its vibrations to all things and beings. Fire erupting in the mineral, vegetable, and zoomorphic fusion of hot tidal waves of lava. One aim; his only aim: escape. To flee the murderous embrace of an infernal stream. The whole family together, if it were somehow possible, or individually if it were not, crashing through the emerald thickets. His father in the lead "Uuuuaaa! Uuuuaaa!" With his black body illuminated by an immense flaming river, a gigantic rainbow-scaled serpent trying to clutch at everything. "Uuuaaa!" Not coils, but countless howling claws of flame, snatching at everything. "Uuuuaaa! Uuuuaa! Uuaa!" Suddenly his panic was very urgent. And if I'm dropped on the burning coals? And if this volcano is not burned out? If its guts begin to churn? If it vomits its incandescent minerals? If its angry explosions destroy my ears? If it breaks loose, pulverizing me? How could I get away? There'd be no escape. These sons of whores have me in a fix. Their threats were nothing compared to what they've actually done. He moved up to the bars. He shook them with all his might. He shinnied up them. He threw himself like a giant trapped wasp against the sides of his cage, as if trying to wreck it.

—God damn! Get me out of here! God damn!

Was he going crazy? He seemed to hear some music. Yes. Those bastards are driving me crazy. Who knows whether they gave me something last night? Maybe that's why I can't remember anything. Surely some kind of drug. The music was getting louder. No. I'm perfectly sane, and in control of my faculties. That's music all right. A popular song. He gazed anxiously in the direction from which it was coming. One almost followed another. Just a few steps from the cage, tilted against the rock wall, was a loudspeaker. That was encouraging. He calmed down, moving as close as he could to the apparatus. He grasped the bars. Listening intently. The music stopped. An announcer's voice came on. Golden Ace himself. It was a report in detail of the festivities in the main square of Babelandia. He listened, hypnotized, until the moment that the four giant parrots set forth the Amautas' conditions for his release. So these are the imbeciles that have kidnapped me! He despaired. What would they give in exchange for me? They might set those prisoners free. And maybe Holofernes would be willing to sacrifice a pound of his bones. But, two hundred first-class burials? Not a chance!

Nobody would expose himself to possible death at the choosing of the Amautas. Anything but that! They'd rather let me rot here in my cage. A victim of the tortures they told me about last night. Including the worst of them all: the torture of Tantalus before the bananas. What chance is there then? What can I do in this cage, hopelessly isolated from my army? Sit here with crossed arms while they make a fool of me? No. There must be some way out. But what? How? At least I can try something. Screaming louder than the first time:

—Get me out of here, goddamit! I'll give you what you want! Do whatever you say! Get me out of here!

He heard a slight noise. He peered toward it. Goose pimples again. The hair of his pom-pom was on end, as if drawn by a magnet. Something unprecedented was happening. Was it an earthquake? Was it the eruption of the volcano that he hoped for? No, it was something else. Before his eyes the rocks were stretching, as if made of modeling clay. Little by little they came to resemble a bas relief. Finally, the wall itself opened. Several individuals emerged from it. Most of them stopped at a distance. Only two approached him. More exactly, neared the cage. The taller one spoke:

—Did you sleep well, General?

He remembered the first voice from the night before. Was about to respond with one of his customary insults. Held himself back. As a part of the plan he was devising, self-control was essential. His fur—as was the case every time he became human again—lightened in color and began to disappear. He forced a smile.

—Just fine. The bed is magnificent.

Then the other one, whose voice he also recognized, asked a question that shook him.

—Are you hungry?

—No, I'm full.

—Sure you wouldn't like a banana?

Undoubtedly they were applying the dreaded torture. Would he react? Would he insult them? I'll tell them to screw their whoring mothers. Would that get him anywhere? At least he'd let off some steam. Self-control, Jonas Pithecanthropus. Self-control. Don't forget who you are, or where you are. Damn it, how discreet I am. But what's happening? Is the fear getting to me? You *are* afraid, General Pithecanthropus. Admit it. Can my balls be shrinking? He got control again. Even if I'm crippled with fear, I won't show it. But maybe I'm not afraid. Maybe I'm just obsessed by the idea of having bananas shoved under my nose without being able to eat them. Probably last night was just a threat. Maybe they've had second thoughts. And realize how dangerous it is to fool around with me. He straightened up as much as he could. Which wasn't very much. That was one of his problems. He almost always oscillated, as if trying to balance himself with his hands. Now he forced another smile.

—You know. I'd die for a banana.

The first one to speak turned to the others:

—The General's bananas.

His subordinates moved toward the rocks, which began to stretch again. They split apart. Bunches of bananas appeared there. They were lifted and brought closer. The fruit was deposited a few steps from the cage. They left.

—A promise is a debt.

Instinctively Pithecanthropus pressed against the bars. He stretched out his arms. As far as he could. Still knowing that it was useless. He stretched. Stretched. A half-inch more and he'd have the bananas. Half an inch more. Just half an inch. Half. But enough to establish a barrier of hunger between his stomach and the fruit.

Twelve

GLEAM and Eneas peered over the edge of the crater. There, far down, they could see Pithecanthropus in his cage. The Amautas surrounded him. The snow shell covering the peak throbbed with colors.

(Gleam had noticed that Theophilus Bright was growing in his memory. From which his world and his life rose up like an apparition. I can still see him. I was going into the church when Theophilus and Polygamo—was it really Polygamo? Or wasn't it? It looked like him. In his recollection, at least—they were fighting. Bright was a mestizo. Tall and bony. Long-armed. With deep, dark circles under his eyes. Eyes of a condor. He too was a priest. As he returned the blows, he explained: he only wanted to say mass. To communicate to the faithful something that could illuminate their minds and hearts. The Gospel was the same. Its meaning had hardly changed. Since he had just returned from the Other Life, he knew that the "Lord's Path" was the right one.)

In the distance, the lamentation of the Babelandians could be heard. A lamentation of conflicting values. Large or small, true or false, depending on one's point of view. A kaleidoscopic basket of vipers or birds.

(Just then, Eneas appeared. Together they forced the combatants apart. They could see that the other priest—was it really Polygamo?—was seething with rage. He pointed at Theophilus and accused him of madness: for assuming that there could be fewer poor people in the world as well as less poverty. And, by the same token, that the rich could be fewer and also less rich. Well, maybe just fewer rich people. Pure demagogy. Was it not clear proof of his madness? For safety's sake, he'd been confined to the villages nearest the jungle. There he revealed further madness: a regeneration of the savages. They'd learn to read, to write, to cultivate the earth, to live under a roof, to cover their nudity, to drink fewer fermented beverages, to fight for their smallest rights. He even expected the bureaucrats and the land owners to be kind and tolerant with the Indians. And still worse: he wanted religion to undertake all this as its main endeavor. To worry about something besides eternal salvation. To make more of this life than of the hereafter. Or at least as much about one as the other. Of course, he was prohibited from exercising his ministry.)

Gleam was in a reminiscent mood. In the remote blue distances, he seemed to find the lost images he was searching for. It was as if he had come to life once again.

(The mestizo priest was crestfallen. Still, he begged again for permission to say mass. The other denied him. Then he asked to borrow the pulpit. Explained that he could say many things that should be known. I exchanged looks with Eneas. Could his madness be real? Bright's rival wasn't mad. It was not just Polygamo. He was hundreds of Polygamos in one—he insulted him with a new term, "apostate." "Crazy Apostate," driven from town after town. Now he'd be a missionary only to the middle of the jungle. Theophilus tried to explain his situation. One day his boat sank in the Amazon. He was devoured by piranhas, together with his companions from the shipwreck. But only he was allowed to return to the world of the living.)

The sun climbed the horizon on its bier of fire. Highlighted great banks of clouds. The ridges of snow were like a procession of macrocosmic alpacas. Down in the crater, clusters of bananas encircled the cage like an enormous golden sunflower suspended over the abyss.

(The parish priest won in the end: Theophilus could neither say mass nor use the pulpit. He was limited to a small hill. There he began to sermonize. Even that was a failure. His adversary organized everyone against him. The fanatics, the pressure groups, the gluttons, and the idiots supported him. Assiduously repeated the accusation of the epithet "crazy apostate." Furthermore, he explained that Bright had been excommunicated. Had worked against God, the Virgin, and the Saints. And clearly also against the people. Wanted no one to be saved. No one to worry about original sin. Heaven and hell could meet right here, as if they were man-made creations. Thus he reduced the importance of a real Hell with its eternal flames. The crowd was infuriated. It howled. It rushed the visiting priest. He tried to reason with them. They would not let him. Eneas and I stepped in to calm the most excited ones. In vain. The hostile priest continued inciting them. Some one bent down. Grabbed a stone. He threw it at Theophilus, who stood his ground. He didn't try to defend himself. Another stone. A trickle of blood on his broad forehead. More stones. Ten, twenty, fifty? We tried to shield him with our bodies. Dissenting from their ancient orthodoxy, we asserted that to us it seemed he was neither an apostate nor a madman. He simply wanted a more direct understanding with God. In vain. Now they also attacked us. Called us infidels and traitors. Stones rained on us too. They pressed closer to us. They formed a kind of monolithic block. We no longer felt the blows. Nor the noise. Nor the shouts. Only numbness. Our senses atrophied. Our human limits had merged with the mineral limits. For how long? How long did it last? Time was meaningless. Did we sleep through it? Was it a temporary withdrawal from conscious life? Suddenly we were free of the stones. We were our organic selves again. It was night. Night. Night. Immense solitude engulfed us. Solitude encircled by interminable strings of stars. We felt a release from our petrified existence. Were men once more. Free yet limited, like all other men. Eneas and I—united again, and of one voice—looked at each other and wondered mutely about the impassioned mestizo cleric. Then from the depths of the crater—we had already risen to the summit of the volcano—came a deep, intense, fraternal voice. It was Theophilus. Theophilus Bright. There he was, eternally alive! Growing. Young, yet as old as the millenia.)

All nature continued awakening. The clouds had vanished. The sky was growing bluer and the land greener. Gleam and Eneas looked below. At their feet, the cage was swinging. It seemed to fill with metallic, thumping sounds. Could they have been blows—desperate blows of Pithecanthropus' head, feet, and fists?

As they left the Palace, Wiley Warhorse told Piggy Rigoletto:

—We'll have to meet without the Dic.

—That's right.

The idea was proposed to the other members of the Cabinet. They approved. Actually, they'd had the same idea. The only problem was finding an appropriate place to meet. Each one offered his own headquarters to the Secretary.

Warhorse dissented. That would be too obvious.

—We need a secluded place. To be at ease. And where nobody will bother us.

Rigoletto suggested:

—The Boll Weevil Club seems good.

The response was unanimous.

—Wonderful!

The high officials found Spongy Sumptuoso taking a bath in tears from his own eyes. The purest sobs. He'd cried so much that, for practicality's sake, he'd installed himself in his bathtub. Naked. fleshly, flatulent, he continued his weeping. Each time the tub filled, he pulled the plug to make room for his new tears. Between sobs he looked up and moaned:

—Isn't it perfectly awful?

Warhorse solemnly replied:

—Indeed it is, don Spongy. General Jonas Pithecanthropus' kidnapping is the worst calamity in Babelandia's history.

Cottonpuss gestured impatiently.

—Of course, of course. But bad as it is, it's nothing compared to something worse.

—Something . . . worse? Like what?

—The cancellation of our party.

—To be sure. Also a terrible thing.

The homunculus was excited. As usual, it was an excitement from the belly button inward. On the outside, his little voice continued to bubble from his anus-like mouth.

—The most terrible of all, señor Secretary of Defense. You don't know—you've no idea—how

how hard we worked preparing it. It would have been, because of that, the crowning glory of my existence. An unprecedented and insuperable achievement.

Piggy Rigoletto interrupted:

—Quit exaggerating, Spongy.

A shower of tears fell into the tub. A wave of emotion spread over his soft white flesh. The plump little hands fondled each other anxiously.

—Exaggerating! How do you define exaggeration now, my never tactful friend? Clearly you're unaware that our performance was beyond the call of duty: importing a gorilla from overseas to serve General Pithecanthropus. An old one but still in good working order. We built a greenhouse to grow bamboo. In this way, the General could pick the shoots for his meals with his own hands. As for the guests' fare, it would be sensational. Needless to say, we got the finest, most exotic foods from all over the world, and the most famous chefs. To dine here tonight would have been a form of worship. A quantity to satisfy Morgante Maggiori.* The quality—as if Lucullus had prepared a banquet for Lucullus. And what wines, Blessed Mother! I revived Ali Baba's forty thieves and contracted with them to bring us the best bottles of every era. The music and dance would have made Harun-al-Rashid's extravaganzas sick by comparison. All was to be lit by living torches. Fifty naked virgins

Translator's Note: The giant in Luigi Pulci's classic narrative poem, *Il Morgante Maggiori* (1483).

with flames leaping from their bodies. Not just from their mouths, like flame throwers. But also from other suggestive places. And tell me if I'm exaggerating, honorable Secretary of the Interior! You're not only unjust, but cruel.

All that emotion had infected his fellow listeners. Piggy Rigoletto was confused, His deepest concern was the sticky question of the amount to be paid for those lavish commitments. Paid? Really, why should they pay? Could it not be treated as an accident, a situation beyond their control? So maybe a clarification would be helpful.

—Believe me, don Spongy, we're truly sorry. We sympathize with you. We realize how hard it's been to see so much effort come to nothing. However, you have to understand it's not our fault. The Amautas are in every case the culprits.

—The Amautas? What do you mean?

—They're the ones who kidnapped the General.

—And what do I have to do with that?

Well, if we were unlucky enough to have to cancel our party, the whole blame would be theirs.

—So?

—Any complaint you have would have to be made to those guerillas.

The pale proboscidian scrutinized him from head to foot. So, the little bastard thinks he can have a field day at my expense. He doesn't suspect what's in store for him. Ignores what I can be like when it comes to protecting my interests. He doesn't know me. If he keeps this up, his skin isn't worth a nickel. We'll see if he understands me! And I wouldn't have to dirty my hands. I'd simply give others the opportunity. So many others are eager to get at him. It's only a matter of egging them on. Still, why is he doing this to me? His money isn't at stake. Why should his belly ache when somebody else eats? The money belongs to the government. And I'll keep it for myself if there isn't any party. Even if I have to throw everything away. Throw it away? Never. I'll use it all little by little. Nothing will be wasted. Who knows whether that's the best way to handle it! Just like getting paid twice for the same thing. Once by the party guests who would have come. Again by the guests of future parties that I can use these supplies for, bit by bit. Amautas! Charge the Amautas for it? This Piggy must be crazy. On the contrary, we'd have to pay them for such a unique opportunity. That would be the limit, Spongy. As soon as these idiots are out of the way you can dry your tears and reorganize everything the way you want. He had decided. Broke his silence:

—Charge the guerillas? How? And where? By what means? If you, with all your power and influence, can't even find them, what could I do? Poor me, who has the Boll Weevil Club walls for his prison.

Wiley Warhorse was getting impatient. This barbarian Rigoletto was already putting his foot in it. He'll stop at nothing. But his greed befuddles his thinking. He wants to eat, at all times, the goose that lays the golden eggs. Doesn't he realize we're in the driver's seat and can pay—including our own part, of course—as much or as little as we want? The cost of a party used to be a set amount. You could tell in advance what this and that would cost. The guests could estimate the price of what was consumed. But now that's a question mark. And the question mark can represent whatever sum, less or more, seems profitable. Of course it's to our advantage to make it more. He broke in, conciliatory:

—We'll take care of that in due course. For now, we have more urgent problems.

Piggy was climbing the Olympus of pesos. Everything had suddenly been transformed into that denomination: the bathroom, the tub, the toilet, all the furniture, the wash basin, the little fat fellow himself. How could he take his colleague seriously? He went on:

—We'll lend you our support, Spongy. You'll see. It'll be easy to get money from the Amautas.

For his part, the person addressed felt like Ulysses tied to the mast during the song of the sirens. Nevertheless unlike Penelope's husband, he was listening to neither Warhorse nor Piggy. He just watched their jaws move, as if they were ruminating cows. He simply said:

—The Amautas. Aren't they something?

—What's that?

He reacted. Returned to his tub and his tears.

—They're like ghosts. They appear and disappear. But we'll find them. We're sure to find them.

Warhorse took Piggy by the arm, forcefully:

—Hurry up, friend. Soon we'll make arrangements with the owner of the Boll Weevil Club. As for now, we have decisions to make. Don't forget that time is money. For one thing, the international delegations are arriving. For another, the deadline for meeting the ransom demands—if we decide to—is fast approaching. We've only got a few hours.

Plácido Hotwheels specified:

—Twenty-two, to be exact.

Twelve

One early evening María and her two friends came home together. No doubt it was the condors' fault. But it was the straw that broke the camel's back. Upper-crust Labyrinthians were bursting beneath their skins. As if their inquisitiveness had swelled the fibers of their muscles. So then, the virgin—their virgin—had reached the limit of defiance! Hadn't her daytime display—on land and in the air—in their enemy's company, been enough? Was she now daring to carry on under the cover of the night? Was she doing it so no one could watch her, even from a distance? Frankly, she had exceeded all limits. They'd have to put an end to the young woman's excesses. Her hymen was in danger! Since they had proposed it, they'd defend it with tooth and nail, if necessary. No sooner had the bell-ringer's disappearance spread a little honey on the bitter-gray life of the town than new adversities presented themselves. And much worse, while Agapetus had assaulted them only with his tongue, Maria was attacking them with something else. Well, that was the limit! They'd react in the best way and as quickly as possible. Their first thought, of course, was to outline the problem to the priest. They decided against it. The truth was that each day Polygamo was leaning closer to the ground. As much because of what he was dragging along like a living penance as because of his acts as a priest and as a man. These had reached excessive proportions. In Labyrinthia many already wanted to call him to account and even to restrict his movements in the community, especially in the wee hours of the morning. Accordingly, they thoroughly discussed it before they finally decided to confront the evil-doer. One of those who most opposed it was Domitilo Mercenarìo. Besides his stated reasons, this one-balled sneak had something else tucked away between the folds of his lower abdomen. He was jealous of the Minister of the Lord. Jealous above all because of the negative ways in which he was forced to express his own deviant sexuality, while the cleric gave evidence quite to the contrary. Out loud he declared he did not believe Polygamo should be allowed a role in those proceedings. As for himself—he concluded—he couldn't care less about the disputes and gossip that that man caused. Anyway, why set fire to the hornet's nest? Why approach someone who was avoided by everybody else? For her part, Pepita San Toro was also adamantly opposed. For two reasons that she kept secret: First, because she was spiteful toward the ecclesiastical satyr. How was it possible that she was the only woman in town who hadn't received a proposition from him? It was public knowledge that she had generous buttocks, designed for the community's well-being. Her pleasurable offerings—whatever they might be called—could supply the whole town. And if Polygamo had sought her out at the beginning, she would have been an enthusiastic witness to the growth, inch by inch, of his organ. Even now there was time. But the haughty one passed her by, indifferent. Just as the first motive was directly related to her own sexuality, the second, of a sentimental nature—in the multi-widow's judgment—was an attachment to Maria's hymen. In this regard she, Pepita, was against the majority. How was it possible in such a civilized community that a woman had maintained her chastity for so long? It seemed to her as if "that" had not fulfilled its purpose and destiny. It was as if someone with a perfectly normal digestive system were forbidden to eat. In the virgin's case it was worse, since not only was she going hungry, so were all the men. Was it a fair comparison? The digestive tract, and sex? Damn! Often she thought her ideas were becoming confused and she shouldn't waste time worrying about "those things." "Those things" were better done than said. While expressing these opinions out loud, she kept her poise and concluded simply that Polygamo was in full decline. A priest couldn't limit himself to only one . . . family. Her listeners looked at one another apprehensively. Was she about to expose Ludivina? In Labyrinthia anything could be said *sotto-voce*. Nothing out loud. San Toro saw before her, like a small cloud, the image of Agapetus. And she suspended her meditations. But soon many others descended upon her. And then? Then they headed—the Bosses of Labyrinthia—for Clench Tremolo's place. Now here was somebody—just as they conjectured—who could lead them to what they desired. The Tremolos lived on the outskirts. Protected on all sides by stone walls. The delegation drew near. Several dogs barked. The door opened. Clench's fox face appeared. He looked at the recent arrivals, and his attitude immediately grew obsequious. The members of the committee, however, were not invited to step in. When they told him the reason for their visit, he broke down in lamentation: Maria had disobeyed him. In vain he had tried to convince her in every way how harmful her relationship with that young man had been. If, under such trying circumstances, providence had still preserved her virginity, she should thank heaven and wait for a better opportunity, or forever. His personal preference was forever. An opinion shared, he insinuated, by his wife, Gymnastia. When they asked about the latter, he replied that she was doing her noble household chores. Since they had not announced their visit, the reception they deserved had not been prepared. On another occasion, it would be. The visitors tried to conceal their scorn. They resented being stopped at the door, while the dogs howled in chorus. Despite everything, they insisted he should be more strict with the immaculate widow. Left the matter in his paternal hands. Were confident that all would be right and that the virgin would continue as such, for the honor and glory of Labyrinthia. As soon as they left, Clench Tremolo went to the back door. Then out to the fresh water well. He began turning the crank coiling the rope that raised the huge bucket up to the rim. Soon a female head appeared. Then a rachitic, wizened body, dismally doused in the dripping cold. Standing in the receptacle, she gave the impression of a frozen insect. A cynical smile flowered on the husband's thin lips.

—You can come out now, Gymnastia.

Thirteen

THE arrival of the small-town newspapers was more vinegar in the mustard. The eight columns had the impact of a bugle blast. An adventurous reporter had gone to Four Vultures Island. It was said that—more islet than island—a strange family had been living there. It consisted solely of sixteen women: a mother and her fifteen daughters. Living without contact with anyone, marginal to all society. Only banana trees had been planted on the island. It was encircled by explosive mines—around the shore and offshore—that made it virtually impregnable. No one could get on or off it. When a ship drew near, it was blown to the winds. And also blown to the winds were its innocent passengers. Then, from the middle of the island, the vultures would rise. These fearsome carnivores had feasts that lasted several days. It was rumored that from time to time a high-ranking officer appeared. Making unimaginable, spectacular leaps. From tree to tree. From island to island. The last leap always left him on Four Vultures Island. He would stay there two or three days and then depart the same way he arrived. Rory Notorioso, author of the article, had suspected for months that something worthy of his pen was going on in that small space. Saying nothing of his suspicions to anyone, he made a helicopter tour of the neighboring islands. From up there he was able to watch, through a wide-angle telescope, the strange traveler's arrival. His suspicions became more intense, until all doubt vanished. It was, no less, General Jonas Pithecanthropus! He was drowning in conjecture. What was this escapee from the jungle looking for here? A seditious act? Impossible. His was the power and the glory. More than it had ever been Verbophile's. Bananas? Absurd. He could have as many as he wanted sent to the Capital. If necessary, he could have them flown in by the National Air Force. Munitions? Weapons? Troops? Still more preposterous. Not only did he have all that in abundance; on Four Vultures there was no symptom of it. Well then? Why rack your brains thinking up asshole explanations? You know perfectly well what he has there. It's a matter of these sixteen women. And what's his relationship with them? Can he be servicing them all? That too would be strange. In the Nation's largest cities he can sleep with as many as he wants. So why should he come to this small island without comforts? I smell a rat. Confused memories began to tumble through his head. First, he began searching his files for stories from the past. Pulled out and put back the massive volumes of the bound periodicals. Leafed hurriedly through pages and pages. Not knowing exactly what he was looking for. His instincts were his only guide. Nothing. One day passed, then another. And nothing. Am I wasting my time with these things? Because I'd be better off writing on other subjects. Maybe I'm imagining it all. Whatever I'm thinking is an illusion. Maybe Four Vultures does not even exist. He was about to throw in the towel when he discovered a photograph. It caught his eye because it was of a wedding. The groom was none other than officer Jonas Pithecanthropus. Flaunting his lieutenant's uniform. The bride—innocent, timid, and mentally retarded—was smiling. He checked a few more newspapers. Lost the trail of the pair of newlyweds. There was no information, no news about them. As if Babelandia had swallowed them up. Bored, he terminated his investigation and devoted his time to easier and more productive affairs. With the news of the kidnapping, his mind had sharpened. He boarded a helicopter. And as dawn broke he was flying over four Vultures. Was about to give up. Having seen not a house, nor a hut, nor a trail, nor anything that would suggest a human presence. Still, he would exhaust the last possibility. What a pity if I had to retrace my steps. If I'm thorough now, really thorough, I'll know there's nothing left to be done. He asked to have the mechanical bird brought down.

Opened the door. Jumped. He'd only taken two steps outside when a shower of rocks stopped him. He looked in the direction they were coming from. He trembled with horror and astonishment. Before him were—dirty, bedraggled, half-naked, and with the appearance of savages—the sixteen women. Well, one woman and fifteen girls. The latter, curiously, were divided into five groups of three each. Each group had a marked similarity with the others, and their constituents seemed of the same age. They behaved, completely, as triplets. Although he believed it impossible that the adult was able to talk, she began to speak:

—What do you want here? Go away! Go away right now!

—Rory Notorioso answered with another question:

—Who are you?

—None of your business! Go away!

—We want to help you.

—With what?

—To change your life. To improve it.

—We're all right the way we are.

—You've no right to keep your daughters in this condition.

—Mind your own business. We don't want help. Whenever we need anything, I ask my husband.

Although Notorioso was virtually certain, he wanted to confirm it.

—Who is your husband?

—Don't you know?

—If I knew, I wouldn't ask.

When she spoke, she assumed a definite air of pride:

—My husband is Jonas Pithecanthropus! And now, get going! If you don't, you'll be sorry.

—Have you heard what's happened to him?

She stared at him defiantly.

—What?

—He was kidnapped last night.

—That's a lie. Nobody could kidnap him.

And with that they began stoning him again. He retreated, running, to the helicopter. Once inside, he took a few pictures. When the girls realized what he was doing, they covered their faces with their hands. Reproductions of precisely those pictures later appeared under glaring eight-column spreads in the local newspapers. When Babelandia's readers picked up their copies, they wrinkled them, animating the black tufts of gorillian hair. The tears at dawn were later replaced by bitter expressions of protest and anger. Popular imagination, excited by what had happened, seasoned all conversations.

—He had them so secluded!

—Practically buried alive.

—Why has he done it?

—Maybe because he was saddled with five sets of triplets.

—So what? That's just a stupid superstition.

—Maybe he's afraid they'll be hurt.

—Them? Why?

—For revenge. For the harm he himself has caused so many people.

—And it seems that they're just like animals.

—So it seems. They walk on all fours. Or swing from branch to branch.

—Their diet is mostly roots and leaves.

—They go around naked.

—They attack anyone who comes near them.

—They can't read or write. They're completely backward and ignorant.

—They defecate on the ground.

—Do they know how to talk.

—Rory Notorioso spoke only with the mother.

—What a man! Having a family like that!

—A man? Can you really call "that" a man?

—He's not the worst.

—No?

The worst are those who follow him. Those who obey all his orders: the ones who seem to control Bab.

—Shut up!

—Isn't it true?

—You'd better keep quiet. There are fifty thousand snakes listening. Maybe there's one in your pocket. Or on some other part of your body. They're living microphones. Don't you realize that?

The whole Cabinet was assembled on the top floor of the Boll Weevil Club. In emergency session. Strangely, Wiley Warhorse began to feel a familiar sensation all over his body. As if he wanted to bend over. To get down on all fours. To saddle himself up with his riding gear. To dash down the gold banistered stairs with ten-meter landings. To get out on the street. To canter right out of the city, or wherever was necessary. And to find the Kidnapped One and serve once again as his mount. Control youself, wretch! If you can't suppress those impulses, tie yourself to a chair, or the leg of a table. Head, body, and limbs. Before it's too late. So that there's no danger you'll start bucking. Nor that you'll succumb to your usual psychic metamorphosis. Also, close your mouth. Before you start to whinny. It was a great effort. He got control of himself. Cleared his throat. Spoke with a distinct trace of importantitis.

—Honorable colleagues. Let's get directly to the point.

Placido Hotwheels continued on his one theme:

—First and foremost, the Transit Plan.

Warhorse looked at him as a fox observes a chicken.

—Just a minute now, Mr. Engineer.

—One billion. . .

Piggy chimed in:

—We'll get to that later, dear colleague. For now there are more urgent matters to discuss.

Onc bill. . .

—Later.

—But. . .

His associates glared at him in unison in such a way that he became smaller and smaller, until he disappeared under the table. Warhorse, as a precaution, felt his jawbone. How reassuring! It had not lengthened, as he feared. Again he spoke:

—I know perfectly well that each and everyone of us has thoroughly analyzed the ransom conditions. Isn't that so?

They answered in unison:

—That's right.

—Well, then, I think that two of the conditions could be easily met. First, the release of political prisoners and university students, so that once the present crisis is over, we can stage a demonstration, a simulated strike, a subversive act, or any other such pretext. Then we could lock them all up again "with just cause." And, if necessary, we could even eliminate a few.

Rigoletto intervened.

—Exactly. Not only a few, but all of them. That way, we'll also save on their prison expenses.

Wiley Warhorse looked at him disdainfully. What a donkey this pig is! Why does he want to cut off his nose to spite his face? Is he so godforsaken that he doesn't understand? If we have fewer expenses, how will the money circulate? And if money doesn't circulate, how can we get our hands on a few extra pesos? Bah! Let him shoot off his mouth, as Verbophile says. Later we'll appeal to reason. When he sees it's to his advantage, he'll accept everything unconditionally. Now let's get down to what concerns us. Glanced all around. It seemed like being in a corral, surrounded by ruminating philosophers. Ruminating? Philosophers? Don't kid yourself, Wiley. Except for Rigoletto, nobody sucks on his fingers around here. He went on:

—As for the second condition, the stage is set. A pound of our dear Dictator's bones is not worthy worrying about. What would he care about one pound of bones, more or less? After all, in the end he has bones to spare. If it were a pound of flesh, well that would be impossible. That would be to hand over all the flesh he has.

Piggy Rigoletto again put in his two cents' worth.

—That depends.

—Depends?

—Of course. It depends on the part of the skeleton the Amautas decide on.

Warhorse felt that his head was beginning to rattle. Damn, this empty eggshell makes me gag like a fishbone caught in my windpipe. Why must he always stick his foot in it up to his neck? Is he, perhaps, all foot? Why does he emit idiotic remarks, one after the other, like inflated balloons? What do we care what the Amautas decide on? That's between Holofernes and them. We have other business. And it's strictly ours. Then he grunted with a certain harshness:

—So?

—Suppose they chose their pound of bones from his cranium?

Another, more aggressive grunt:

—So?

—How could he go on being Dictator, without a head?

Warhorse was resolute. I'm going to put the quietus on this microbe. I've had it up to here with him. If I followed my instincts, I'd pull down his pants. Stretch him out on the conference table. And have every one of us slap his buttocks. That would cure his myopic spirit and body.

—Mr. Secretary of the Interior. To put you at ease, let me say that in such a case two things could happen, First, our Dictator would want to continue governing without a head.

—That would be ridiculous.

—Not so much as you think, dear colleague. To be sure, many countries have rulers with something on their shoulders that resembles a head. Or that's what they call it. It's only an excess of optimism. Sometimes the noun "head" is badly employed: Or there's no head, but only a coarse imitation, or even if it's the real thing, it might as well not be. After all, if you have no brains in it, what good is it?

—Ah yes, of course! I understand.

—The second possibility is that our government would be unwilling or unable to continue. Then, what a magnificent opportunity we'd have! We could call a special election. We could make sure that the electoral machinery functions to our taste. That is, to our advantage. The Chameleonic Congress would draft another amendment to the Constitution. Since that wretched document is so much amended, no one would notice. And if all this came to pass, who knows whether one of us—maybe you yourself, my dear colleague—could be anointed by the populace! How does "Your Excellency Piggy Rigoletto, Constitutional President of Babelandia" sound to you?

The latter felt himself rising and falling as if on a ferris wheel. His eyes grew clouded. *In mente* he was seated in the Chair. With the presidential sash wrapping him in its chromatic embrace. He gave a strange gurgle. Squirming, he stated:

—You're entirely right. As usual, you speak just like an oracle.

Wiley continued:

—The true problem is the Amautas' third condition: the two hundred first first-class funerals.

Drunk from vanity at his future presidential possibilities, Piggy aruged:

—That's the least of it. What do we care about losing the terrestrial company of a few inhabitants of Babelandia?

The leader of this chorus scratched the back of his head. Once again, dead head, follow me? Patience, Wiley. Patience. Consider, with all you've told this cretin, how already his donkey ears have sprouted like wings. Likely, he's already no longer with us. Thanks to their flapping power he's probably already landed at the Palace and is savoring what he'll be devouring when he becomes the Highest Dignitary of the Nation. Ha, ha, ha! Ha, ha, ha! I wouldn't be known as Wiley or Warhorse if I didn't know how to cook this sucker's goose. He made an effort. Looked at him understandingly.

—The two hundred first-class funerals would be no big deal if the future dead were chosen by us! That's not the case. The Amautas insist that the choice remain in their hands. And that we don't want.

—Why not?

His interlocutor spoke with an emotionless, incisive, and final tone:

—Because if that happened, who could assure you, illustrious and most prudent Mr. Secretary of the Interior, that we ourselves would not be at the head of the Amautas' list? Probably in their eyes we have established ourselves as the leading candidates. So then, how could you fulfill your own most righteous political aspirations? How could we help you with your presidential campaign? You know better than anyone: the dead can't vote or be voted for. Don't you agree, distinguished attorney?

Every "You" sounded like a vote for President. A match was lit in the dark recesses of his brain.

—That's right. You're entirely right. And then what?

'That's what we have to talk about. What are we able to do? How can we safeguard our lives and our endangered noble interests? I believe every one of us is ready to sacrifice all for the salvation of the Fatherland . . . Our Nation has called! We cannot deny her the treasure of our human values, the purity of our principles, the sterling defense of our democracy!

Fourteen

POLYGAMO'S sexual organ had grown several meters. It seemed like a forlorn, wrinkled hawser bumping along the ground. In his eagerness to conceal how large it was, he tied it in several knots, some of which he already dragged beneath his cassock. A number of women crossed themselves as they passed, quickening their steps. Others, finding the temptation irresistible, looked at him askance. Among the latter was the San Toro woman, who trembled and sighed. A few didn't notice him at all. The men already stared at him threateningly. He—even when it was cold—was bathed in a sticky sweat. A sweat of anguish, wrath, and helplessness. Several times he attempted to escape from this milieu. To free himself from the urban dilemma. To hide himself in some cave where he could find refuge from everybody and everything. That was the purpose behind his nocturnal walks. He took little clothing. Abandoned his vestments and everything that might identify him as a cleric. Then he'd set forth. The dogs that barked in the shadows crept up, trying to nip that which he towed along with so much difficulty. He woke the neighbors. Hid himself. After a little while—when the windows closed and the dog barks lapsed into yawns—he would continue on his way. Until he reached the point where there were no longer houses. It seemed, finally, that he'd escaped. He walked still faster. Suddenly a group of the local young toughs would appear and start wisecracking. Sometimes they were not satisfied with that. Approached him. Tried to trample his gigantic member. Its owner would attempt to defend himself. In vain. Would start running to break through their encirclement. But he was unable to penetrate the city's limits. The church itself was watching, through its ironic, steeple-clock eye. And suddenly a procession of severe, ghost-like priests blocked his path, pointing back toward the temple. They'd force him to back up, all the way to the atrium. Then they'd vanish in the mist. His many attempts to escape were useless. The result was always the same. The fence of menacing priests impeded him. Were they forcing his return to celibacy? Was that really possible? Were they actually priests? Or devils disguised as priests? If so, why were they working to return him to the fold? And he, he himself, what had he changed into?

Sometimes it seemed to him that another being inhabited his body. A contradictory being who on occasion fought with him, argued with him, or gave him absurd reasons for this strange behavior. In truth, he went about as if in a sinking whirlpool of darkness. The only thing he was sure of was his organ. That organ that kept growing. And of the insatiable libido that kept him revolving constantly around that organ.

People, for their part, never stopped talking about it.

—It must be a penance, don't you think?

—Could be. God knows how many he owes.

—There was a time when he didn't even look at women.

—Now he respects neither their age nor social position.

—He's made it with some of them.

—Of course. He's a priest. Visits all the homes.

—Used to visit. Now most of them are on their guard. Afraid of the monster.

—Sometimes it seems that he's the Devil.

—Ah! Probably he is. Tangled up in his own tail.

—Hail Mary Immaculate!

—Conceived without sin.

—He's changed so much. When he says mass or delivers sermons, even though he says them just as before, they sound so different!

—Worse each time.

There'd be a pause. And then they would speak more softly.

—And when will *the thing* stop growing?

—Yes. When?

—They say that when God decides to give. . .

—God ? You believe He's involved in these things?

—If it isn't God, why can't anybody stop what's going on in this town?

—Maybe the Lord hasn't set the date yet for Judgment Day.

—That must be the reason.

Fourteen

Ludivina provided more venom for the vipers' tongues. The pumpkin was already swelling. She didn't go out at all. "She can't go out. It shows too much." She and her mother were arguing night and day. At first doña Prudencia had tried to cover up the misdeed.

—You're not the first, and won't be the last. Besides, many people don't like to blaze the trail. I know what I'm talking about.

—Please don't talk like that, Mamá.

—. . .Without going much further, there's don Lindo Mollejón, owner of the bakery. He's one of the rich ones. And he's always ready for you, whatever your state.

—Ay, Mama!

—If you let me, I can fix everything.

The girl was desperate. She retorted:

—The way you "fixed" my disgrace?

—Don't say that. Who could have guessed you'd end up pregnant?

—That's the least of it. The worst is the treachery against Eneas. Letting that damned hypocritical priest slobber over me. And it's all your fault!

—Don't talk like that. I haven't the slightest idea how it happened. That Polygamo turned out to be a bastard. I never would have dreamed it. Before, he was different. He changed overnight. Probably what they are saying is true. That he's no longer a priest, but the Devil. That the Devil got into his body and kicked the real Polygamo out.

—And you believe that?

—I don't know if I believe or not. I'm not sure of anything. Sometimes I feel different myself. As if I too had the Devil in me.

—And I?

—You, what about you?

—How should I feel?

—If you like, we could call in a midwife. There's one on the outskirts of the city. We'd get rid of the baby and. . .

—Stop it! And stop "fixing" my affairs. What a fool I was to listen to you.

Who knows if the Devil was moving your lips? Only lies and tricks. It's clear you aren't the only one to blame. It's more my fault that it went as far as it went. I should have fought in every way, with all my strength against the fire that began to consume me. And against your words and your "help". Why did you do it, Mother? Was it because you were really on his side? Or was it because I'm so bad—I—too—that I couldn't or wouldn't defend myself? Or was it that no defense was possible? I didn't tell Eneas a single thing. He could have helped. Or at least he would have realized what was happening to me. And perhaps would have understood.

In the meantime Eneas had discovered something that unsettled him and left him dissatisfied with himself. Absorbed in his own problems, he had neglected or had not realized what was going on in Labyrinthia. There were serious developments that in different circumstances would have made him tense and excited from the beginning. For example, the Bell Ringer's experience. The Bel Ringer. Since he left, no one had seen him return. Not a trace of him. Still less had anyone mentioned the subject of his mutilation. His tongue. As if nothing had happened, absolutely nothing. As if the poor creature had never existed. Or as if everybody had attempted to forget him, or to erase him forever from the town's memory. When Eneas began to think of these things, he felt a sudden remorse. That tongue. Curiously, before he'd had the impression that he was dreaming. In full wakefulness he was aware only of what was going on in his life. That tongue. His remorse culminated in a growing indignation. Was the crime to go unpunished? Wouldn't they at least manage to identify the culprit so that there could be a trial? For him—as he thought over the situation—it seemed more important and painful than for others. He had chatted with Agapetus almost daily. The tongue. Up there, so near the clouds. And he had been chatting when the Bell Ringer left his tower, as if released from earth's embrace, from wingless alcohol, from certain little wormlike people around him, from all that joined him to macro-digestive systems and to micro-brained ruminants. And the more he thought about all that, the guiltier and more responsible he felt. The tongue. At the outset, he tried to get Gleam to help him investigate the circumstances that had culminated in this atrocious act. With lucid discernment, his young friend would help him clarify his conjectures. Had it been a collective crime? Had most of the community taken part? Or had only the local owners of people and property acted? At the least, there was probably no lack of accomplices. But undoubtedly one alone had torn out or cut off the precious organ. He soon discarded the idea of involving Gleam in his deliberations. His friend already had enough on his hands with his fight against Labyrinthia. He fully realized that most of its inhabitants—on their own or someone else's initiative—persisted in protecting Maria from that liaison. They were eager to keep her immaculate. Charlatans! As if love didn't purify whatever it touches. Thus he did not even discuss this with his friend, and he, he alone began a pilgrimage in quest of the truth. His first call was on the Political Boss. Listening to his presentation of the case, Domitilo Mercenario assumed the air of a crow disguised as a lily. Like someone fallen from the moon. So Agapetus had disappeared? No wonder the bells hadn't sounded for several days. A new bell ringer would have to be found. And how had it happened? On what date? Ah! The same day he had shown his tongueless mouth? Was the organist sure of what he said? As for himself, in his position of authority and knowledge about what was going on, this was the first he'd heard of it! How strange! No? Why hadn't he been told earlier? Why had no one complained? Could it be that people were making it up? Was he sure of what they said? Couldn't the Bell Ringer have gotten drunker than usual and be wandering through the countryside, lost to reality? He would certainly investigate—of course he would investigate what ever had happened. He would investigate until he knew the whereabouts of Agapetus. If what the organist was saying turned out to be true, the guilty ones would pay. He would punish them with an iron hand. No one could make fun of Domitilo Mercenario and his justice! Eneas, sensing what was to be expected from that justice and that single-testicled jackal—that's why he was called a *chiclán*—began consulting some of the other more notorious Labyrinthians. They all acted like crippled hogs circling around their troughs. The tongue? No one knew anything. No one had seen or heard anything. Worse still, they did not wish to become involved in the matter. They shrugged their shoulders. Looked at him mockingly. The tongue? Bah! The tongue! And they'd change the subject, asking about Ludivina. They were "candid, innocent, uninsinuating" questions. They were simply about Ludivina. Had he seen her? About Ludivina.

She was getting very pretty. About Ludivina. She was getting fat. About Ludi. Fatter every day. About Lu. Ludivina. Ludivi, Ludi, Lu. Other Labyrinthians—just a few—advised him in good faith not to stick his nose into that scorpions' nest. Or did he want to lose his own tongue, just like the Bell Ringer? Or did he seriously think he could clarify anything? Nothing could be done there against the four rats—enormous rats hungrier than Pantagruel—who divided among themselves all the cheese in Labyrinthia. The only way to go on living was to bow one's head and resign onself. What could the poor organist do? A quiet rage burned in his belly. His helplessness grieved him and filled him with an urge for revenge. Oblivious to the priest, oblivious to the congregation, oblivious to everyone, he climbed up to the organ and commenced to play. Residents in the vicinity leaned out of their windows or headed for the church. It seemed to be transfigured. It swelled with music. Became a palace of vibrations. The altars, the saints, the pews, and the faithful were under a spell. They were as one with that climax of sounds. Suddenly the organ grew wings. It rose above the center aisle. It drew close to the scarce and paltry stained-glass windows, as if yearning to destroy them. It floated up to the highest vaults and inscriptions. Then it danced about the towers like an iridescent butterfly dispersed broken hearts. It became a swan on lakes of atomized grief, on a circular musical score that rose to the bells. And there at the organ, Eneas, creator of the dreams grafted on the visages of the worshippers, himself a delirious arpeggio that all felt tingling up the backs of their bowed heads. Ending its winged excursion, the gigantic instrument returned to its choir crypt shrouded in sobs. Then its own throat was a deep, muted sob, a descending dew-mist of tears.

Fourteen

Gleam, meanwhile, remained deaf and blind to reality. His beloved was all he could see or hear. Each day his horizons shrank. Now they were ending at Maria's silhouette. Desperate, in great confusion, a compass without its magnetic needle, he scattered his tremulous steps across the mountain peaks. Against this panorama, he listlessly helped his father with his chores. Scarcely talking to him. And when he did, it was just small talk, usually about work. But she was always there. She, in a double exposure. Now in the foreground. She. He was beginning to stare at her in an absurd fashion. Was the collectivc psychosis contagious? Now she was at the altar. Surrounded by golden ornaments. Illuminated by hundreds of candles. As if removed from life and confined to the church forever. Was Maria no longer "his" Maria? A kind of trance extracted him from the surrounding world. He began, too, to review the coincidences. Was he delirious and seeing things differently from what they were in reality. No. That couldn't be. His Maria was the same as ever. Only circumstances had made her a widow and virgin. The rest was a collective aberration. Defending her virginity were those who had the least right to defend it. Easy does it, Gleam. Look at things as they are. Otherwise you'll lose what little sanity's left to you. And fight. Fight with everything you can. Disregard the ignorance and selfishness of others. Stay together with your beloved. You've got to surmount all obstacles. Including her, since she's apprehensive and complains that you are around so much. Didn't she tell you that a few times? Were the words hers? Or did you dream them up yourself. "We'd better see less of each other, Gleam. We're exposing ourselves needlessly. The men watch me like prison guards. Moreover, it seems that they want to pierce me with their eyes. That they are eager to see through my underthings to make sure you haven't touched me yet. The women, for their part, simmer with hate when I pass. They who've already given everything, or are eager to give it—can't understand why most of those in the town who wear trousers are so obsessed with keeping me immaculate. So darling, there's no solution. We can't marry, or be lovers, or even friends. Anyway, who'd believe we're just friends? And, as I've told you many times, we'd better not see each other any more, or speak, or even look at each other . . . He—consciously or unconsciously—had insisted that to stop seeing each other was impossible. On the other hand, hadn't he noticed that things were beginning to change? A big sector of town—the poor, the defeated, and the grieving—didn't very much like the direction that the bosses were giving the course of events. And even if events had been different, nothing and no one could have kept him from seeing her. Because of this, when he went down to the town, he would always look for her. She, despite her arguments to the contrary, would come out to meet him. Of course, she was deliberately late. At first she made an effort to overcome her feelings. No. Today I won't show up. He'll get tired of waiting. He'll go away. That'll be best for all concerned. I'll leave him waiting in front of my house. Hours will pass. Afternoon will come. Night will fall. He'll have to leave. And if the condors come? And if one of them finds my bedroom window and carries me off to him? The condors are his friends. Surely now they're my friends too. But they'll continue being more his friends. They know what's going on between us. They'll seize us with their claws and fly us off to who knows where. I'm afraid. Afraid of losing my self-control. Of embracing him. Of pressing against him. Of covering him with kisses. Of feeling him so close as to lose all restraint. Of forgetting where I cease to exist and where he begins. I want to live in him. And also him to live in me. Only that is just, human, natural, and true. The rest is pure sham, injustice, and falsity. Together we're life. Separated, we're death. I'm afraid. Then, a vertiginous wave of two tumbled, intertwined beings. A vortex of flame-creatures. A rapture of anxiety and bliss. The beginning and end of everything. Two and one together. And suddenly, the voices. The same voices that had recently begun to resound in her ears. "With or without the flowering hymen? "Is the hymen worth so much?" "Are you any purer for not having been touched at all?" "Is that really the foundation and ultimate goal of virginity?" "Are you entirely sure you are one?" "And if for some reason—aside from any contact with a man—you lost it?" "Maybe you're defending—or rather, others are defending for you—something that doesn't exist. And if it does exist, is it worth it?" "Anyway, it's ridiculous for a whole town to be protecting it for you." Well then, why did religion convert it into a symbol? What'll I do? Doubt consumes me. Doubt and love. I'm burning. If Gleam were here now, I'd probably wrap him in my flames. Like two conflagrations we'd go racing out. All the way to the main square. Inundate it with shouts: "Look! Here I am! Now nobody needs to watch over me. I'm free at last! " . . . While daydreaming she dressed up and prepared herself to face Clench. He had been watching the girl's preparations in a silent rage. He had said nothing while she was preparing. Only when she was ready and on the point of leaving did he set off a barrage of words.

—Where are you going?

—You know.

—Remember what Labyrinthia is like.

—This is worse.

—You're afraid because you want to be. It's your own fault.

—Aren't you ashamed of yourself?

—I'm a man. Have you forgotten?

—You're despicable.

—You'd better not go anywhere.

—Try and stop me!

—Careful!

Behind them, Gymnastia's voice sprang up. Sweet, calm, but firm:

—Yes. I dare you to stop her!

Clench half turned. And Maria, once again, had set out to meet her lover.

Fourteen

That morning airplanes began arriving in Babelandia from every corner of the earth. The sky was full of them, as if flocks of migrating birds had suddenly gone mad. The din of their engines was nearly incessant. They emerged anarchically from behind the mountains. As they neared the airport, they moved into formation. Landed in order, one after the other. They taxied in. Scarcely had the stairways been attached to the doors, when the passengers disembarked. They were military delegations invited to that evening's ceremonies. Most of them knew about the kidnapping. They'd been informed in flight or just before take-off. For their part, they assumed that, given the importance of the event that was about to take place, the ransom for General Pithecanthropus would be paid. Period. Only after arriving and hearing about the conditions demanded by Amautas did they begin to have doubts. Truly, they never had suspected anything like that. They had thought as in most previous cases, it was just a matter of money. Or, at the most, of freeing the government's enemies and possibly providing them safe conduct out of the country. But, a pound of the Dictator's bones and two hundred first-class burials—that was a novelty they hadn't expected! Some even regretted having taken the trip. And *in mente* they studied the possibility of turning back right then. What was the point of staying on? It would be useless. They'd have to return later anyway, ill-humored, in their noisy crates, to where they had come from. And yet any reasoning and decision right now seemed premature. They'd hope. Certain optimists thought there was a chance of reaching an understanding with the guerillas. Thus things would follow their normal course. The airport was seething with uniforms, epaulets, ribbons, and speeches. Numerous officials and their staffs were welcoming the newly arrived. Attempts were made to soothe them. No words were spared. That's what would happen. It would be only a matter of hours. Perhaps of minutes. The Armed Forces of the Nation and all the Police had been mobilized. Energetic searches were taking place in the cities, along the rivers, and in the mountains. A truly minute combing, foot-by-foot, of the entire territory of the fatherland. As if that weren't enough, a generous reward had been offered for any information about the hostage or his abductors. Highways, bridges, harbors, and airports were subjected to a strict vigilance. Anyone could enter, no one could exit. And the fifty thousand serpents carried out a millimeter by millimeter inspection, house-by-house, bed-by-bed, of the whole Nation.

Roundups of suspects were numerous. Since most enemies of the state were already behind bars, they now invented a few new scapegoats to demonstrate the strength of the Strongmen of Babelandia. Only as a last resort would thought be given to complying with the conditions set by the kidnappers. Or who knows if at that very moment negotiations were beginning? The matter proved most urgent! The Secretary of Defense was very clever and so friendly with the eminent hostages. Maybe he, in person, was beginning to shuffle the cards! For their part, the newspapers from the provinces were flooding the airport, Rory Notorioso's report had signaled them with the black banners of its eight columns. The visitors bought up numerous copies. Scarcely were they touched than the newspapers took on gorilla faces. And they stared up at them, ironically, from those skins tattooed by an anarchic alphabet. Then they had voices:

—Look. This is the general you came to pay homage to. Does he please you? Is he worthy of your homage? And how about his woman? Look at her, half-naked throwing rocks at the camera. Isn't that a charming spectacle? Look at his daughters. These five sets of triplets that constitute his daughters. Aren't they marvelous? And take in the atmosphere. It's an island. Not amounting to much. More like an islet. "Four Vultures." Covered with banana trees. Beautiful, isn't it? The sixteen women, do they eat only bananas? There isn't a house to be seen. Do the inhabitants of "Four Vultures" sleep in trees? Or on the bare ground? Rory Notorioso says that the only way to get there is by helicopter. And only by landing exactly in the middle of the island. Because its perimeters—on land and sea—are heavily mined with hair-triggered explosives. The man is on the alert. Man? Can that really be called a man?

The top-ranked officers receiving the guests did their best to erase the latters' doubts. It was yellow journals—they asserted—who were feeding on the worst sources. They would have to close them down. The pockets of their owners could be filled with banknotes of the highest denomination. Or give them a permanent sleep six feet under. In any case, who'd take Notorioso seriously? He was a peripatetic water closet, oozing infamy. If it weren't for the fact that he'd escaped with time to spare to another country, he'd now be getting paid just what he deserves. But you should really forget all that. You'd see how eveything could change in Bab—in just a few hours. How Babelandia was almost the Promised Land.

Fifteen

THE Skeleton Disguised as a Man had calmed down. After all, he was as old as Methuselah. And used to the worst abominations. Anything, that is, except being prevented from making speeches. That represented the greatest punishment that could be inflicted on him. Happily, the Amautas didn't know that. No one knew it. Not even Harpitune. Only he. Without speeches life would cease. It would be like tearing out his heart. By contrast, a pound of bones more or less, could scarcely affect his fortune. In any case, they could easily be replaced by plastic, platinum, or whatever fits. As simple as that! Moreover, the bone quota being demanded of him, with all its implications, signified that his life was out of danger: the guerillas, for the moment, were not including him among those marked for the two hundred first-class burials. Almost jubilantly he retreated to his study. With great emotion he joined his three Magic Brains. They were spongelike. With malleable bones—really more like cartilage than bones. They had rachitic bodies. Their heads were their truly distinguishing features. Protruding bug eyes. Trumpet ears. Bloodhound noses. Fox faces. Moreover, their brains defied zoological classification. They were actually computer cells, micrometric nests of springs, wheels, and wires. That seemed to bulge from their crania. Sparks jumping from one place to another. Phosphorescences. Curious little noises. Peristaltic movements. Their great heads contrasted with their dwarfish torsos and limbs. They moved with the lethargic steps and gestures of somnolent marmots. Spoke not a word. Simply hoped. As on previous occasions, the Dictator indicated the topics of his future harangues. They looked at each other. Seemed to come to life. Picked a few books sticking out from the shelves. Their eyes emerged still further, spectacles on the end of a hose. Scanning and scrutinizing pages as if breathing in their meaning. Then they went to the writing desk. Sat down one after the other. The first one fired a few neurons. They merged with those of the second, and these in turn with those of the third. The current had formed a kind of circuit among the three. The third one began to work on the typewriter. It went with dizzying speed. Each time a page was finished, he handed it to Holofernes, who read it avidly. Four speeches were turned out that way. The fifth had been started when they were interrupted in their task by three knocks on the door. Verbophile jumped. His reaction was angry. Who had dared disturb him? Don't they know my time here is sacred? Not even Harpitune is allowed to stick her nose in this place. Pity whoever it is! I'll pulverize him! Again three knocks. He wondered if it was something important. If it weren't, nobody would have faced the perils of an interruption. He called out in a loudly:

—Just a minute!

Quick as a flash, he opened one of the bookcases. A secret door appeared. The Three Magical Mentalities disappeared through it, vibrating. He drew the tape recorder from his thorax. Placed it on the desk. Seated himself before the typewriter, as if he'd been using it all along. With his left hand he held a written page. In his right, the microphone. Commanded:

—Come in!

Slithering underneath the door came Bacchus the Groveler. Recognizing him, the Dictator dropped his pose and snorted,

—You!

—Yes, your Excellency.

—You know that right now I'm in the throes of inspiration. So get lost. *Ipso facto.*

—I can't, your Excellency.

—What?

—The vital forces of the nation. Its party leaders. They're there. They've invaded the Palace.

He ordered vehemently:

—Well. let them un-invade. Why weren't they stopped at the door?

—Who could have dared? Everybody knows they're the Government's pillars of strength.

He reacted immediately.

—Of course. Show them in.

—There isn't room. They're too many.

He smiled, satisfied. Of course, how could there be just a few? I have so few adversaries. Besides, even they are out of circulation. Piggy Rigoletto has seen to that. We know where they are. More exactly, they're nowhere. He bared his teeth. Was he laughing? In keeping with his skeletal self-esteem, he seemed to be constantly laughing.

—Then show in as many as will fit.

No sooner had he spoken than the room was filled with his supporters. His supporters' leaders, that is. They dispensed with greetings. Elbowed their way toward him in disarray. All talking at once, producing a rumble like that of a wall caving in.

Attempting to control them, he shouted:

—Silence!

They paid no attention. Their babble rose and fell in consecutive waves. Blablabla. Blablabla. Rude smirks, brusque gestures. Pushing against each other to get closer to him. Many were touching him. As they gestured, they struck him. As they spoke they made exploratory nibbles at his bony protuberances. Holofernes could take no more. He took the initiative. And dispersed himself like a floating jigsaw puzzle in the air. When they tried to pick up the pieces of the puzzle, he commenced to reassemble his scattered self and soon stood integrated atop his desk, dominating them. The feat was so unexpected, that the Verbophiles fell silent, staring at him in astonishment. The calcareous acrobat growled:

—One at a time!

Again, a hundred voices. He raised a finger.

—One! he roared.

The leader of the bankers spoke. He had magnetized clothes. Because of that, he was covered with coins. Instinctively—without giving it a thought—he picked them up in passing: off the street, out of people's pockets, at cashiers' windows from wherever they were to be found. He expounded:

—Supreme leader: uncertainty engulfs us.

Holofernes bowed compassionately. Rubbed his eye sockets against the noses of those nearest him.

—Tell me your cares!

The Banker got right to the point.

—Will the Amautas' conditions be accepted?

—We're studying them.

—Time is getting short. Just a few hours to comply with the deadline. You should have reached a decision by now.

—We have to know the results of our investigations.

—What is your own idea of the conditions?

—It's all premature.

His questioner shrugged, making a strange jingle with his cloak of coins.

—Excellency, consider our predicament. We can't continue in the dark. You have to give us something to go on. We demand it!

His associates chorused:

—Yes. We demand it!

The skeleton shrugged his shoulder blades. He repeated the objection that everybody now knew by heart.

—Of the Amautas' demands, the only stumbling block is the 200 first-class funerals.

They all looked at one another. Repeated in unison:

—It's the only stumbling block!

Holofernes increased the volume of his voice:

—Especially, because the Amautas want personally to select their own candidates.

The Banker growled:

—Ridiculous!

He chorused again:

—Absurd!

—Possibly the best in the country would become candidates. Especially, all here present.

He repeated:

—All here present!

Holofernes assented:

—All here present.

All here present. And also, the great majority of Babelandians. But not everyone, because many of them are accomplices of these criminals. Criminals? Hold on. Don't get carried away. Don't forget they're Verbophilists. That they are made in your image and likeness. Well. Not exactly. I am as I am because of my sacred concern for the fatherland and my oratory. If, in order to maintain power, or to keep on making speeches, it was necessary to eliminate them, I wouldn't satisfy myself with 200 funerals, as the Amautas want. I'd bring back death by the garrote. And I'd break the necks of several thousand in the main square. They're all just wicked egoists. Only wanting to satisfy the obsessive triangle: bags of gold, sexual organs, and the digestive apparatus. The irony is that most of them already are so decrepit. Still, they whine about what they can't enjoy but is accessible to others. Unfortunately I'm a victim of these circumstances. I can do nothing without them, or without the noble and most prudent military. And he repeated with conviction:

—All here present!

The Banker arose. Stared at him in anguish.

—That's just why we have to do something.

—Something. But what?

The Spokesman of the Verbophilists seemed to have a bomb beneath his buttocks. And so did his associates. Would they let them explode? Never. The silence was ominous. Only Holofernes' creaking ivories and the digestive gurgles of his visitors could be heard. The Banker arose. The Calcareous One bowed, aware that it was a confidential matter that required a very low voice. And that it was, effectively. His interlocutor proposed, almost in a whisper:

—Why don't we abandon him to his fate?

The Skeleton exhibited his most innocent smile.

—I don't understand. To his fate? Who?

—The General.

His jaw trembled like an electric mixer. Affected by the Banker's tone, as if whispering in secret.

—Do you mean General Pithecanthropus?

—Of course.

He raised his voice:

—Impossible!

—Why?

He grew ultraserious:

—He's the guardian of the peace. Of order. Of national security.

A Junior*—privileged by the wealth of three generations of ancestors—shook his curly locks and, rolling his eyes, intoned in a flute-voice:

—The only security we care about is our own. We're ready to defend it at any cost.

The Skeleton quivered. He launched into a series of aerial pirouettes. Then stood on his head. How absurd his supporters looked! They seemed like human stalagmites hanging from the ground. He reasoned:

—Even assuming that to be true, to abandon him would set a bad precedent. Nobody would be loyal. Nobody would have confidence in the Gov-

*Translator's Note: *i.e.*, a junior member of the Chamber of Commerce.

ernment. People would realize that the greatest of their servants could be betrayed, abandoned, at any moment. A banker half-leaned on the desk to be closer to his colleague. With some severity, he stated:

—For you to give up 200 first-class citizens at the guerillas' whim would be worse.

Holofernes stood up with a leap. Assumed a Demosthenean tone:

—On the other hand, what would be left of our international prestige? You know that the commemorative festival tonight—if it takes place, ay, if it takes place!—will include delegations from all over the world. We'd have an extraordinary party, never before seen. Guests are already arriving. Our airport can't accomodate all the planes. It will be a great opportunity to lay the foundations for our future. To obtain pacts with those governments that would be advantageous to us. To increase our foreign trade.

The Banker smiled like a rabbit before an undefended field of alfalfa.

—And who's preventing the achievement of these things? It's a case of force majeure. You, your Excellency, didn't capture General Pithecanthropus. He was captured by the Amautas. You're doing everything you can to rescue him. You've also offered a substantial reward to anyone providing information about the abductors or their victim. It's all you can do. You're not going to sacrifice so many Babelandians for just one, even on the hypothesis that he's the most valuable of all. Nor should you again release all the intellectual, academic, and political prisoners. They were jailed precisely because of their criminal activities against society and the magnificent and profitable democracy we all enjoy. And neither should you surrender a pound of your precious bones. You're our Leader, and we want to keep you intact. We need you with all your parts.

The Dictator bowed his head. Straining to force a teardrop from his eyes. But he couldn't. In the first place he was aware of his "disinterested" partisans' motives, and secondly, his eye sockets had been dry for a long time. In his lachrymal impotence, he murmured:

—Many thanks, dear supporters.

The Banker was not satisfied. He went on:

—Finally, if the party takes place and there is no Jonas Pithecanthropus, who will be the main attraction?

Holofernes took on the innocence of a lamb about to be slaughtered. He whirled twice around his coccyx.

—Who will it be?

He was not answered by words. They simply pointed at him with their index fingers. And he saw himself on the highest altar of patriotism. He did not reply. Bowed his head. Modest. Pure. Annointed. Profound. A tide of satisfaction ran through him, like an arpeggio up and down his spine. When I tell Harpie about this, the poetess and Melopea will dance with joy. The palace will resound with her rhythmic prancing. Or, maybe as in happier times, she'll start reciting. Who knows if perhaps she might even compose more poetry! Or better, she might want to get drunk. That's what she usually does when infinite sorrow or joy grip her with their fickle fingers. Especially when she thinks Sinbad might be involved. Or better still, that it would hasten his return. I'll have to hide all the liquor. Even though I know it's useless. She'll find it. Besides, she has several bottles stashed away in secret places in the Palace. And sometimes inside the cotton of the stuffed boa. When she takes to drinking, no one can stop her. She imbibes alone. Usually while strolling with that enormous reptile skin. It wasn't always like that. She was brilliant, and liked nothing so much as poetry. Saved a great deal of it, unpublished. Little by little she was rewriting, revising, and polishing it. She wanted to publish a book. An anthology of her finest efforts. Because of that, she'd never forgive Pithy for what he'd done to her. And because of that, she'd be elated to hear what the Verbophilists said about him. I'll take them literally. Perhaps in the cold light of their egotism they see things more objectively. And why, through self-sacrifice, should I deprive the nation of everything he stood for? Why not transform into something positive—positive for Bab—a kidnapping that once seemed so ill-fated? In the end it might benefit me as well. Again I'd be in sole possession of power. Alone, holding the Scepter. On the throne. Wrapped in the presidential sash. Anticipating what will happen, I'll record another tape. Just as soon as they leave. Who can assure me that I won't need it tonight?

Sixteen

AS the hours passed the bananas became more and more tantalizing to the eyes and nose of Jonas Pithecanthropus. Had he not become all nostrils? Now the fruit no longer lay in a circle around his cage. It had stood up. Had begun to march around him. It was trembling and releasing more of its fragrance. But no. They're not really bananas. They're guerillas that look like bananas. They've disguised themselves to add to my humiliation. They know that bananas are my weakness. And that today my hunger multiplies their presence. They're laughing at me with their yellow mouths and writhing stems. They're moving closer to the cage. I'll touch them. I'll grab at least one. One. Just one. He leaped against the bars. Struck his face, his legs, his torso. Damn! I can't get at the sons of whores. And now? What are they doing now? Are they eating each other? Were they the guerillas? If that's so, they don't look like cannibals. And so? So what's going on, Goddamnit? goddamn! Are they demolishing my brains? Have they stuck a propeller in there? Or did they just inject me with a little of the fruit? He screamed in desperation.

—Get me out of here!

He was sweating. His fur was dripping. His little eyes were flaming vermillion. Everything was beginning to swim around him. Was it because the cage had wings and swayed, on the point of rising in flight? Were they winding it up like a colossal spinning top? Were they dragging it along? Had they suspended it over the abyss? Would they let it plummet? Would they throw it against the walls of the crater like a pinwheel? His questions formed another cage superimposed on the iron one. He shouted:

—Don't take them away! Please! At least leave one bunch! Or a handful! Or one banana. At least a banana. Just one!

A stern voice set him trembling.

—Give him one.

—But . . .

—One!

The prisoner turned. All the accumulated hatred in the world began to show on his face.

—You!

Facing the cage in all his serenity was Captain Gleam.

—Yes, me.

Pithecanthropus growled, with a certain desperation:

—It had to be!

He turned. Walked to the other end of the cage. Gave him his back. Continued:

—I might have guessed.

He felt the light thud of the banana falling on the iron floor as if it were on his belly. Despite this, he stayed put. A second passed. Whiffs of the fruity aroma beckoned to him with a hundred invisible hands. He held back. Five seconds passed. The fragrance had become thousands of lips kissing him ceaselessly. Ten seconds passed. He held his breath. Opened his mouth. Moved his very dry tongue over his lips. The perfume he could almost eat tickled all his taste buds. He gripped the bars in order to avoid turning. I won't give the Amautas the satisfaction. Still less, Captain Gleam. But, the banana is ripe. I'll stay right here. I'll close my eyes, my mouth. I'll try to block out my sense of smell. Can I? Its pulp is soft, creamy, flavorsome. There it is, within my reach. They left it for me. Don't think about it, stupid. You'll go crazy. That's what they want. Control yourself. I could peel it slowly. Eat it in little bites, so it would last. How long? How long could a banana last eaten a millimeter at a time? The hair on my head is rising. One more effort. Uuua! Uuuua! I can't stand it any longer. I feel that the banana is winning. Instead of bananas, I should be fighting Amautas. And I could fight them even without weapons. Uuuua! Uuuua! Uuuuaaaa! The banana. It's getting to me. The banana. He made an acrobatic leap. Or better, a gorilla leap. Came down on all fours. Crawled toward the fruit. For an instant everything was forgotten. As if only he and the golden marvel existed. He straightened up. With meticulous care he began peeling it. He raised it to his mouth. Took the first bite. Ate slowly. Very slowly. Opened his eyes only when the last morsel was finished. Reality returned. He took note of his surroundings. Of the people around him. Of the conditions that he faced. He went to the bars of the cage. Grasped them. Shook them with fury. "Uuua! Uuuuaaa!" Gleam watched him in fascination. Now he sensed how his free will was battling his darkest instincts. Considering the latter, he shouldn't have given even one banana to the savage Monster. Nevertheless, his conscience rejected these methods. But in war, anything goes. Don't forget it! The enemy must be defeated by any means possible. Anyway, we're not at war. Oh no? And even if we were, there are degrees of war. To the end we must respect humanity. It's not winning or losing that matters. Then what does matter? The cause of humanity. The triumph of principles that promote the majority's best survival. All right, Gleam. All these theories are magnificent. Nonetheless, theories are irrelevant here. We're faced with a caged beast. Isn't he going to pay for any of what he's done? Is he already paying? Let him undergo, at least, one day without food. He who feeds on other people's suffering. We can't do that. That's just the way he is. We're different. He raised his voice:

—Give him all the bananas he wants.

An Amauta objected.

—Does that seem just?

—No. But give them to him anyway.

—As you wish.

They began to cut the fruits. Then they started throwing them through the bars, one by one. At first he didn't eat. He didn't try to get near them. Broken in spirit, he watched them land in the cage. He couldn't believe his eyes. Surely he wasn't seeing what he believed he saw. Still less did he believe his nostrils. Neither was he smelling what he was smelling. It was all a product of his imagination. His sense organs were deceiving him. Suddenly he grew still, as if he'd been hypnotized. His eyes were open, but unseeing. His legs were in a crouch. Now he lowered himself to a squat. Stretched out his hand. Felt about. Yes. He was touching bananas. Nervously he appeared to pick one out. Selected it. Grasped it. Raised it to his lips. Sank his teeth into it. Savored it. Wolfed it down. Felt its long descent through his digestive tube. A wave of happiness commenced to scintillate through his whole being.

Three knocks sounded in the make-shift conference room of the Boll Weevil Club. Without waiting for permission to enter, Spongy Sumptuoso poked in his little head. The tears had vanished from his face. On it began to appear, instead, infinite sweetness and tranquility. He suggested the image of a plucked turkey, oven-ready. Piggy Rigoletto—possibly already imagining himself the Constitutional President of the Republic—looked down from the heights of the Chair.

—Why are you interrupting us? What do you want?

Soggy Spongy oozed the rest of himself in. His hands swirled benedictions like an abbot's. He started to bow. But his spinal column couldn't cope with its own fleshy adversary. His thick layer of fat proved to be a straitjacket. He smiled meekly.

—Excuse me. I just wanted to offer you some drinks and sandwiches. If you'll pardon the intrusion.

The Secretary of the Interior changed his tone. Accepted immediately.

—Bring them. And thank you.

When the Fat One had left, Warhorse grumbled:

—That walking pumpkin wants to stick his nose into everything . . . Well, let's get down to business. As I was saying, we have to protect ourselves in retreat.

Placido Hotwheels persisted:

—One thousand . . .

The Secretary of Defense confronted him angrily.

—Quit fooling around.

—But I . . .

—Saving our skins is what we're talking about.

Piggy suggested:

—We could arrange diplomatic immunity.

—Impossible.

—Why?

—That way we could only save our lives. And only if the Amautas didn't kick us out of here, which is most unlikely. It seems they'll stop at nothing. Besides, who knows if, in the end, the army of the Verbophilists will back them, just to save Pithecanthropus. But worst of all is that there'll be no "immunity" for our assets.

—Then what do you propose?

Warhorse turned to Panfilo Wincewing.

—Could we count on ten aircraft?

—I suppose so.

—I mean planes that can fly. That can really get us to the Antipodes from here.

Panfilo scratched his head. Made a few calculations.

—In that case, I'm afraid not.

—Then how many can we definitely count on?

—Really good ones?

—Yes, damn it!

—Three.

Well, it could be worse. We'll leave on the best one. In the second-best will go our valuables, jewelry, and cash. In the third, our less important possessions. Of course we'll submit to a strict apportionment. There'll be no favoritism.

—How about our families?

—They can take the "probable" planes. After all, we're the important people.

Knocks on the door again. Spongy entered with several waiters who placed food and liquor on the improvised conference table.

—Thank you, thank you.

The club owner left. Warhorse once again assumed the floor.

—All right, the plane must be loaded. And be ready to take off when we give the order.

The Secretary of the Air Force promised:

—That's my responsibility.

If any of these plans I'm proposing fails, we'll leave *ipso facto,* as the Dictator would say.

Impatience was devouring Rigoletto.

—Perfect. And now, we're all ears.

—First, we'll ask for an interview with the Amautas.

—With the A-mau-tas?

—If we obtain it, then after they accept the first two conditions, we'll propose that the 200 first-class funerals be increased to 1000.

—That's ridiculous!

—Not really, because it will be us who will choose the candidates.

—Ahah! And if they refuse?

—We will give them the 200 that they ask, as long as we're not included among them.

—And if they don't accept that either?

—Then our only recourse will be to get on the planes and say goodby to Bab forever.

—There's no alternative?

—None. So if this afternoon we don't find the hostage or his abductors, we'll just leave things as they are and, without waiting any longer, board the planes. And fly off to a far-away place! I've had reports that the Armed Forces want to rebel. That they're throwing the blame on us for everything. We've got to act before it's too late.

Just then Spongy Sumptuoso's head reappeared. Smiling more congenially than ever.

—You'll keep me up to date on everything, won't you? I'll probably need a seat on that plane, too. Unless by that time you've paid off the last cent you owe me.

The impetuous Piggy Rigoletto was indignant.

—How dare you!

His interlocutor replied in his sweetest voice. Seemed to be a snake clothed in a canary's feathers.

—So we'll all be together to the last moments. How very sad it would be if certain Babelandians should discover your escape plans.

Seventeen

LUDIVINA herself was the first to be frightened. Everything that was happening to her was incredible. A monster seemed to be growing in her womb. From time to time, to the rhythm of her heartbeats, she felt sharp abdominal pains. Way inside. At first they were only sporadic and she didn't take them too seriously. No doubt something in her system had broken down or was out of order. Or was it just her imagination, a product of her frazzled nerves? After several days she was convinced it was real, because the pains were twice as bad. They began like a drill from the inside. Soon it felt as if they had nearly reached the outer skin, almost to the point of puncturing it. No longer did she doubt. There's a monster in my belly. She trembled in anguish. Could her child—hers and Polygamo's—be the Devil's offspring as well as the priest's? Were Polygamo and the Devil really the same person? And if they were, would I have to give birth at the natural time? Or should I take action right now? Should I get rid of it once and for all? She was afraid to tell her mother. But one evening, obsessed with the Green Child nested within her—that's how she imagined him, sulfur green—she could no longer keep the secret. Anxiously she grasped her by the arm and shook her.

—Haven't you noticed?

—What dear?

—What I'm trying to show you.

—Let me see.

She uncovered her swollen abdomen. Below the navel the skin resembled a miniature circus tent with two poles. Doña Prudencia genuflected.

—Virgin Mary! Why didn't you tell me?

—Feel it.

The mother came closer. Placed her hand on the critical area. She could easily feel the protruding points beneath the skin. She was disturbed. Fell on her knees. Wept. Began to pray.

—Hail Mary. Full of grace. The Lord is with thee . . .

Her daughter strangely serene, interrupted her.

—It's no time for tears or prayers. Besides, I'm convinced you've never really believed in them.

Doña Prudencia, suddenly transformed, unfazed by her offspring's words, stood up. She wiped her tears.

—Do you realize what "that" is?

—How could I have known?

—What a horror! And what can we do now?

Her daughter looked at her. Anxiously. Disconsolate.

—What can I do, mama?

Mama perked up. Ready for action.

—For the time being, get out of sight. And look for a midwife.

Ludivina was on an imaginary see-saw. Not knowing what to do. All consequences aside, wasn't it her child? Could she bear extracting and destroying it? As the mother of such a strange creature, could she hate it and rid herself of it? And if it really was a monster? Poor thing! No doubt about it. She knew it was a punishment. For her weak will. Had she ever been able to use her will power? Hadn't she been swept along by some current? She was also paying for her betrayal of Eneas. Why hadn't she told him in time? He might have protected her. Could he have? Could anyone have defended her? Eneas. Eneas, first of all. And Eneas was now seen near the house only once in a while. There he was in spite of himself, as if by inertia. Clutching a lost hope, he denied reality. Was it all a frightful nightmare? Maybe she'd come out the way she used to. Maybe he'd have another chance to come over and talk to her. But her door and window remained closed. And the vicious gossip still throbbed in her ears. Especially the lines of a jingle from who knows where:

Guess, if you can guess,
Whose is the Egg in Ludivina's nest.
Who might be the author
Of her pain and ruin. Guess!

Well, he wouldn't have to guess. He knew the "who" in the verse. Come on, Eneas. Enough of acting the fool. You know the saying, "where there's smoke, there's fire." So resign yourself. Still, the poem, like a slip knot, was tightening around his neck. Especially the first two lines.

Guess, if you can guess,
Whose is the Egg in Ludivina's nest

But for now, Labyrinthia's conversation piece was the Priest, who scarcely dared leave the Church. Each night, his Monstrous Member slipped like an endless coiling serpent across town. It reached Ludivina's house. It slithered through the window. It sought out the young woman. And it satisfied itself with her. How was this remote-control intercourse achieved? By what stimulus? In what way? Seemingly, it was impossible. Nevertheless, Labyrinthians contributed details. They told how, at first, they had tripped over that Elastic Organ, just like rubber. Had danced on it. On occasion they had even tried to squash it. To cut it. A vain hope. The Undulating Member climbed rooftops, adorning them with its infinite loops. Or remained dangling from the trees, finally descending directly on Ludivina's house. Or disappeared. Others swore it was true that the Organ penetrated the house. Likewise, it was certain that it easily reached the Pregnant One's bed. But it didn't penetrate her you-know-what. It simply coiled around her waist. It dressed her in its multiple rings and swept her off to its own bed—the priest's, that is—there in the Sacristy. Returned her in the same way when the sun was scarcely licking the highest mountains. Others maintained that whether the erotic encounters took place in his bed or hers, it was certain that Ludivina resisted them. The Member then would go into a rage. And begin to thrash her until she fell half dead. At times it was unsatisfied with its metamorphosis into a whip. It would wrap itself around her feet. And lift her up, threatening to fling her against the walls. The worst thing—they concluded—was that Polygamo's member seemed to have gone crazy. Or was that its libido was growing in proportion to its great size. Was beginning to act independently of its owner. Besides its adventures with Ludivina, it thrust its way into other houses. In a ceaseless, indiscriminate search for other females. As the news of this surged through the town, a smoldering wrath invaded the hearts of its inhabitants. A desire for punishment and vengeance was visible on most of their faces. Action against the Satyr would have to be agreed upon. Moreover, day by day a terrible certainty was growing in all their minds: the priest was not the priest. So then? Could he be the Lord of Darkness in person? Or was he only a maleficent entity that had taken up residence in Polygamo's body? God knows! It was some time since the Malignant One had possessed anyone around here. And now, of all places, he was doing it in the bedroom of the parish priest. Maybe the Bellringer—crazy and drunken as he was—had hit on the truth: Fire and shit would rain on the Labyrinthians for their wickedness. Eneas, for his part, felt a great claw squeezing his heart, piercing him. And I? What's my role in all this? What should I do? A noise nearby interrupted his thoughts. It came from her house. He peered in that direction. The door to the street opened. Two women came out stealthily. He shivered with anguish. They were Doña Prudencia and her daughter. He shouted:

—Ludivina!

The young woman turned quickly.

—Eneas!

He approached her resolutely.

—Where are you going at this time of night?

The girl did not dare look at him. She was ashamed and confused, and wanted to disappear.

The Organist persisted:

—Where are you going?

Her mother answered:

—That's none of your business. He took Ludivina by the arm. Shook her.

—You're not leaving until you tell me everything.

—Let me go!

—Tell me the truth.

—You're hurting me.

Doña Prudencia intervened again.

—Let her go! Can't you hear?

He paid no attention.

—If you don't talk, you can't leave.

She tried to shake him off. No use. His hand was a vise. A muscled vise that kept closing. She desperately realized she was helpless. What could be done? Moreover, time was running out. Day would soon break. The neighbors would begin to get up. They'd see what was going on. Perhaps try to block her escape. Who knew if Polygamo's protrusion might also appear. How could they fend it off? It might encircle and batter the three of them, just as it had done with her. It was useless. She had to resign herself. Poor Eneas, how he'll suffer! But that you should have thought of before. Not to have been so weak-willed. Nor such an easy catch for the Priest.

—All right. If that's what you want.

She told him in a few words. He denied it, hopelessly.

—You're lying!

—Look!

She displayed her stomach. Naked, shining, swollen, it exhibited the presence of the two horns. His vision dimmed. A flame enveloped him. He had the sensation of riding on a carousel. The multicolored horses were all mounted by a Polygamo. Many Polygamos. As if multiplied by a game of mirrors. Each Polygamo armed with a great phallic spear. All constantly jabbing at them as the platform turned. He had no clear notion of what was happening. Were his senses momentarily paralyzed? He had only a very simple idea: kill her. I have to do it. Even if I tried to avoid it, I could not. Death. My obligation is to kill her. Death. Death is all she deserves. "Yes, Eneas. Kill me! It's for the best. Kill me!" He felt something moving between his hands. Something that seemed to have convulsions. How strange! It looked like her head. Like her neck. Was he strangling her? Death. Death is all she deserves. I'll kill her. He attempted several blows to her head. Am I killing her? He stared at his hands. Clenched. Rigid. They were a living gallows. Encircling Ludivina's neck. Now she was almost lifeless. Yes. He was strangling her! Was she dead? She must be dead. Yes . . . Doña Prudencia, meanwhile, was striking him again and again.

—Beast! Don't you see the state she's in? You're killing the mother and the child. Let her go!

Let her go! He made an effort. Was it too late? The first step was to remove his hands. It was difficult. They seemed to have turned into steel. He tried again. Could he? He was doing it slowly. Very slowly. A sob rose from him. An inward rainstorm ascending. He'd lock it within him. And she? He had to release her. He was letting her go. She was free. They were falling. Would her mother hold her? What did it matter? What did anything matter? Ludivina and all these things began to recede. Or was he the one? He was. He was fleeing. Coward, Idiot. Out of control. Fleeing.

When Ludivina recovered her senses, they started out again. They left town. Had they been seen? Maybe no one tried to stop them. If they cleared out, so much the better. Nobody wanted the plague. And they had it. First they'd look for the midwife. She lived in a nearby hut. Later they'd decide where to go. Away from Labyrinthia? Could they ever get out of Labyrinthia? For the Pregnant One it was becoming more and more difficult to keep going. Each step taken was a little victory. She felt faint. I ought to stop here. To hope for death. What a blessing death would be! For all this to end at once. And not to run the risk of encountering Polygamo again. Or his cursed erection. Sharp pains seized her abdomen. The pointed horns were almost piercing it.

—Mama, I can't stand it anymore!

—Hold on. We'll soon be there.

Around them the trees were transformed. They were Devils. With all the traits of the most devilish Devils. Hand in hand they formed a circle and began to dance around them, making them stop. Doña Prudencia tried to encourage her.

—We have to keep going.

—The Devils won't let us.

—Calm down and let's go!

The creature she carried within also started turning. At the same time it kicked her. Thrusting its horns further out. Convulsing, she embraced her mother.

—I can't.

—We're almost there.

—Really. I can't.

She sat down. Her mother tired to lift her. Impossible.

—Get up!

—Leave me alone!

—Come on. Let's go!

—What's the use?

The woman fell to her knees. As always in her difficult hours, she prayed.

—Hail Mary. Full of grace. Blessed art thou amongst women. And blessed is the fruit of thy womb, Jesus . . .

—Ay! Ay!

She clutched her daughter in anguish.

—My little darling!

The young woman fell back.

—Mother, I'm dying.

—No, dear, no!

—Ay!

Her skin was stretching. Stretching. Soon it burst in a shower of blood and bits of muscle. First one horn stuck out. Then the other. They tossed from one side to the other. Tore a gap, wider and wider, in her abdomen. She no longer complained. Her glassy eyes had a fixed stare. The horns continued their frenetic contortions. The strange creature's body emerged. It was green—sulfur green—from ears to tail. It finished freeing itself. Leaped in the air and hopped away on its only foot. Doña Prudencia, in shock, still held her daughter.

—Ludivina! Ludivina!

She wasn't listening. She'd never listen again.

Eighteen

MORE and more people were coming to the crater. Pithecanthropus—having eaten his fill—had retired to a corner of his cage. He stared incredulously at the crowd surrounding him. He was worried. Confusing sentiments and ideas were interwoven in his being. One thing he couldn't understand was Gleam's order to give him bananas. If I'd been in his shoes, I wouldn't have given the enemy as much as the skins. What does this bastard have in mind? Maybe he's testing me, to see if I'll give in. It's strange. In that case he would have denied me everything. No. That's not what he's after. Probably he did it so that when he does deprive me, I'll suffer more. Yes that must be it. Meanwhile, the Amautas continued arriving. As always, so to speak, they sprouted from the volcanic walls. They were all ages, from the very young to the very old. Of diverse condition: Sloppily dressed with abundant hair and a bohemian appearance. In blue-jean overalls, with a military air, armed with submachine guns. In normal clothes, balding, scholarly, and dignified in manner. Most were men, although there were also several women. More than a hundred had gathered. Captain Gleam presided. They settled around him. Some seated. Others on their feet, leaning against the rocks. The Great Parrots had unexpecedly appeared. Each was perched on an Amauta's shoulder, on either side of Gleam. The latter was about to speak, when he heard the raucous music on the loudspeaker increase in volume. All were listening as the musical curtain fell, followed immediately by the familiar voice of Golden Ace.

—Attention! Attention! We now transmit an urgent bulletin. Attention! Attention! No trace has yet been found of General Jonas Pithecanthropus, Commander-in-Chief of the Armed Forces of Babelandia. All airports, border points, and seaports remain closed. Anyone can enter, but no one can leave. Investigations so far have produced no results, despite the continuing nationwide search by 50,000 serpents. The 500,000 peso reward to the person who provides information about the Amautas or their Hostage still stands. Guests for this evening's festivities are still arriving from north and south, east and west. In the meantime, reward yourself with a Golden One. Drink it! Drink it anytime! No beer can compare with Golden, nor any liquor with Whichever, nor any cigaret with

Whatever. The myth that alcohol brutalizes or degenerates its users and their descendants, or that cigarets cause cancer was invented by disruptive, extremist enemies of the nation, of private property, the law, and religion. Ignore them! Drink your Golden as you smoke your Whatever! Preparations continue at the Boll Weevil Club. The *crème de la crème* of Babelandian Society is dressing formally for the most memorable event of this century. We all have hope that the Number One Citizen of our Country—second only to our president, that is—will soon be free and able to attend the homage being prepared for him. But now for something most important. Drink your Golden while we tell you! The most important news is that here in the Presidential Palace, where we are broadcasting, is Doña Telésfora de Pithecanthropus, the General's wife. And with her, their daughters, their five adorable sets of triplets . . .

—Damn them!

The prisoner's ancestral howl had drowned out the Announcer's words. Again he gripped the bars—half-ape once more—frothing at the mouth. His sinister eyes shone. In vain he tried to rock the cage. Over and over he repeated:

—Damn them, damn them, damn them! Uuuuuaaaa!

The Announcer went on without interruption:

—Our Secretary of Defense, Wiley Warhorse, sent a helicopter to Four Vultures Island to pick them up. They haven't stopped weeping since their arrival. They're anxious to know if there's any hope of seeing their near and dear one again. And if that person is alive and in good health. We appeal to the Amautas. Why can't they provide some evidence of that? Sixteen feminine hearts would be eternally grateful. Are you listening, Amautas? If you are, don't fail us. We ask it in the name of humanity.

Again they heard the musical interlude. Fading in, fading out, then totally disappearing. Seizing on a sudden idea, Gleam approached the cage. He beckoned to the two Amautas with the Giant Parrots to follow him. So they did. Pithecanthropus was still gripping the bars. Was still consumed by his rage. Saw his enemy coming. A kind of rabid satisfaction flooded through him. Come! Come closer! Let me get my hands on your neck. I'll twist it like a rag in the wringer. Come closer! When he figured he had him within reach, he thrust his arms violently through the bars. Captain Gleam scarcely had time to step back. The tyrannical fingers reached within a half-inch of his jaw. The Apeman, seeing that he'd failed again, turned away towards the other side of the cage:

—Jonas!

His answer was silence. A hostile silence that seemed to increase before the thousand, nearly inaudible voices in the volcano. The rest of the Amautas also moved quietly closer, trying not to break those delicate crystals of silence. Gleam repeated:

—Jonas. Listen to me!

His back still turned, he replied:

—Go away!

The Captain hesitated for a moment. After all, why should he worry so much? This wretch deserves everything that's happening to him. And a lot more. Of course, it's his family I'm thinking about, not him. His wife and daughters, that is. Right, Gleam? Are you becoming a hangman? Are passion and hate getting the better of you? Didn't you always say feelings were irrelevant in these matters? In spite of everything, Pithecanthropus is a man too. A man? Do you believe that this beast can be called a man? Well. We haven't much time to clarify that. I think my first duty right now is to insist.

—It's a question of your loved ones.

Jonas half-turned. His anger had totally transformed him. His fur was reddish. Was it on fire? His thick, slightly parted lips trembled. Between them, his fearsome teeth thrust out.

—You can't respect even them. You bastards!

—Take it easy.

He didn't seem to be listening. His voice sounded strangulated.

—I thought they'd be safe on that island.

Gleam almost involuntarily murmured:

—I'm sorry.

Was he listening? Did he hear him at all? He continued:

—I thought they'd always be safe there from men's evil. Why can't you take it out on me? They're innocent. Why should they pay for others' guilt? Why?

Gleam tried to keep calm. But it wasn't easy. His recollection of the prisoner's criminal acts began to clash with his compassionate sentiments. Nevertheless, he continued to control himself.

—Calm down and listen to me!

Pithecanthropus' wrath was reaching its climax.

—You're the guilty ones.

—Not of this.

—Of everything. If you hadn't kidnapped me, nobody would have known anything about my wife and daughters. I could have protected them against anything or anybody.

The Captain controlled himself. Coldly replied:

—You won't listen. It's your own fault.

He turned away. And, followed by his partisans, began to walk off. Now, it was the prisoner who was trying to calm down. Why don't you listen, imbecile? You're in his hands. He probably has a worthwhile offer. Besides, you know Gleam. He's your enemy. But a man of integrity. Don't lose this opportunity. Control yourself. He controlled himself.

—All right. Tell me.

He came back.

—Don't you want to be in touch with them?

—What for?

—To reassure them. To tell them you're well. In a place where no one can ever find you. Where you're not being mistreated. To say the ransom we insist on should be paid very soon. So that we'll set you free immediately and you can go to the party tonight.

—That's useless.

—As you wish.

—Besides, how could I transmit that message to them? Could I write them? They don't know my handwriting. I've never written them. Or do you have a tape recorder?

—Better than that: our feathered green emissaries. Whatever you tell them, they'll repeat it exactly. Better than any machine. And not in a mechanical way. How could they? It will be as if you were talking in person.

—It's impossible.

In unison the Giant Parrots repeated:

—It's impossible.

There wasn't the slightest difference in their expressions of these words. It actually seemed that Pithecanthropus had repeated it himself. So he gave in.

—All right. I'll do it, for their sake.

In a voice strained by emotion—his human qualities had suddenly returned—he began:

—Telésfora: don't worry. We'll soon see each other . . .

Piggy Rigoletto walked without touching the floor. Or walked without stepping on it. As if it had been carpeted with eggshells. The prospect of being President of Babelandia—he could see it very near—had perturbed his senses. This had led, undoubtedly, to the greatest mistake of his life. He had forgotten Voracia, his fearsome spouse. At the same time as he neared his mansion—the hour approached to render homage to Lucullus—the lady's image was becoming more tangible. Her minute size, outweighed by her rapacious hunger for money, was threatening him more and more. How will she react when I tell her in detail what had been going on and what decisions have been made? And if I tell her nothing? Impossible. That would be worse. When she found it out—in case she didn't know it already—she'd turn into a basilisk. And first, she'd denounce us. Especially if she could get several thousand for herself in the process. Really, why is she so crazy about money? I've never known anybody so hungry for it. Hunger. Physical hunger in the most literal sense. It's absurd, but so it is. Some people accumulate money to spend it. To buy everything they want. Others go after it just to possess it. To be or to feel powerful. Still others, simply assure themselves that what's in their bank account, in a treasure chest deep in the ground, or in a hole in a mattress, will grow from day to day. Not Voracilla. Voracilla doesn't accumulate. She tries to pick it up wherever and however she can. Never satisfied. And she never saves a cent. Neither in her pocketbook nor anywhere else. She devours it! She serves it to herself on a platter. She seasons it with spicy sauces. She cuts it in little pieces. And she eats it. Each time she does her face lights up. Her lips attest to an indescribable joy. She breathes faster. Her satisfaction grows in proportion to the amounts she swallows. From her viewpoint, she doesn't really eat what she eats. That is, mere pieces of printed paper. Often dirty, greasy, and repulsive in every way, having been in who knows what hands and places. No. She "eats" all the goods she could have acquired with the pesos she gulps. It's a genuine exercise of her brazen imagination. If the amount is small, it's a dress, a pair of shoes, a piece of jewelry. If it's large, it's a piano, a car, a house. "Just think, Rigo? this morning I ate a washing machine." "Guess what, Rigo? I've eaten half a chest of drawers." He's often told her she shouldn't do that. That it's extravagant nonsense. Maybe madness. And besides, unsanitary. She could even aquire some incurable disease. Voracia just listens and smiles at him. An understanding smile seasoned with scorn and compassion. "Don't be a tightwad, Rigo. It's my only pleasure. Why do you want to take it away from me?" I have to accept everything. To put up with her. Who knows for how long? It's clear that one of these days I'll be fed up, and give her a death worthy of her. I've thought about it several times. I know how to kill her. Have planned it in all its details. Know how to kill her already. I'll change several thousands into one-peso bills. I'll strip her completely. Then I'll proceed to stuff the bills in her mouth, her nose, her ears, her anus and vagina. Until she can't take in even one more. "Isn't that what you wanted, Voracilla? Eat, eat, eat. Until you explode!" We're there already. "Eat, eat, eat. Until you've satiated all the money-hunger you've had!'' We're here, Mr. Secretary, we're here.

—We're here, Mr. Secretary.

—Ah yes, of course. Thank you.

He got out of the car. Entered the house. It was a good house. Of little use to him to be sure. He couldn't use it to its full advantage. First, because he had locked his own father upstairs. An attractive and comfortable prison, but a prison nonetheless. So much time passed since his incarceration that he'd forgotten his reasons for it. Of course the Old Man was no trouble. Voracia was the problem. Naturally he'd have to carry out her execution via the bills before he ascended to the supreme office. How could he maintain his relationship with the female money gobbler? Imagine her, Piggy! On her golden anniversary trying to wolf down all the bills in the treasury. Listen, why don't you buy her a little printing press that could turn out bills all day long? Don't joke about it; it's a very serious matter, Rigoletto. She must be eliminated. The sooner, the better. By swallowing thousands of bills. He entered. His wife was already waiting for him. Her lips puckered. Curses! And on top of everything, I have to kiss her. But, before I'm President . . .

—Do you know, Rigo? For dinner I'm going to treat myself to a new dining room set. Look!

She showed him a roll of big ones.

Nineteen

ENEAS was becoming an instrument. He grew metallic, an organ of a thousand voices. Vibrated in its notes, broadcasting the whole coda of his lament to the four winds. Felt himself a sensitive transparency through which all creation was visible. Was he standing? Flying? Walking? Melodies, not words, were his medium of expression. In them he told, in intimate detail, his misfortune. Because of having misunderstood Ludivina. Because he'd failed her in her time of need. Rather than consoling her. When he should have been her most complete and trusting friend, he had turned his back on her, before and after her death. Was all that love? Isn't love a song of triumph that transcends even the indifference of the beloved? He had turned his back on her! That was worse than murdering her. Of course. But it wasn't his fault. Who was it, then? Polygamo's! You would have worked wonders to save her, had it not been for his nauseating organ. The shotgun! That degenerate priest is the guilty one; he gave in to the lowest wordly pleasures. It was he who was causing all your misfortune. The shotgun. That's it. The shotgun. It has two barrels. Yes. The shotgun. Load them with shotgun shells. To perforate him from head to foot. This way, just as he lived several lives, he'll die several deaths all at once. The shotgun! But soon. He'd get it. He didn't return until night had fallen over the church towers. He walked through the courtyard. Stood before the great wooden doors. Shouted:

—Polygamo!

Silence was his only answer. He drew closer. Pounded with his fists. Insisted:

—Polygamo! Polygamo!

From inside came a sleep-muffled voice.

—I'm coming!

Soon the rusty locks were groaning.

—Who is it?

—Eneas.

—Ah.

One of the doors opened a crack. The Priest. In his underwear. Most conspicuous was the Phallus. It was now totally unmanageable. He pulled it laboriously along with him, with all its loops and rolls, like an oversized fire hose. Rather than an organ attached to a Man, he seemed to see a man attached to an Organ. Suddenly he had misgivings. The poor fellow appeared helpless. Surely he's dominated by his instrument. Dominated? This priest? Hadn't he always worked against everyone's well-being? Wasn't he always on the side of the exploiters and evil-doers? I'll close my eyes and execute him. Nothing, nobody, must prevent it. This antireligious cleric has to be stopped in time. Why take on the role of Providence and hangman? You know you're eager for vengeance. If it weren't for Ludivina, what would you care about his swindling the poor? Still less would you fret about his promise of eternal salvation, just so in this Vale of Tears only they would shed tears. No. I'm neither God nor a hangman. Actually I'm just another one of those who have suffered. One of those who'd like to do away with him right now. Not just for my own sake. Above all I want to protect those who haven't been hurt yet. It's my good fortune that I'm here with the shotgun. He was almost calm in confrontation.

—Say a prayer.

—Which one?

—Take your choice.

—To save a soul?

—That's right. Your own.

—I don't understand.

—Your time has come.

He didn't seem frightened. Rather, he showed signs of relief. Tranquilly he replied:

—I'm prepared to die.

—That's good!

—I've been ready for some time now.

—Really?

—I've sought death many times. But death eludes me.

—This time is different.

A double-barreled shotgun. He took aim. Hesitated a second. Not about killing him. But about where to hit him. His head, or the head of his penis? There was a problem. Where was the weak spot in the penis? Could he face it? By contrast the head was visible. And the forehead. The forehead was his ideal target. The man was motionless. If his face had been clearly visible, its expression would have been a surprise. It was one of satisfaction. Almost pleasure. As if he were about to seduce a new virgin. His eyes rested patiently on the weapon. Eneas squeezed the trigger. The shot sounded. Curiously, just as the charge emerged, one of the shotgun's barrels twisted violently. Its fistful of pellets flew off at an angle. The priest implored him:

—I'm cold. Hurry up!

He loaded the other barrel. Fired. The long tube, just like the first one, bent away. A shower of pellets fell on the field nearby. The Priest was desperate. Knelt down. Grasped the organist's legs.

—Don't do this to me.

—What?

—Have mercy. Kill me!

His answer was almost mechanical.

—There were only two shells.

—Then get more. I'll wait. I don't want to lose this opportunity.

—Do you really want to die?

—It's my only salvation, I can't bear the load on my shoulders any longer. I mean, the load I'm dragging. Well, really, that's dragging me.

As if to confirm his words, the Phallus acted. It gave him a tremendous shaking. He couldn't stay on his feet. Remained stretched out on the ground. He was starting to get up when it knocked him down again still harder. He cried out in anguish:

—Kill me! I beg you!

—I told you. I only had two shells.

—See that? I haven't any luck.

He was about to ask him to elaborate. But he didn't get the chance. The Member was impatient. It began to toss Polygamo about continuously. Then it dragged him to the village square. Suspended him in mid-air. When Eneas tried to intervene, the priest and his bizarre master had already disappeared. Now what? Should he pursue them? Better not. The lecher's new attitude had disarmed him. By now he was nearly convinced he couldn't kill him. Something was preventing it. Was it that this satyr was invulnerable? Or was his life no worse punishment than death? No doubt that was it. It must be horrible to be at the mercy of one's own dominating and insatiable organ. Would alleviation from that domination be beneficial, even at the cost of one's existence? A serene voice spoke nearby. A voice accustomed to dealing with problems on a more transcendent level.

—Creation is the answer.

—Theophilus Bright!

The Volcano-priest was resplendent.
—You don't recognize me yet.
Eneas was mildly remonstrative.
—You made the shotgun miss. Right?
He stared attentively.
—Yes.
—Why?
—Crime doesn't pay.
—I committed another before that.
—You're mistaken.
—I killed Ludivina.
—That's what you think.
He brightened.
—She's alive?
—No.
He darkened again.
—Then what happened?
—It was her baby.
—I don't get it.
—It killed her at birth.

The Organ continued to drag Polygamo about. All the sorrowful, the poor, and the hopeless confronted the priest. Armed with clubs, rocks, or knives, they set upon him. They didn't strike his head or his body or his limbs. They hit directly at the vital spot. The Organ. They battered it until they were exhausted. And the Organ—to their astonishment—was dying, dying, dying. Little by little. It had a few convulsions. At times it seemed it would revive. Evade the blows. And maybe even return them. But no. Undoubtedly it's strength was spent. Or maybe the priest was affecting it. Who knows if he was actually waging an internal battle against that untiring sexual instrument? At the end, his will was victorious. The long, fat-headed member withered and stiffened, taking on the appearance of a stretched-out twig. At the same time the lascivious priest withered and stiffened. Seeing both of them inert, people moved closer. Timidly they wondered what to do. For a few seconds they stood in their tracks. Then they came to life. Touched them. Could they really be dead? And even dead, couldn't they still react in some way? They grew quiet. Were the dead "faking it"? Now they felt them. No. They were really dead. They lifted them. They carried them to Lindorio Necropolo's funeral parlor. Obtained two caskets. One for the priest, another for his Member. Would they amputate the latter in belated recognition of its autonomy? Someone expressed an objection, putting forward a strange reason:

—In spite of everything, he was a man.

—Right. You can doubt anything else, but not that.

—Yes. And no man should be deprived of his thing.

—You said it. We can cut off even his balls. But this thing, never.

The others agreed with this reasoning. The Deceased was placed in one casket, and in the other, his ten-meter Penis. They rolled it up so it would fit properly. Then they moved the caskets, side by side, to a site near the Church. A deep ditch was dug. And the boxes were unceremoniously dropped to the bottom. They dumped sufficient soil on top. Tamped it down with their feet. There were no prayers or flowers or farewells. Only silence, accompanied by the descending loose earth. Once the task was finished, they turned their backs on the tomb and walked away. But a strange noise stopped them. They turned in its direction. Paid attention. The noise seemed to emanate from the Deceased's new abode. The Deceased in the plural, should we say? Had they returned to life? Weren't they completely dead? Or was it another ploy of the indomitable Member? That was it. The Organ was opening a crevice in the tamped-down soil. First the bulbous tip showed. Soon the whole great thing was out. The astonished witnesses were terrified. Was it going to chase them? Would it make them pay—maybe at a hundred-to-one—for what they'd done?

—Let's get away!
—Yes, let's go!
—What good will it do?
—Nothing works against "that."
—Hurry up!
—Before it's too late.
—Let's get going!
—Let's go!

They didn't wait for the decision of the resurrected thing. Of the resurrected Organ. To a man they fled in all directions. A few seconds passed. They hadn't seen or heard anything unusual, so they stopped. Looked around. The Member hadn't pursued them. So what had happened?

—Maybe we're kidding ourselves?

—Right. Maybe imagining something absurd.

—Everything's absurd.

—But nothing has happened.

—That's right. Polygamo's instrument must be still buried.

—And it always will be.

—Always?

—Maybe we'd better make sure.

—Let's go.

—Let's go.

They retraced their steps. Slowly. Stealthily. Fearing at each instant they'd be facing the Monster. Apparently their fears were unfounded. The Member was still underground. It could not escape now. Once more they were beside the grave. They were stupefied. Were they deceived? No. The Phallus was re-emerging. Curiously, it was no longer flesh. It had become a plant. It extended to the Church. In the form of strange intertwined crowns of thorns. It had fastened itself onto the century-old stones. Its muscles, now woody, climbed the walls. The silence had swelled into dissonant arpeggios. In turn, light limned the darkness. All silhouetted things had a golden edge, as if kissed by Inti Ilugshina, the Rising Sun. Suddenly a chorus of bronze bells filled the air. Had the Bellringer returned? Most probably. No doubt he was drunk. Embalmed in his own alcohol—alcohol that swung his body and soul—howling north winds. Soon sleep seemed to overtake him. The bells had begun to harmonize with his feelings. Their voice was now less distinct and more confused. But, as if within that voice, the tubal organ melodies surged. It was not the Bellringer. It was he, Eneas, telling the world the episodes of his unrequited love and of his desire to save all men, his brothers. There was the spark of another love. Love that encompassed the diapason of restraint, but which sustained an inner glow of hope. He longed for reunion, not only for himself, but for all. The search for a new direction in life. It seemed that he had been given wings of steel. Or that the condors—his new friends from the heights—were about to carry him over new horizons.

Nineteen

Later that morning Gleam realized what had happened. Although Labyrinthia was sizzling with commentary under the arches, in the bars, barber shops, drugstores, and markets, he hadn't stopped to hear what it was about. For the first time in some while, nobody seemed to notice him. He moved among them like an invisible spirit. He didn't have to wait for Maria, as he'd usually had to do. This time the young woman was waiting for him. Without losing a moment, she told him all that had gone on at daybreak and gave him some other information: the leaders of Labyrinthia were beside themselves with rage. Even at home Clench mouthed curses and obscenities. He was shocked that the most impoverished Labyrinthians had attacked the Priest. Especially a priest who—in spite of his flaws or his covenant with the Devil—was the friend of those who wielded the power and made the decisions in Labyrinthia. The bad thing, according to this angry man, was that the crime was collective, committed by a thousand hands or maybe even by a majority of the town's inhabitants. "But," he avowed—piercing her with his little dagger-point eyes—"we'll find the culprit. The intellectual author of the murder. This crime will not go unpunished. The Political Leader, Domitilo Mercenario—who was always just—has conferred with all us respectable and important people, to exchange ideas on the matter. Later a complete investigation will be conducted, until the criminal is found. We'll pass judgment on him. Give him the punishment he deserves. We have several clues. All lead to the same suspect." She asked him who that was. The Old Waspnest Face smiled a spine-chilling smile. "You'll soon find out, Maria. You'll soon find out." And off he went to his appointment. When she told Gleam, she implored him with her eyes.

—We'd better stop seeing each other.

—Impossible.

—At least for a while.

He eyed her reproachfully.

—Do you love him?

—No, I don't love him.

—So then?

—Any pretext could be used to harm you.

—They wouldn't bother with me. I haven't even been around.

—When they want to get rid of somebody they'll do anything. They'll frame you. You know that.

She was overwrought, and he gave in.

—All right then. All right.

The girl wanted to stay no longer. She was also afraid for herself. Above all, for her mother. How could it be any other way? Clench could come back at any moment. And if she weren't there he'd beat Gymnastia. Or he'd drop her back in the well. Gleam didn't try to stop her. Watched her from a distance. Beautiful. More and more beautiful. Her suffering became her. She moved away. Her steps were small but rapid. Now she had merged with others. Far off. Very far. Soon she disappeared around the corner. He remained, like a spinning top in its last gyrations. Turning and wobbling. Or was everything else turning? What to do now? Where could he go? And should he look for Eneas? No. What for? He'd walk. And keep walking. Walk to the point of exhaustion. Soon he was out of town. Aimlessly. Walking. Perhaps towards the mountains. Or toward the banks of some river. Some roaring stream that descends to the low plains. What difference did it make where? The important thing was to walk. To keep walking. He had the sensation of being followed. Maybe by one of Domitilo's thugs. Maybe by Clench himself? He stopped. Startled, he turned. He'd been wrong. Beside him in brotherly silence was Theophilus

Shining-Volcano. It wasn't the first time they'd walked together. On the contrary, several times when he'd returned from the peaks he was accompanied by the resurrected priest. They'd talk for hours. He admired him more and more. Recognized in him an exceptional person whose natural calling was to help others. That's why he wasn't satisfied with mineralogical chores and geological transformations. His role as a volcano was but one of his functions. His principal calling was the salvation of human beings. Not only in the hereafter. Also in this life. That morning he asked Gleam candidly:

—And you, what are you going to do?

He was disconcerted. For a second. Responded.

—When?

—In the future.

—Live.

—Living isn't an end in itself. One lives for something. Especially someone like you.

—All right. I'll help my father with his work. And I'll go on loving Maria. Loving her is my self-fulfillment.

Theophilus Bright emitted a cloud of vapor. And he trembled. Impatience? Were his entrails burning?

—You can always love Maria, even though it's a love with serious limitations right now. But you can have other loves. Including loves who will make you more and more worthy of her.

—What do you mean?

—For example, a love for all this world's creatures. Not just so they can lead better lives. But also so they can transcend themselves.

—I'm not religiously inclined. Is that what you're getting at?

—Any good cause is worthy.

—Even when weapons are involved?

—Do you maybe love them?

—Who can love an instrument of destruction? But—from the little that I've seen and read—I guess sometimes they're necessary. Though many of us shun violence, others feel it's preferable. And because of that the only effective counteraction is also violence. We can't recite poetry while a tank vomits flame at us. Furthermore, people have always had to fight for the few gains they've won.

—So then?

—You may be right. My life is incomplete. Thanks for showing me a little light. It's strange. Now I feel as if I'd always been on this path. As if over the centuries past I'd fought in innumerable such battles.

Twenty

WHEN Clench arrived at Epifanio San Toro's house, almost all Labyrinthia's leaders were there. His host came out hesitantly to meet him. A ball-of-cheese wearing a milk-white milky smile.

—We thought you weren't coming.

—How could I miss a meeting like this?

—Evil tongues say you can never find time for anything.

The recent arrival's nose quivered. It always quivered when he was indecisive.

—Really?

His visitor stared at him steadily. It made him sleepy. What could he say? It was as if he had heard a lullaby.

Sleep, baby, sleep;
There's just too much to do:
Dirty diapers to wash
And cooking and sewing for you.

What was he going to say, dammit? He remembered. Control yourself, Epifanio. We're not in a milking stable. You're in your home. And for a solemn purpose. He adopted that air.

—You must be the fruitiest of all Fairies.

Should he give him a swift kick in the belly? He was so flabby that if he did his foot would probably come out on the backside. Or should he knock him down and start dancing on him? That would be like trying to flatten a mudball on a bed of quicksand. But the consequences? Wasn't he the true owner of all properties and persons in Labyrinthia? The prudent thing was to close his eyes. Act the fool. Lay bare one cheek of his buttocks as a sign of self-sacrifice, if necessary.

—Ah, you're the limit, Don Epi! That's pure gossip. People's tongues are scorpion tails.

—I'm glad, Clenchy-wenchy. And you'd better not forget.

—What?

—All we know about the virgin is taboo. Everybody's and nobody's business at the same time. Especially right now.

—I understand.

—The town's on the verge of tearing itself apart. Everyone's thirsting for blood. Even ourselves. Look at us! It would be hard to hold us back!

—So I see.

—All right, then. Come in.

He greeted those present. It seemed like an assembly of sharks. Well, wasn't he one himself? Undoubtedly, but maybe not as much as the others. In other circumstances, he wouldn't have given a cent for his own skin. But that morning conditions favored only him. Conditions that focused his greed on other victims. Otherwise, by now they would have jumped on him and devoured him. Well, drawn and quartered him, at least. Domitilo Mercenario promptly had the floor. He gave an account of the Priest's murder. Spoke in such minute detail that it seemed he'd witnessed the criminal act. Could he have? If so, it must have been from a distance. Or, with his curiosity, maybe he had used the same telescope with which he spied on nude women bathing in the river. He told everything, just as it happened. The only thing that he changed was the number of participants. According to him, few people had taken part. They had taken advantage of the sleeping neighborhood. They had ambushed the holy father. No doubt the latter had been urgently called to hear a dying sinner's confession. As he returned to the church, they attacked from behind, beating him to death. That he deduced from the state of the recently interred remains. They were mangled. Not a bone was left unbroken. According to this improvising speaker, the first news had come from Lindorio Necropolo, the gravedigger. Said that he'd sold two caskets. "The required steps were immediately taken in the case," stressed Domitilo. They went directly to the rich section. It didn't take long to find them. To discover the graves that had been opened near the church. They dug. When they opened the first one, they shook with fear. It was empty. They were confused. Began again. Continued their chore until they located the second one. There was Polygamo. Well, what was left of him.

He declared:

—As I said, he'd taken a beating. When we lifted him out—pardon the comparison—he looked like a blob of phlegm. But that was nothing.

—Nothing?

—Nothing. The worst was, they'd cut off his prick, the whole thing.

—How vile, no! Why was that?

—That, it seems, is the meat in the sausage.

—And what did they do with the—thing?

—Who knows? They may have buried it elsewhere. Or taken it away. No one has found it. The search goes on.

—But where?

—Everywhere. Even in people's houses.

Now San Toro, bursting to talk, broke in.

—But in church something appeared that's never been there: a great many crowns of thorns burst out from the walls.

Domitilo once again was speaking.

—In my opinion it's another miracle. Labyrinthia is becoming a city of miracles.

Epifanio felt obligated to support this interpretation. Making an effort, he fell to his knees. Crossed himself. Murmured: "Amen." The rest followed suit. The Cheese-Balloon-Ball—his fragrance hung over him like a halo—arose with still greater effort. Again, the rest followed suit. The Political Leader, unwilling to yield the floor, continued.

—But there's more.

Surprise was written on his listeners' faces. San Toro himself frowned.

—More?

—Yes, another dead man. Rather, a dead woman.

This was completely unexpected. The group drew near. Surrounded him.

—Who?

He paused, as if to give emphasis. Then he released it, like a shot.

—Ludivina!

—No!

—That's impossible.

—Yesterday she was home.

—Even last night. We saw her.

Domitilo cut them short.

—You can say anything you want. The dead one is completely dead. I have the cadaver. Am holding her wake. Nevertheless, there's still something more. Doña Prudencia.

—Was she also murdered?

—No.

—So then?

—She's disappeared.

A sigh of relief came from the breasts of his colleagues. After all, it was one less death. Clench studied their faces again. Could these sharks also sigh? No time to think about that now. Mercenario didn't want to let them go yet. He enjoyed keeping them in suspense..

—The odd thing is that Ludivina didn't die a natural death.

—Really?

—No. She too was murdered. They performed a kind of Caesarian section on her. Except that instead of making an incision with a scalpel, they seem to have perforated her with a pickaxe, a crowbar, or a drill. All her abdomen was torn to pieces.

—What savages! And the baby?

—What baby?

—Didn't everybody say she was going to hve a baby?

—God knows! We found nothing.

—Maybe the mother took it with her.

—Maybe.

In spite of himself San Toro exclaimed:

—This is getting tough to take. Some miracles are too miraculous.

Again he crossed himself, though this time he didn't kneel. It was getting to be too much for all his kilos. The preceding time he'd gotten bruised all over. The others imitated this most powerful man in Labyrinthia.

—Now—concluded Mercenario—all that's left to do is to locate the culprits.

Already San Toro was breathing a fighting bull's breath:

—It's obvious that the holy Father's murder—may God preserve him in His glory—wasn't part of an attempt to rob him.

Again Domitilo cut in.

—Neither was Ludivina's. They found the belongings of both intact.

Now Clench felt the obligation to intervene.

—It was revenge.

The others repeated in unison:

—Who can doubt it? Revenge.

The Political Leader again took the floor. Nobody could ever persuade him that such a thing was not a function of his position. Besides, the occasions turned up very infrequently.

—And who had motives against the deceased?

Stretching his neck like an accordion, Epifanio lowered his head as if taking a wide-angle photo of everyone.

—Right. Who?

Even though they were on everybody's mind, nobody dared to pronounce the names. They named them without naming.

—The ones we all know.

Authority once more asserted itself. As if they were on trial, a series of questions was asked:

—Who was furious over what happened to Ludivina?

—They were.

—And to Maria?

—They were.

—And who—without justification, of course—were enemies of the Priest?

—They were.

—Therefore, who were the ones who wanted revenge?

—They were, and nobody else!

San Toro pulled his head back straight. Was he strutting like a rooster or snorting like a bull?

—Of course! They were the ones! United to help each other. They're the only culprits.

—But the rest?

—They were accomplices. We'll punish them too. But You-Know-Who are to receive exemplary punishment. And with that we'll eliminate crime in Labyrinthia.

—What are we waiting for, then?

—Yes. What are we waiting for?

—Let's hunt them down!

—Let's find them before it's too late!

As they left, they heard a spine-chilling laugh. They were paralyzed in the grip of their conflicting emotions—horror, fear, and nausea. Immediately they saw a pack of stampeding dogs in a howling tumult. Running on bleeding stumps. Leaving small trails of blood in the street. And several severed paws. In front of the house, oozing with sperm, Quindolo Sheepbang was masturbating. The Leaders paused. Suddenly an idea crossed their minds. Suppose they included the idiot among the culprits? They restrained their impulse. Impossible! They might be committing filicide. Quindolo might be the offspring of any of them. For hadn't his mother, old tramp that she was, always granted each one of them—in happier times—her most intimiate favors?

The verdict of the sharks' tribunal spread all over town. And it was natural that it also promptly reached Maria's ears. She couldn't believe it. It was much too cynical and treacherous. Clench soon arrived and confirmed it. He had such a triumphal, self-satisfied air that she had not the least doubt. All they were saying was true. Particularly when the Old Man began to enjoy her anxiety. Not satisfied with telling her in detail about the conclusions reached, he went further. He outlined a possible plan of punishment that they would impose on—he said the names—Gleam and Eneas. These punishments could include anything from imprisonment with daily tortures up to mutilation or application of the "escape law." Did she know what the escape law was? Simply, assassinating someone from behind on the pretext that he's tried to escape. Anyway, she might as well start saying goodby in her imagination, for she'd never see that person again. "Now do you realize how you'll suffer for ignoring what I said? I warned you. Sooner or later you had to pay for what you did to me." Still and all, if she wanted, he could intervene. Maybe he could help protect Gleam. She could invent an alibi: For example, that the night before he had invited him over to his house out of good will to call attention to his behavior, to ask him to leave her in peace if he did not wish to suffer the consequences. Or that he had gone up to the mountains to tell the young man his patience was running out, that he ought to leave his daughter alone—up there no one knew that she was actually his stepdaughter—that they had talked till dawn, and that only then had he returned. In other words, when the murders had already been committed. Maria protested that Gleam had nothing to do with any of it. Only in the morning did he find these things out. That was the truth. Clench smiled sarcastically:

—What does the truth matter? The owners of Labyrinthia are out to slake their thirst for revenge. Who knows whether or not the organist is important to them. But Gleam is. He'll pay the price for being your favorite.

Restraining herself—even though sensing what it would cost her—the girl proposed:

—If you save him, I'll forgive you for what you've done to us, and I'll thank you for it the rest of my life.

—Do you promise me never to see him again?

It seemed to her that an invisible serpent began to coil around her neck. What could she do? It would be impossible to get free of it.

—I . . . Yes. I promise.

A glimmer of jubilation showed on his hateful face.

—Then only one condition remains.

—What?

—You already know.

She continued looking at him. Without hate. Or scorn. Or rage. She just looked at him. A cold stare. Why answer him? Continued looking at him. Stared expressionlessly, absently, lifelessly. Looking. Looked through him. Toward time. At bygone days. How had she withstood so long the presence of this monster? Why hadn't she escaped from his house when she was still a little girl? Why hadn't she killed him long ago in his sleep, smashing his head with a rock? Several times she'd been on the verge of doing it. He was so evil! Especially with her mother. Perhaps it was because of her that she had never acted. She had accepted everything. For her mother, and through inertia. Had let the days and events pass. Her mother. Poor Gymnastita. As far back as she could remember Clench had changed her name. From Gina to Gymnastita. Having heard it so much, she answered only to the latter. Gymnastita. Her first memories of Gymnastita were happy. Smiling, beautiful, delicate, petite. Little by little, maybe because of her husband's mistreatment, she lost the first two attributes. She became taciturn, bitter, and rather sharp-edged. Without doubt, she still had the patience of a saint. Took everything Clench dished out. Drunken, shiftless, lecherous, murderous, the man had but one asset—asset?: He could play the guitar and sing with half-closed eyes. That's why, even though he did the most horrible things, whenever his wife saw and heard him performing, she lost her senses. Her heart became her harness. And already she was at his mercy. The sly troubadour knew it. Behaved like a horsebreaker. Instead of reins, spurs, and a whip, he crooned his languid musical ardor and shortly his wife not only forgave him, but slavishly lowered her neck and accepted everything. There was only one thing she refused to tolerate: the step-father's treatment of Maria. From the first he showed only relentless hate. The pretext that he put forward was jealousy. He wouldn't tolerate even the child's presence. He forced her to do exhausting chores. Humiliated her day and night. Insulted her for the least of reasons. That's what went on in the first house they lived in. When circumstances reached the breaking point, Gymnastita—with Clench's blessings—sent Maria off to the capital of Babelandia. There she had a sister who took the child in. By the time she returned, she was an adolescent. Their next step was to move to Labyrinthia. Here they presented her as the daughter of both. From that time on, the man began to change spectacularly. He frequented the bars less. He didn't chase—or appeared not to chase—other women. He got a job with San Toro—Saint Ox, as he was popularly baptized—and began to fix up the house they lived in. He went to bed early and tried to keep everything in order. He dressed better than was his custom. And of course, everytime he could, he strummed the guitar, rolled his eyes, and sang sugared melodies in his ladykilling style. For Gymnastita, he was glory personified. And Maria—why deny it?—also felt some happiness. She hadn't forgotten her stepfather's earlier behavior, but now she had no reason to complain. Much less so, observing her mother's happiness. Still, most often at night, a strange uneasiness assaulted her. Despite the transformation of the master of the house, there was something—she couldn't put her finger on it—inexplicable in the old fox's new attitude. He looked at her too much. And not candidly and openly, at her eyes. No. He looked at her body, which was beginning to bloom as if she no longer fit within herself. Something else disturbed her still more: the man showed these passionate looks and attitudes only when they were alone. Whenever Gymnatista appeared, he assumed a reserved appearance, modest and grave. He even spoke in a different tone. That was only the beginning. Soon the sensual stares were matched by words of the same kind: "You're getting very pretty." "You have the loveliest eyes in the world." "Your cheeks are like apples." Her mouth was this. Her body, that. And to demonstrate his affection and respect, he gave her presents every payday. Of course, he also gave presents to Gymnastita. That was part of his scheme. But he found ways of insinuating to the girl that he did it for her. For her only. As one might expect, the inevitable came to pass. One Sunday—after several drinks—he returned early. Much earlier than usual. Taking advantage of the time his wife had gone to market. Maria was alone. He approached her, beginning with his usual flattery. She reacted nervously. He moved closer. Stared at her in such a way that the girl recoiled instinctively. Still advancing, he was almost touching her. Frightened, she tried to escape. Looked everywhere in desperation. Where could she go? He had her cornered. Before she decided, he had already grabbed her. She tried to fend him off. Impossible. He was a man. With strength that his desire multiplied. He pressed her to his chest. Trembling, Maria pleaded:

—Don't hurt me.

He did not respond. Was trying to kiss her. The girl resisted. Tried to shake loose.

—Let me go. I'll scream.

Without drawing back from his aim, he warned:

—Nobody'll hear you.

His grip tightened. Tighter. He smothered her with kisses. Wherever he could. On her mouth. Her cheeks. Her shoulder. Her neck. She struggled in anguish. Was beginning to see shadows. Felt herself in a fantasy world. In her confusion she couldn't believe what was happening. It was all unreal. Treated it as a horrible nightmare. An undulating nightmare among oozing cottons. Curiously, she was powerless. Was unable to react, even within this mightmare. Was gelatinous, stretchable, clay-like. Subjugated to a will that gave it whatever form and movement it wanted. She heard her own words echoing like someone else's voice in her ears: "Don't hurt me, don't hurt me, don't hurt me." Just as always happens in a nightmare, it was impossible to escape. And if she screamed, why didn't the screams wake her up? At last she was able to scream. Nevertheless she was still a prisoner. Not only a prisoner, but also bound by multiple shackles. "Let her go!" This couldn't go on. Unreal as it seemed, the torture was too much. "Let her go! Let her go, you beast!" Clench felt blows on his head. At the same time he was aware that another head had slumped on his shoulder. Maria! Had she been struck too? "Let her go, you beast!" Another blow. He staggered. Let her fall from his grasp. She slumped to the ground. He turned. It was his wife.

—Beast!

He was disconcerted. Stammered:

—I . . . Gymnastita . . . I . . .

Her blazing eyes, two bullets, shot through him.

—If you touch her again—I swear to God—I'll kill you!

He did not touch her again. Or her mother either. Or even his guitar. Instead, he returned to his old habits. Drunken, shiftless, lecherous, and murderous, he scarcely showed his face at home. When he did, he was like a zombie. Stumbling and leaning against the walls, avoiding encounters with the two women as much as possible. Several times Maria wanted to leave home. She suggested it to her mother. Gave a series of reasons. Her main thesis: maybe the man would change if she were gone. She was the only cause of discord in the family. Her absence would bring back order and tranquility in their home. As for her, she'd move back to her aunt's house in the Capitol. It wasn't far. She'd find a job. She'd return for a visit as often as possible. The author of her days did not accept this. What was the use? It would be the same . . . or maybe worse. "The man realizes now that there are limits; he can't persist any longer. Besides, between him and me, everything is finished." They were separated by a wall of hatred, that neither could now break through. Fortunately, this hatred was seldom expressed. At least in front of Maria. Only when the girl was out did he return to aggressiveness. Insult her. Mistreat her. And end up forcing her into the wet hole of the well. Why did he do that? From sadism? Did he think that this would be a new way to dominate her? Did he believe that this would one day persuade her to let him renew his "affair" with the girl? His procedure was to lower Gymnastita on a rope down to water level. Not to submerge her completely. Just up to the neck. She didn't complain. She didn't struggle. She said not a single word. She lived in perennial lethargy and sleepiness. Nevertheless, it seemed that this was a part of the price that had to be paid. That way he wouldn't molest her daughter again. She confided none of this. Simply, she transmitted her impression that Clench had become a ghost. No more than an apparition that drifted between them. Things continued that way until the carpenter widower invaded their lives. Start the man of the house made his intentions clear. And in this he had his spouse's support. For the first time in a long time, communication was restored. Now he spoke of the multiple blessings of matrimony. Notwithstanding his ripe old age, the hard-working and honorable carpenter was one of the best catches in town. To Gymnastita, all the reasons advanced made sense. Undoubtedly the most convincing part was the thought that her daughter, without leaving Labyrinthia, was nearly out of danger. The danger was Clench. Nevertheless, with this new appearance of change, it was always possible he'd return to his old ways. Who could tell if by force or criminal methods he'd try to trap the girl again? All considered, she was worried about her husband's new attitude. How come he had suddenly hatched that marriage scheme? Did he want to free himself from temptation? Did he plan to take some kind of advantage of so hasty a union? Who could know! As for Maria, she was against the wedding. She had always thought of marriage as something special. The culmination of love, which she hadn't yet experienced, that would make her view the world as a new discovery at each instant. But what was she to do now? What could she do? What future could she expect in that house? To grow old under her step-father's domination? Even if he was no longer manifesting his intentions so obviously, she was sure he'd be after her, like an animal stalking its prey. He'd wait for the proper moment to pounce on her and possess her by any means possible. Also, the old obsession remained: wouldn't she continue to constitute an obstacle between her mother and this man? In spite of everything, Gina had loved him. Still loved him. That was clearly noticeable on those days that he played the guitar again and sang with half-closed eyes. So maybe with her marriage the pernicious one would change and the situation would improve, giving her mother some few moments of happiness. So they? What could she do? Did she have some other course in sight? She resigned herself like a lamb that—with no choice—is led to sacrifice, and although each day her heart grew heavier, she did her best to insure that her anguish began and ended with her. Besides, down deep she had a dim hope. An absurd hope, to be sure. The hope that moments before her marriage to the widower was to take place, a horseman would appear. Would arrive from who knows where. Would take her in his arms. Would sweep her away from this place forever. She thought this continually—with intensifying hope—right up to the wedding day. The day of the wedding was another nightmare. From the instant she was pronounced that man's wife until—a few seconds later—she became his widow. It all happened as if it were to someone else. Or, at least, as if what was going on were not of this world. Even now, as she was recalling it, she seemed to be dreaming it, that it had never happened. Real life, true life, only commenced with her love for Gleam.

Twenty-One

THE Skeleton-disguised-as-a-Man flew out the window. As always, on his winged ass. He wanted to mix with "his people." Hear their comments. Surprise them on their jobs. Sense the public reaction to the kidnapping. Pithy must be having a hard time of it. He'll have to pay for all he's done. It's his own fault for ignoring my advice. "Don't run roughshod over people, Pithy. You'll regret it. You've sown much hatred and rancor. Why don't you proceed objectively, without sadism, rejecting force whenever possible?" The Apeman only laughed. "Don't be an asshole, Holie! Terror is the best weapon against our enemies. That way no one dares stick his neck out. You'll see in the end that I was right." Now he must be the one trembling in his boots. I'll never forget that. If we pay his ransom and they actually return him, there won't be much left of him. Fortunately, we won't pay his ransom. We'll leave him with the Amautas. Personally, if I were in their place, I'd rip the skin from his belly and use it for a drumhead. That way Bacchus could accompany my musical inspirations. I'd play the ocarina while he'd beat the stretched-out Pithy-skin. I wonder what his skin would sound like, anyway. But quit the pipedreams. Think about more important things. Don't be carried away by the automatic regulating device in your cranium. It's no time to be fooling around. You've got to face up to the problems caused by Jonas' absence. He must be replaced. Find someone who will be less difficult. He was always giving you trouble. That's for sure. He wore my patience thin. He acted as if it were he who was making the decisions in the palace. That was too embarrassing for me. Any day he could have pulled a fast one on me. Then I would've had to retire him from the army. His pension would have cost a fortune. And perhaps, since he's so influential among the military, he'd have organized a revolt against me. Paradoxically, the Amautas are inadvertently helping me through this crisis. How blind I was! I even ignored Harpitune and wanted to give them a pound of my bones. The Verbophilists had to clarify it for me. They wanted me whole, without a single ounce missing. They sound like good supporters. Good? Aren't they just thinking of themselves? Bah! So what? Who doesn't act in self-interest? Besides, the problem's almost solved. We have to look to the future. And especially to know how to deal with the Amautas.

It won't be easy. Their attitude confuses me. Who ever thought of bones, cadavers, and prisoners as conditions of ransom? When I heard the kidnapping was real, I panicked. I imagined that with such a prize they'd demand millions, or power, or something like that. And then came the shocker. Well, soon, the anonymous will be identified and our doubts will finally disappear. Maybe the Amautas are only idealists or fugitives from an insane asylum. If they are, I certainly wouldn't want to be in Jonas' skin. But what's happening to me now? I'm getting aerostatic. Have I become a kite? Am I rising on the wind? That must be it. There's no saddle under my butt. Still less can I feel a donkey's belly between my femora and tibiae. What can it be? What can it be? See what you get for thinking foolishness? It wasn't foolishness. Good. Anyway, this isn't the time or the place for it. For now, calm down! Easy does it, Holofernes! If you want a better idea of what's going on. He looked around. Nothing but sky and clouds. He looked down. Saw the electrocardiogram silhouette of the capital of the Republic. With its arbitrary skyscrapers, its outcroppings of poverty, and its vast expanses without a house. The blinking of the anarchic beehive of its inhabitants. The innumerable ostrich-neck steeples of its churches. The mysterious lullaby of the mountains, grasping in their broad, diamond- and opal-studded hands of the vertical shafts of the sun. And his donkey? Flying at roof level. And he himself? Way up here. For now he was many parts. His vertebrae disintegrated. He was a scattering of bones. Many fingers hurled in the air by the toss of a colossal dice cup. He made a special effort. Sharpened his senses. Hurry up, Holofernes. Be careful not to lose any parts. Later you're not likely to find anything. He extended the tips of his phalanges and began to rejoin his vertebrae in the throes of a feverish self-integration. Was stuffing them inside his clothes, jiggling them into place. In this reassembled state he called his donkey. The latter turned his long-jawed head. Stared with mocking eyes. Smiled, showing his perfectly symmetrical teeth. He came near as rapidly as he could. But Holofernes wasn't satisfied.

—Hurry up!

When once again he straddled his docile steed, he ordered:

—Let's go down!

The ass obeyed. In a flash they were on the most impoverished streets. The Bony One took out the mask of a beggar. Put it on. To keep his phalanges and phalanx tips from showing him up, he pulled on gloves. Turned the suit he was wearing inside-out. As on other crucial occasions, he covered his skinless cranium with a Chaplin-style derby. In that imposing outfit he bent himself over and struck up a conversation with the first people he met. They were two half-naked men, hitched to a yoke and pulling a wooden plow. They scrabbled over the hard earth on all fours so that the primitive machine might break it. Undoubtedly their sweat would help fertilize it. They had the vacant stare and stiffness of escapees from this life. To talk with them he had to follow their unending trek along the furrows. Without stopping, they took turns answering him.

—What do you think of the kidnapping?

—We eat only roasted corn, sir. Once a day. Every day of our lives.

—No. Kidnapping means carrying somebody off.

—Ten years ago I tried to carry off Anafra, sir. There was no way. Neither money, nor time, nor anything. I'll be dead before I can carry her off.

—You don't seem to understand. It's something else. It's a general. They have abducted a general.

—What's a general, sir?

—Someone who commands soldiers.

—And what are soldiers?

—Soldiers are the ones who protect their country, law and order, and justice.

—When you have one of them to spare, send him here, sir. Even though we don't understand this, anything that can protect us is fine. Nobody ever protected us human oxen.

—And what do you think of the Government?

—Yes sir. Sunrise to sunset. We come and go. Sometimes our dead ancestors take pity and give us a hand. But they already died of exhaustion. And can't help us for long. We have to go on. Indefinitely. From sunrise to sunset, sir. That's why we were born oxen, sir.

Later he quizzed an old tailor in the outskirts. One who accompanied his work with whistled tunes. And made rhythmic stitches. He was eager to talk to anyone. From time to time he snipped a thread in the air. When he saw Holofernes on the donkey, he invited him to step in and sit down. The Skeleton-disguised-as-a-man replied:

—I'm already sitting.

The tailor corrected him:

—You're mounted, which is different.

—Anyway, I don't need anything mended.

The other one eyed him professionally.

—Your suit needs to be turned. Shall we turn it?

—No.

—Then, suppose we exchange it for another?

—Neither. I only wanted to ask you a question.

—Shoot.

—What do you think of the Government?

—What Government?

—This one, our country's.

—When has there been a government in Bab? What we have had—and continue having—is misgovernment. A mafia of thieves and criminals who have taken the country over. They're only out to fill their pockets, while the rest of us die of hunger.

The Calcareous One bit bone.

—Verbophile is honest.

—Honest? Could be. But he's a fool. Those around him take advantage of him and the country.

Disconcerted, and just to say something, he murmured:

—Isn't that the limit?

The tailor showed him a lit candle under his workbench.

—I keep praying to the Virgin. That this misgovernment will fall as soon as possible!

—What party do you belong to?

—POP.

—POP?

—Yes. The Perpetual Opposition Party. The party of all those who want this regime and each of its successors to fall . . . Personally, this is what I'd like to do to every offical of our government, so!

He gave a scissor-cut that made a good portion of threads fly from the cloth.

—This!

He repeated the earlier act.

—This, this, and this!

Each succeeding utterance was accompanied by a fiercer snip. The Calcareous Horseman and his steed took advantage of the tailor's frenzy to put a prudent distance between them. On moving, they found themselves swept away on an irrepressible wave of young people. Students, no doubt. Some carried books or notebooks in their arms. Clean-shaven and bearded. Hair in all lengths and styles. Clothes in varied condition. A mixture of male and female. They seemed united by a single passion to transport the numerous coffins on several wagons. Holofernes dismounted from the donkey. And, on the march, questioned the nearest participant:

—Whose are the bodies?

—What bodies?

—The ones you're carrying.

The other looked at him mockingly.

—There aren't any corpses.

—And these coffins?

—They're empty.

—I don't understand.

—They're for the 200 burials the Amautas requested.

—Do you believe that they'll take place?

The student or whatever he was became serious.

—The only thing that we can lose is our hope.

—How can you say that?

—Don't you agree it would be healthy for our country?

Holofernes changed the subject.

—And what do you think of the kidnapping?

—It's wonerful!

—A terrorist act, wonderful?

—All those opportunists should be kidnapped. And kept kidnapped for good.

Later he came upon another young group. They were entertaining themselves in a public park. From closer up he got a clearer idea. Strange-smelling cigarets. Was it pot? Beer in abundance. To which powders were added. Cocaine? Some played instruments. They improvised many kinds of songs. Only the harmony remained the same. Others beat time in a quite awkward way, in an almost gymnastic ballet. Still others were sprawled indifferently on the ground. The expressions and gestures of most of them came out in slow motion. It was difficult for him to distinguish which belonged to one sex or the other. Suddenly a few of the sleepy eyes noticed him. With slow, vague movements, their arms began to sway. He was pushed. Other arms received him. Then he was given a fresh push. The first group repeated their movement. And so on, successively. The game continued, punctuated by raucous laughter.

—Keep time, Dome Head.

He stammered:

—But I . . .

They paid him no attention. He repeated still more forcefully.

—I . . .

—Leave him alone!

They obeyed. He looked at the one who'd spoken. He was a huge—huge imbecile?—muscular man. Before he hadn't noticed him. He was dressed like the others but, strangely, he wasn't drinking, or smoking, or singing, or dancing, or playing any instrument. Was he the pusher of the drugs and drinks? They all gave him their respectful attention. He gazed fixedly at Holofernes. The latter right away seized the opportunity to ask him:

—What do you think of the kidnapping?

—Not worth two cents.

—And the government?

—Not worth two cents either. Nothing's worth two cents. Life is short and we ought to enjoy it.

Then he asked him how much stuff he wanted. But since Holofernes couldn't understand the jargon that the other began using, the latter became furious. "Is that all you interrupted us for, you bastard?" He turned to the others.

—Tune him in.

He was unable to protest or to say anything. Nobody would have heeded him anyway. Strident music sounded. Increased in volume. The dance went on. He was twirled. round and round. Began to feel seasick. Was he on a boat? Or was it a carousel? Maybe both. A merry-go-round on a ship. Or a ship on a merry-go-round. Ship? Ship? The image of a ship evoked his Sinbad. Sinbad. He tried to erase the memory, just as always. He couldn't. Again he'd appeared, just as the last time. Sinbad. Sinbad. Fool that I was to let you go! Why did I try to impose my will at all costs? Sinbad, my son. You were about to inherit control of Babelandia. And you went away. You refused even to consider it. "You must benefit from what I've built"—I told you—"You ought to carry on my work." But you didn't care. "Dictatorship for life," you called it. You wanted to be free. To dedicate yourself to poetry. And to embroider beauty with your own blood, if necessary. To make a poem of your life and your creations. I was blind. I took Pithecanthropus' advice: "Sinbad has to be toughened.

Make him a soldier. Tear up his verse, as well as Harpitune's." And that's what he had done. With his own hands. Then I washed them, like Pilate. Sinbad's disillusionment culminated in his departure. Forever. His eyes dissolved into a sea. And on that sea—sails to the sky—he sailed away.

Twenty-Two

THEY were arrested very quickly. Not knowing what they were being charged with, they neither fled nor hid. One patrol got Eneas while he was playing the organ. He didn't ask the reason for his apprehension. Nor did he offer resistance. Did they suspect he'd killed Ludivina? No doubt there had been witnesses—behind the window curtains—to the violent scene. Or was it because of the priest? Had they heard the shots? Had he been seen using the shotgun? His conscience, to be sure, was not clear. In both cases homicide had been forestalled. Right. But only chance stopped him from strangling the girl, and his buckshot from eliminating the parish priest. The surprising thing was that they also arrested others. Had something occurred that he didn't know about? He resigned himself. In the end, he'd soon know what was what. Gleam, on the other hand, didn't give up so easily. Those who went after him found him half-way home. Their spokesman gave the order:

—Come with us!

Bewildered, he asked:

—Me? But why?

—You'll be told in Labyrinthia.

He broke away. The other came after him, followed by his party, shouting:

—Stop . . . or I'll shoot!

Since he didn't obey, the threat was carried out. The rifle bullet whistled past the young man's ear. He halted. They caught up with him. Surrounded him.

—Don't be a fool, Gleam. Why risk your skin?

They started to handcuff him. He protested.

—Let me loose, I'll walk alone.

—But don't try to escape. You'll regret it.

They started out again. Suddenly Gleam stopped. So did the others. The Leader came up. Seized him by the shirt. Raised his first to strike him. Held back.

—Goddamnit! Again?

The wounded one stared fixedly. With serenity.

—Let me go!

The other released him. The young man continued:

—I told you I'd go along. And I will. If I didn't feel like it, I wouldn't budge from here. Even to save my life. All I want is to notify my father.

—Impossible. You have to come with us. They're expecting you. We'll notify him later.

—Is that a promise?

—Yes.

—Let's go then.

The walk toward the town began once more. They'd gone just a few steps when Gleam asked:

—Can you tell me what's going on?

—Don't take me for a fool. You know perfectly well.

Without breaking stride, he turned. He was surprised.

—I swear I don't.

—I'll refresh your memory. Today before dawn Eneas and you, with help from others, murdered Ludivina and Father Polygamo.

Still more bewildered, he stammered:

—Ludivina and the priest . . . us?

—If you can't prove you didn't, things will be rough for you.

Epifanio San Toro hadn't figured on wasting time. All was in order: the imprisonment of the culprits, the trial, the sentence, the clandestine meetings, the consultations he'd offer, the visitors he'd receive, etc. But time? These things would make him waste a lot of time. And now, as always—but especially now—his time was gold. Because of a new project: Napoleon. A phenomenal bull. He had just arrived. From abroad. And he was administering the semen of this new emperor of his corrals as efficiently as possible. No one could replace him in this delicate work. He personally attended to his bovine's smallest sexual details. Furthermore, he adored Napoleon. He couldn't help it. He'd hung the ruminant's pedigree in a gold frame on his livingroom wall. The enormous macho image haunted him day and night. The mere thought of him in spectacular copulation caused a tingle in his own genitourinary tract—more urinary than genital, to be sure. He personally selected Napoleon's lucky cow. Led her to Napoleon. Then he encouraged him with words and gestures that he judged stimulating. He found a way to arouse the progenitor's virility. The truth is that the animal was sometimes bored or bothered. The biological role that he exercised, noble and significant as it was, did not automatically please him. Maybe he'd have preferred a different mate. Or was masticating a sweet clump of grass that led him to other thoughts. Or maybe he was in his I-don't-give-a-damn mood. Just because I'm a breeder-bull, must I always be subjected to the whim of this Cheese Ball? But San Toro was not to be denied. He topped off his encouragement with stronger expressions. "Get on her, you bastard! Don't be a mule. I didn't pay a fortune for this stubborness. Perform!" Sometimes Napoleon seemed to understand. But not always. Then he'd stand by impassively, continuing the rhythmic movement of his jaws. His dark-mirror gaze losing itself in intangible worlds. That's when San Toro would give up speeches and gestures. Began to take decisive acts. With his hands he'd begin to stimulate the prize stud's potent genitals. Only this simulacrum of masturbation would win over the namesake of the Waterloo loser. He stowed his grassy clump in his cheek for later leisure. Started to tremble. More precisely, to vibrate. And then to arms. As Napoleon's climax neared, Epifanio's muscles began to quake like frightened swine in a pig-sty. How could this man, to the detriment of his sacred interests and fascinating pastimes, bother about two dead people and a few prisoners? Of course he might leave these delicate tasks in the hands of Pepita. She was dying to do them. Always accompanied him. She too trembled as she excitedly watched her father's work. Especially enjoying Napoleon plunging and dipping his pestle in the female's chocolate pot. Of course the multi-widow's agitation was a vicarious experience. When insertion was achieved—a little earthquake of undulating flesh branding the damp pastures with fire—she clutched Epifanio's arm. With a nervous squeeze. Momentarily crazed, she would imagine herself competing with the cow for the impetuous Napoleon's ardor. Of course she wouldn't await, cow-like, the vigorous macho charge. She saw herself naked—would this be important to the bovine? Vagina up or vagina down?—in voluptuous peristalsis on the soft grassy bed. When she was ready to put in practice these tremendous experiences and was on the point of stripping off her clothes and leaping over the fence, she'd get hold of herself. How crazy she was! Crazy-crazy-crazy! How could she sexually confront that 500-kilo zoological machine? Or could she? Her father watched her askance. Knowing her as well as he knew her, he thought it would be risky and dangerous to leave her alone with the bull. Not that he cared much what such a confrontation might do to her. The bull was what concerned him. His Napoleon. And if the latter, facing his "little girl's" wiles, petered out in the same way as the parade of men who preceded him? Perish the thought. It was like leaving a lamb in a tiger's care. Pepita was a pip of a pussy pumper. Probably she'd finally do the bull in. And those 500 kilos would be reduced to skin and bones. Because of all this, then, once more he'd have nothing to do with assassins, with their presumed judges, with the victims, with Maria, with Pepita, and even with himself in any role connected with such a tragicomedy.

Meanwhile, Labyrinthia reverberated with gossip. Very few were working. Most kept busy enough slipping messages with their loose tongues into each other's ears. The whole town seemed a tapestry woven of tongues and ears.

—They were tied and dragged in.

—Where were they taken?

—Where do you think? Domitilo's house. The jail's there. Well, one of the jails.

—Are there many?

—Two. Didn't you know? Where have you been?

—The bakery.

—What do you mean?

—I work there. Night shift. While you're all sleeping. I sleep during the day, while you're awake.

—Well, yes. There are two jails. One in Epifanio's house and the other in that of the Political Leader.

—Two jails for such a small town?

—Why does that surprise you? Those arrested for minor crimes get a few days at Epifanio's. If they have no money they pay their sentences in work, in the corrals or cheese factories of the Dairy. At Domitilo's they stay much longer—months, years, the rest of their lives. Those are the ones sent to break rocks in the mountain quarries.

—Some news, this news! I didn't know that either.

—So now you're learning something.

—Then do you think that Gleam, Eneas, and the others will be behind bars for a long time?

—Of course.

—But almost all Labyrinthia says they aren't guilty.

—Right.

—And the Bosses don't know it?

—Better than anybody.

—So then?

—They want to get rid of Gleam. Because of Maria.

—But why Eneas?

—They're close friends.

—And the others?

—They're still in the way.

—Hell! It makes me angry that they take it out on the innocent.

—Do you need your tongue?

—What?

—Your tongue. Do you want to keep it?

—Who doesn't?

—Remember Agapetus!

—Ah, right! Still, we have to do something. Those who imprisoned them are really the guilty ones.

—Good bye, Professor. It's easy to see you sleep while the rest are awake. I hope you can keep on talking for a long time!

Twenty-Two

A little later, Labyrinthia—the town of a thousand alleys, easy to enter, hard to get out of, network of hungry stomachs and imprisoned minds—joined in a monolog. Thousands of voices became one. Even though a figurative distance separated one from the other, even though fear glazed their eyes and stained their underpants, people conversed, breaking the heavy silence that filled the streets. A silence of solitude, anguish, and death.

—Something must be done.

—We can't let those with sulfuric acid for blood be the only winners. Their tentacles of excrement smother the best in all of us.

—Right. We've got to do something.

—But what?

—That's it. What?

It wasn't necessary to open their mouths. Or to hear themselves. Or to look at one another. The talk traveled on invisible filaments. From house to house, from one street to the other, from one plaza to another. Dialog sprang up like a transparent elastic reed bearing thoughts. Only those listened who had to listen. The others were shaded and isolated by the intangible walls of themselves.

—You, Maria. What would you do to save them?

—Anything at all.

—For example, what?

—I . . . Well . . . I'd kidnap Pepita. I'd only return her to her father in exchange for the prisoners.

—Ha, ha, ha!

—Ha, ha, ha!

—Ha, ha, ha!

—What's so funny?

—That would make Cheese Ball's pot rich. He'd practically melt with gratitude if someone carried off his daughter. But no one's hero enough to take charge of that broad.

—Then . . . I think I've got it.

—What?

—Let's kidnap Napoleon!

—The seed bull? Now that's an idea!

—Don Epifanio would offer anything for his bull.

—There's no time to waste. Let's find him!

—Things are done right or they don't get done. We'll go get him later tonight, when it's darker.

That's what they did. With two blows they put the peon guards out of commission. The dogs barked. Were about to attack. They were asked to be quiet and listen. The canines acceded. They were convinced that it was an act of justice. The noble animals understood. They quieted down. And, raising their tails, full of curiosity, they prepared themselves for an unprecedented event: an act of justice in Labyrinthia! Napoleon was dreaming about a bovine Eden where cows didn't exist. And where—in slow motion—he alone moved through always green pastures. Hearing the commotion, he woke up:

—Another cow?

—No.

He yawned.

—In that case, in principle anyway, your visit interests me.

He stretched.

—What can I do for you?

—You have to come with us.

—Where?

—On a little trip.

—Fine. But on one condition.

—What's that?

—If we run into a cow, I'm coming back. I only have daytime obligations to them. Nothing at night.

—Agreed.

He became spontaneously talkative and mooed a confidence:

—You don't know what it takes to face rear ends, and more rear ends, all day long. I see that end of my females so much that if I were to approach a mare and a cow from the front, I couldn't tell one from the other. Do cows still have horns?

—They still do.

When the corral gates opened and they had moved slowly away from the place and its persistent characteristic aroma, Napoleon underwent a transition. Joy filled his heart. He re-experienced freedom. He stopped talking. Full of exhiliration, he pranced in a playful trot that his kidnappers had a hard time keeping up with.

Twenty-Two

At dawn, Epifanio, as usual, peered out the window at his corrals. His vision was blurred and his blood frozen. Was he seeing what he was seeing, or more likely, was he seeing what he was not seeing? Between sobs he tearfully shouted,

—Napoleon! My Napoleon!

Soon he was rolling in short ball-bounces down the stairs. Bounce-a-ball-boom-boom-down-the-steps. Rolling toward the shelter of his most precious possession. Damn it all! He was gone! In his place was a written message, tacked to a post.

—Leave Maria in peace and free the prisoners. In exchange we'll return Napoleon. If you don't, we'll still return him, but castrated.

He tore off the message. With it clutched in his hand he rolled in more ball-bounces along the street. Went to the plaza, bounce-a-ball boom-boom. Wrapped in a whirlwind of whines, tears, and urine. Giving off a sour manifestation of his rage and bewilderment. In this state he appeared before Mercenario. Showed him the note.

—You've got to give them what they ask.

—Impossible.

—And Maria must have her way.

—But, Epifanio.

—Stop epiphanizing me, and all the other screwing around. I want my bull, understand? I want my Napoleon. Intact. Now. Immediately!

—And if someone objects?

—Send him to me. I'll make him a capon.

—And if it's Clench?

—Chop him up. Kill him. Make him disappear. Whatever you want. But you have to send them what they want immediately. I want my bull. I need my bull. I cannot be without my Bull. My bull! My Napoleon!

—All right. All right.

Later, time and space—instruments multiplied in the symphony of history—came and went in swirls, always returning to the same point. The fugitive butterflies were drinking in speed, light, and hopefulness. Gone from Labyrinthia in search of their true selves. The route of their destiny. Apprenticeship. Formation. The renewed struggle against everyone and everything. Always the struggle. The struggle between those who want to dress the world in smiles and those who want to perpetuate its tragic and bitter grimace. And the zig-zag, especially for Gleam, from past to present and present to past. The soldier in other times battling for liberation. The soldier today battling in the same cause.

Twenty-Three

PITHECANTHROPUS was reassured by the radio broadcast of the message to his wife when he heard it. He sat on the floor of the cage with his hands on his knees. Watched the Amautas as they spoke. Gleam presided, with Eneas at his side. Now he had a sudden urge to begin a conversation with them. That would clarify a few doubts and, at the same time, let him air a few opinions. He himself was surprised at this impulse. Is my predicament affecting me? Or is it just the need to talk to somebody—whoever it may be? Control yourself, Jonas. Don't give in. Remember they're your enemies. Anything you say will be held against you. And if they revealed something that could help me elaborate an escape plan? Escape? Don't be stupid, General. The only way you'll leave here is feet first.

If that's the case, maybe there's nothing to lose! Make up your mind. Of course, if I antagonize them they'll treat me still worse, until my time comes. Could anything be worse than another few minutes of Tantalus's tortures? Nothing could be more trying or horrible than that. It looks as though I'd better give them a piece of my mind. If they don't like it, that's their problem.

Almost shouting:

—It's unbelievable!

Gleam was surprised.

—What is?

—It's unbelievable that officers like you and Lt. Eneas Pioneer could behave like that.

Gleam's tone of voice was scornful.

—And just how do we behave?

—In the first place, you run around with outlaws, like these people.

While speaking, he made a derogatory gesture toward the group. The Captain was ruffled. A flicker of anger showed in his eyes. But, as usual, he controlled himself. Stated serenely:

—I won't let you talk like that about the Amautas. Intelligent, and cultured, each one embodies the highest virtues of his activities, conscience, and profession. Above all, their humanity is insuperable. They've given as much as they could to the struggle. Their only guiding principle is the common good. They're prepared for death—and even those things worse than death—for the triumph of our cause.

In ape fashion, the other raised his arms.

—All right. All right.

The Captain had difficulty controlling himself. Nevertheless, he made an effort. Once more mastered himself. Thought personally that nothing could be lost in trying to give the prisoner a lesson. And for that, it was best to introduce him to a few Amautas. He turned to the group and called out:

—Theophilus Bright.

And the Volcano-Priest appeared. Modest, serene, he seemed very distant from his strange dual role. The sight of him astonished Jonas.

—You! But you don't exist. You're just a legend.

The Priest fixed his clear eyes on him.

—Sometimes legend is truer than the testimony of the senses. The truth—my truth—is that I live, I die, I return to life, and return to death, and am resurrected in unending succession.

—Ahh!

Gleam added:

—And each of those resurrections is double.

—Double?

—Right. He is who he is. But he's also the volcano we're in right now.

Jonas scratched his head.

—I don't understand. I can't understand.

—It's hard. But that's not all.

Distraught, uneasy, as if repentent at having started this exchange of words in which he found less and less security, he no longer attempted to conceal his astonishment.

—Really?

For an instant, happiness radiated from Gleam's face.

—For example, the wonderful women that accompany us.

He called unctuously:

—Maria!

Prominent in the group, the beauty raised her eyes. Advanced a step. Her image radiated self-reliance. Her beautiful smile showed solidarity with Gleam and his followers. Pithecanthropus stared at her. Then at the captain and the others. He got to his feet. Approached the bars. Shook them. Banged them twice with his jaw. It hurt. Proved that he wasn't sleeping. But dreaming. What he'd been seeing was false. The resurrected priest didn't exist. Much less was there a volcano-priest. And they weren't in a mountain, suspended inside its crater. How could a man be animal and mineral at the same time? Nothing was true. And least of all—in such circumstances—was the presence of that incomparable woman true. Nevertheless, something inside provoked and obliged him to accept those truths in a strange way. Possibly obeying a more mechanical instinct than his already exhausted will power, he wanted to be convinced. Babbled:

—And you . . . you too . . . are an . . . Amauta?

She responded, modestly:

—We all want to take part in a worthy project.

But his preconception persisted.

—I don't think women should be mixed up in these things.

—As for me, there's nothing strange. Gleam and I will always collaborate. By every means possible. By contrast, many of our female companions only pursue an ideal.

Pithecanthropus was itching to hurl a few epithets. That would sting their ears, sentiments, and sensibilities. He held back, Doubt gnawed at his spleen from all sides. No. It's not possible. It must be psychological torture. They're tormenting me with unreal images invented by specialists in parapsychology. Or maybe with electronic procedures still unknown. Besides, if the priest and the women are genuine, how can they be associated with these guerillas?

—How can you go off with those guerillas?

Pedro had asked Maria that some time ago. The old Fisherman was disturbed. Twenty centuries of life in the sky had led him to ignore many earthly happenings. Furthermore, the planet of his birth repelled him. There had been so many inventions that to try to keep up with them was an invitation to madness. Men seemed to have been born with an irrepressible wanderlust. Already they were traveling at astronomical speeds that were still increasing. Their progress had already eroded the romanticism of the Moon, and soon they'd arrange tours to the stars. But their sentiments and ambitions haven't improved. They're still no better or worse than when human beings first walked in their world. They'll spend billions on wars or on equipping cosmonauts, but next-to-nothing on self-enlightenment. They're more interested in atomic bombs than in cancer. In technology than in living conditions. Happily there are people like Maria. Maria! Maria with her generous instincts. The bad thing now is that she wants to be a guerilla. If he didn't know her, he'd think she was on the verge of losing her sanity. A little respect, Pedro! Such ideas shouldn't cross your mind. And what if it isn't really She, as she herself assures you? If you, obsessed with your fishing, have forgotten the true nature of things? If old age—is it 2000 years now?—kept you from seeing clearly what's going on around you? But then Maria—this Maria—has already told you: Gleam isn't just Gleam. Is that how she put it? Gleam is also humanity. Through his spirit—impartially—she loves everyone. All human beings are worthy of love. Even the foreign bloodsuckers? All have a right to salvation. But, according to Maria, she must be with those who most need her love. Not to save them for the Hereafter—she isn't so presumptuous—but right here: in order to find some way to help improve the society they live in. Still, he persisted:

—How can you go off with those guerillas?

—It's easy to see you've lost your memory, Pedro. Have you forgotten Joseph was a carpenter?

—No, I haven't.

—And that because of his poverty Jesus had no place to be born?

—Who could ignore that?

—And that He came to this world—He who was to sacrifice himself to save us—from a manger?

—Enough, Maria.

—That the rich and the powerful began to persecute Him from the time He was born? That a King, Herod, in order to kill Him, ordered the killing of all children under two years of age in Bethlehem? That, because of this, the Holy Family had to flee to Egypt? That He spent all his life with the poor, the sick, and with those who hungered and thirsted for justice? That the beneficiaries of this life were those who judged, condemned, and crucified him?

—I know, Maria. I know.

—Then why does it surprise you that I—who share only Her name—am with those who fight to help and save his brethren? Isn't that what He did, as a Man? Since there won't be a Second Coming, we all have to contribute to the fulfillment of His work.

He had to hurry to gather in his fish.

—You're quite right, Maria. I'm the one still afflicted with doubt and hesitation. Maybe I should be asked, "Quo vadis Domine?" Just as I asked the Lord that time.

Pithecanthropus was getting jumpier and jumpier. I'm sure they're out to trick me. They'd like to turn me into an idiot or a madman. To destroy my sense of proportion and reality. I'll defend myself. At least I'll tell them what I think and feel about them. Besides, despite the illusions I may be suffering, there are some things I can't fail to see.

Again he told Gleam:

—You can say and do what you like. Some things still don't convince me.

—What, for example?

—Why do you oppose the Government, Law and Order, the Nation and, above all, your own brothers-in-arms?

Gleam tried to keep his temper. So that his words would have a minimum charge of passion and violence.

—What government? The Dictator and his clique? The people who have delivered on schedule almost all our national wealth to the overdeveloped Octopus Countries? The ones who divide only among their own supporters whatever's left over?

—But the Nation has progressed. There are highways, bridges, buildings. More and more public works, more . . .

He interrupted:

—That's the pretext and justification of all Dictatorships! And what kind of order? The silence and immobility of prisons and graves? The physical and mental castration of anyone with ideals or a desire to improve the human condition? That of the satisified, who exploit the energy, intelligence, and labor of others? That of the powerful who, in order to subsist, need to grind the helpless to dust?

—No officer should talk like that.

—And what Nation? One that hides its misery behind its demagogy? One that uses the defense of its borders as an excuse for internal oppression?

—Everything you say . . . is treason!

Gleam looked at him as if he wanted to run him through. Would it be worth the trouble to make him eat his words? Right now, while holding him captive, behind the bars of a cage? That would be contemptible. So he continued restraining himself.

—As for us, we believe in our country. A great country, whole and transcendent. A country for all. Not just for those who exploit, strangle, and devour it.

—Are there two countries?

—Just one. Ours. The real one. The one we want to share in the world's progress, and to become part of. A country to live in. Not to die in, like the one you people are benefiting from.

—I still don't get it.

Gleam looked at him with impassive eyes. He had overcome his momentary anger. Even his voice was softer.

—And what Law? That of hunger for the hungry, thirst for the thirsty, cold for the shivering? The law that protects millionaire-thieves and assassins for hire while liquidating those who steal a pittance or kill for passion or revenge? The law that helps the one-in-a-thousand who has everything and prosecutes the nine-hundred-ninety-nine who lack the most elementary things?

—I see it's useless trying to tell you anything.

He seemed not to hear. Continued:

—As for brothers-in-arms . . . in what army?

Pithecanthropus' jaw was trembling. It was too much. He said, cholerically:

—Are there also several armies?

—Haven't you heard? It's clear there are several armies. On one side are those who attack and subdue; it belongs to the tyrants; the corrupt; those who usurp Power turn their weapons against the people, the students, and the best citizens; the infamous; those who always join the negative and regressive forces. On the other side are those who struggle to improve the society they live in; the progressives; the idealists; those who fight for the political and economic independence of their country; those who serve noble causes. Eneas, other officers, and I belong to this last army. We're those who fight under the command of Hidalgo, Morelos, San Martín, O'Higgins, Bolívar, and other such heroes, and we'll continue to be until we erase the Spaniards from our soil. Those who continue to struggle for our second independence. And against the inept satraps within who are still serving the enemy. Against you, for example, who are one of them. We're an army that hates violence, paradoxical as it sounds. That only declares wars in order to abolish war. Always in the name of peace, solidarity, and love. That's the only reason we can't passively allow so much injustice, so much misery, and so much crime.

Pithecanthropus was surprised by his own question:

—And when you gain control—if some day you're able to—then what?

Gleam responded deliberately, weighing his words.

—There are wise, just, and progressive people among us. They have been preparing for centuries. Never have they had an opportunity to act. Some day they'll have it. They'll put our ideals into practice. So everyone will have an education. And enough to eat, and a place to work, and a home.

The hostage scanned the group. He was growing more and more distraught. Too much was incomprehensible. Most of it seemed absurd. He shrugged.

—Bah!

Just then the voice came louder through the speaker. It was a sentinel of the Amautas.

—Captain Gleam: thousands of serpents left Babelandia a short while ago. We captured one. It was carrying a message for us. It said the others all had a copy. The message is from Wiley Warhorse and urges, on behalf of the government, that we communicate with him.

The hostage's eyes shone.

—Well! They responded sooner than I expected. No doubt I'll be freed any minute.

The loudspeaker sounded again:

—The viper awaits a reply. What'll we say?

Gleam thought for a moment. He glanced at his companions. On their faces he read consent.

—We'll be in touch right away.

Twenty-Four

IF it hadn't been for the donkey, Holofernes would have lost all his bones then and there, or at least a good part of them. The winged ass realized what was going on. The Dictator swerving from one side to another—the music's frenetic impulse—like an ivory fan. It was clear that a few seconds later he'd spill his osseous humanity on the floor. The donkey didn't think twice. He confronted those who amused themselves at the bony rider's expense. The aggressors were confused by this unexpected challenge. They tried to fend off the good-natured quadruped, assuming he was like the rest of his species. They were wrong. This was a donkey, of course, but a donkey with wings. Only at this moment he seemed to have wings on all four limbs. Because they beat in a way that awed the revelers. The spark-striking hooves were more like a hundred than just four as they trampled the flaccid bodies. In a matter of seconds the hairy hippies—some throwing off their wigs—abandoned their instruments, bottles, and packets of cigarets on the battlefield, and took it on the lam. In addition to his hooves, the donkey, now drunk with triumph, allowed himself the pleasure of nipping at some of the dancers' buttocks. As trophies of this part of the struggle, various fragments of torn cloth remained in his teeth. The vanquished withdrew rapidly, their nibbled rears forcibly ventilated. Peace restored, the loyal donkey began his search for the disjointed Dictator. Couldn't find him. Had the pranksters carried him off, bone by bone? That would be a spicy kettle of fish. How could I explain it to Harpie? How am I to explain that while he was debating with the inhuman contortionists they carried him off—one took a vertebra, one a tibia, one a fibula, one the skull, etc.—from her husband's handful of parts. Of course I only obey orders. Carry out my functions as a beast of burden down to the last detail. The only one to blame is the Dictator himself. But she'll never accept that. My misfortune is not my conduct, however bad that may be. My misfortune is having been born a burro. More exactly, a burro with wings. Naturally, that created a series of peculiar situations for me. I can't win. He half-turned and was about to return to the palace and face the people. For the last time he surveyed the scene of his exploits. Eureka! Over there was a little pile of rags with a Chaplinesque derby on top. He went up to it. Lifted it. Put it all together. Just as he suspected, it was Holofernes! The empty sockets gave him a distant look of gratitude. He practically had to lift him on his shoulder, like a sack of kindling wood. In a cavernous voice rising from who knows where, the Bony One sighed:

—Thank you, good steed.

—At your service, Dic. And now what?

He shrugged in such a way that his bones sounded plink plunk like a marimba. He mumbled:

—We'll just carry on.

—But your Excellency, what bones will you use for the soup?

—How's that?

—Nothing. Where are we going?

—Wherever the wind carries us.

He imagined himself a D'Artignan. Wringing out his pharynx, he brought up a droplet of saliva. Licked his right index finger to dampen it. Raised it. Gave himself a turn. When it felt cold, he declared:

—To the northeast!

Instantly the noble beast—less a beast than many rational beings—leapt toward the clouds. He cantered past them, as befits a proud winged thoroughbred. Found the correct route. When they'd reached the point above their destination he deftly descended like a parachute. It was the finest suburb in Bab. Modern houses like hard candy, with limousines out front. Once in the street, they were surrounded by children on bikes, skates, and motor scooters. They stared at the donkey and its rider as if studying characters escaped from a comic strip. Holofernes tried to ignore them. He approached the first door he encountered along the way. Rang the bell. A butler—vertical, like solidified vinegar—examined the preposterous figure from head to foot. Allowing no time for an introduction, he banged the door shut in his face, at the same time saying:

—We only give charity on Saturdays.

Holofernes was not discouraged. Did not even show surprise. Knocked on the door of the next house. The maid who opened stared at him transfixed. Suddenly began to laugh in a hysterical manner. A woman's voice cried out from inside:

—Who is it?

—It's a clown, madame.

—What are you waiting for? We put up with them only on TV. Unleash the dogs!

Soon he heard the barking of the pack. And a second or two later four snarling canines launched an attack. Again the ass saved him. Burst into a gallop. Put his head between his legs. Half-lowered his back like a saddle. And off they were to the clouds once more!

—Let's go down.

—Can't you see it's worse each time?

—I must take the pulse of public opinion.

The donkey flattened his ears. And in no time they were in another section of the elegant suburb. Holofernes knocked, No one answered. But someone was watching from behind a curtain. A woman with a strong foreign accent shouted:

—A crazy man! A crazy man!

The act was repeated at other doors. Varied only by the sex, the age, and the vocabulary of those who observed him.

—A thief! Call the squad car.

In view of the results obtained, the skeptical donkey suggested:

—Excellency, we'd better clear out. Why put your head in the tiger's mouth to see its eye teeth? We already know, more or less, what people think.

—Just one more visit.

—I'll take your word, Dic. Where will it be?

—To the southeast. To the slums. They're more hospitable.

—All right. We're in God's hands, Let's go.

Up to the clouds. And down again. A bar. Drinking. Noise. Language to make the bottles blush. Holofernes sat down among the clientele. Across from his winged companion. Right away he spoke to the nearest one.

—Well, what do you think about . . . ?

Felt a tapping on his shoulder. The man he was trying to talk to squinted at him from eyes humid with alcohol. Did not answer. Took another swallow. Turned his back. The tapping on his shoulder again. Mechanically, he tried to shrug off the hand that was striking him.

Repented:

—And what do you think . . . ?

The man shook his head.

—It's horrible to be drunk! But more horrible not to be, and to see what's going on in Bab.

Again the shoulder taps.

—Donkey, don't bother me. We'll leave in a minute.

When there was no answer, he turned. It wasn't the ass. It was a serpent. It was smiling.

—Don't worry, Excellency. I'm on your side.

—What's up?

—Get going as soon as possible. A few minutes ago, two were stabbed just for mentioning the General, and well . . . you. If you're recognized here, there won't be enough of your bones for souvenirs.

He meditated briefly. Decided:

—Maybe you're right.

—Besides, the foreign delegates who want to meet you are all arriving at the Palace.

—That's true. I'd forgotten.

And zip! On his winged ass he was soon entering his office window.

Twenty-Four

—If there's any news on the Amautas, tell me right away.

Wiley Warhorse was alone, sitting on the revolving chair behind the great desk. Mechanically doodling dollar signs on a sheet of paper. From time to time he glanced at the clock on the back wall. Each tick of the second hand seemed to gouge his scalp. Damned time plays tricks on us. How brief is existence and how long our minutes! Above all when we wait as I'm waiting right now. Has my message been transmitted to the Amautas? Probably not. It's my own fault for taking Rigoletto's advice. How was I to depend on a bunch of vipers? Even ten thousand vipers? Suppose they'd been a million. I should have equipped all the military vehicles with loudspeakers. After having covered all the roads they certainly could have located some guerillas. Or at least somebody who'd notify them. Well, what's done is done. All I can do now is wait. Clearly I'll wait as long as it's prudent. If the Amautas delay their response, I'll peddle my wares someplace else. By the way, I wonder if the planes are ready? Have they already loaded our treasures? Have they taken the proper precautions to keep everything secret? He nervously doodled more dollar signs. From time to time he nibbled on his fingernails. Calm down! Easy does it, idiot. If not, you're going to make people suspicious. And in that case, how can you rely on the reactions of your employees? Do you think they'll let you go and abandon them, throwing you flowers, giving you thanks? How naive can you get? It's likely you'll pay a high price for that. Possibly your life. He could not restrain himself. Furiously pressed the buzzer. The Subsecretary, a colonel, came right in. Stood at attention

—At your orders, Mr. Secretary.

—Hasn't anyone called or arrived to see me?

—No sir.

—As soon as you get news, you're to tell me.

—Yes, Mr. Secretary.

Again he came to attention. Asked permission to leave. Went out. Warhorse continued his visit. In order to take visual stock of his office. It was very large. Big enough to stage a bullfight. He liked it. He was going to miss it very much. Just to amuse himself and kill time, he began to look at everything around him. He stumbled across Generalissimo Holofernes Verbophile's official portrait. Nervously laughed. That portrait would fit better in an osteological classroom. Back to his paper. To his pen. To his dollar signs. Sweating. A tremendous fatigue made his muscles ache. Even in his comfortable revolving chair. There he was. Then suddenly he wasn't. Not there, not seated. He was hanging in the air. Was he flying? He saw all was dark. Could distinguish nothing. Was it night time? Had he fallen asleep? Was he dreaming he was blind? Was he really losing his sight?. Surely that was it. Stupified, he reached to sound the buzzer. What buzzer? His hand touched thin air. He shouted:

—Sr. Subsecretary!

No one responded. He shouted still louder:

—Sr. Subsecretary!

Not even his echo for an answer. Suddenly suspicious, he passed his hand over his eyes. He was tightly blindfolded. When had it been done? How? It was inexplicable. He tried to pull it off. His efforts were fruitless. He abandoned the idea. Felt as if he were being suspended from big hooks. He touched them. They weren't hooks but claws. His suspicion began to take hold in his mind. He tried to work loose from the claws. Could not move them. They felt as strong as steel. Suspicion became certainty. Aloud he said:

—The Amautas.

In a rapid transition, his tone became flattering.

—I have a proposition to offer.

He was deposited on the ground. Heard a powerful flapping fading away. No doubt about it, Warhorse, your ingenuity is now being tested. He pictured for a moment the faces of Jonas, Holofernes, and his fellow Cabinet members if they knew what he would propose to the guerillas. He made no attempt to remove the blindfold. For what? What was at stake was too important to risk.

Moments before, Gleam had spoken to Pithecanthropus.

—Surely they'll put up your ransom.

The hostage squirmed. Said, as if to himself:

—I'd like to hear how much.

Gleam looked at him a few seconds. Acceded.

—That's easy. There'll be microphones all over. I'll have a speaker connected. So you can hear everything.

Jonas, in spite of himself, mumbled:

—Thanks.

Warhorse, on the other hand, was distraught. What was happening to him? He raised his arms. Touched his ears. They were growing. He felt his jaw. The same thing. He noted that downy hair was sprouting in waves along it. As if that weren't enough, now he experienced an irrepressible urge to get down on all fours. Could it be . . . .? Yes. It could be nothing else. Pithecanthropus was undoubtedly nearby. Which meant the General was in Amauta territory. But now, so are you. Do you realize that? You'll have to use every ounce of your wile and skill. Otherwise, instead of one hostage, the abductors will have two. Of course I wouldn't be an additional prize for them. Nobody'd give a cent for me. Well. Not quite. Somebody might offer a few pesos. Just a few pesos. And no more. He heard steps approaching. They stopped. It was Gleam. With a calm voice, he ordered:

—Speak.

That voice. Where have I heard it? I'd swear it was just yesterday. Where? The voice persisted:

—We're waiting.

He responded. Said hastily:

—Could I ask a few questions?

—As many as you want.

—Well, who are you?

—That's none of your business.

—Are you the Amautas' leader?

—Why?

—I want to deal with the decision-maker.

—Deal with me.

—Are we alone?

—What difference does it make?

—I'd like to discuss this matter in confidence.

—We keep no secrets here.

Warhorse wanted to test his own strength, to negotiate with aces in his hand.

—In that case, no deal.

—That's up to you. Meanwhile, you're to stay with us.

—How long?

—That remains to be decided. Maybe for you we'll demand a cash ransom.

Warhorse had already decided what he'd say, but he feigned thought. Appeared to decide.

—All right. It's my fault. I've put all the cards in your hands.

—So you have.

—Fine, then. The ransom conditions will be met.

—All of them?

—All. Delivery of the Dictator, so you can help yourselves to all the bones you want.

—Only one pound.

—Setting free all the prisoners you've asked for.

—Marvelous!

—Handing over the people you want for the funerals. And if you decide you want a few more, no problem.

—Magnificent!

—Furthermore, so that we will be able to act with a more or less free hand, I'll order all the batallions stationed in the capital to leave it and march to the borders.

—Well! Well! I never imagined that Pithecanthropus had such faithful friends.

—It's not for him that I'm doing this.

—Really?

—I'm doing it for me.

If he could have disconnected the loudspeaker, would he have done It? Probably. Wiley Warhorse was nauseating.

—I don't get it.

—It's simple enough. The condition to my offer is my safe conduct out of the country with all my belongings.

—Is anyone stopping you?

—I need special conditions.

—What are they?

—On the pretext of a collective interview with you, I'll gather the Dictator, the top military brass, the Big Wheels of Bab and of course, my cabinet colleagues. I'll fix it so we'll all be arrested. I'll satisfy immediately all your demands. And while the others are still in custody, I'll be released. I'll have aircraft ready.

—Now I get it. You'll appear the innocent victim, with no one preventing your escape.

—If I'm stopped, there'll be no escape.

—Of course. They'll liquidate you beforehand.

—So what's your decision?

—You'll find out.

—When?

—Soon enough.

There was a pause. Then the Captain looked at him sharply.

—And Pithecanthropus?

—It would be best . . . .if he were never heard from again!

Twenty-Five

ONCE again Narcissus Vaselino nuzzled his chin between the Fat Chef's neck and shoulder.

—I'm desperate.

—Calm down. Sooner or later all meat softens.

—You don't realize what's going on.

—I'm dying to know, Narci. Tell me.

—Harpie's about to break protocol. She wants to receive the foreign delegation before the Dictator does.

—Why?

—Who can guess that? But this is the last time. Tomorrow, I quit, I quit, I quit.

Onions and grief had filled Disgusteaux's eyes with tears.

—You're leaving me here, all by myself?

He cocked his head. Twitched like a broody hen.

—You're the one keeping me here. You know it, ingrate!

His arrogant chin jutted forth. Then he took the shape of an Egyptian figurine. And sidestepped out of the room, prepared to solve any problems he might encounter. Arrived in time to receive the foreign delegates. Trembled with emotion before so many uniforms, medals, and epaulets. Having regained his composure, he explained that due to circumstances connected with the kidnapping, His Excellency, Holofernes Verbophile, would be a few minutes late. The First Lady, meanwhile, would receive them. The delegates looked at one another a bit uneasily. Certain criteria unified their thoughts. They had to accept everything. They were in an underdeveloped country. Well, "developing," as they would say now. On entering the reception hall, they were stunned, and some even frightened. Moreover, the spectacle was unprecedented among the social trappings of such places. Harpitune had encapsulated herself in the coils of Melopea, whom she'd transformed into a cylinder almost two meters high. The enormous triangular head swayed at face level in front of the guests. The Dictatrix was seated on the Constrictor, as if it were a throne. They exchanged greeting protocols. And immediately the serpent's confidante got right to the point.

—Have you seen Sinbad?

The delegates' spokesman answered:

—Who's Sinbad?

—The poet.

—The Sinbad we know is a sailor.

—That's another one. I mean my son. He left home long ago.

They tried to make the best of the circumstances.

—Since we did not know of his absence, we didn't know you were referring to him.

—Please look for him. Wherever you go, look for him. Do you want a description, some clue? It's very simple. Wherever you hear a beautiful word, he's there! Whenever a courser flowers on the sea, that is he. He is the only human who can navigate without a ship. He embarks on his own eyes. His eyes are the sea.

—With clues like that, how can we miss?

Her pupils radiated hope.

—Tell him that for my part I'm building a bridge of poetry in order to reach him. All I have to know is where he is. As soon as I find out, I'll run to his side.

The delegates bowed, not knowing quite what to make of that. Then they eyed one another quizzically. In their world of digestion, decrees, and gold-clinking, Harpitune's words were like carnations drowned by beetles.

Pithecanthropus listened to Gleam's and the Secretary of Defense's whole conversation. Confirmed what he'd suspected for a long time. Wiley Warhorse was a bastard. Moreover, the truth is that he had good reasons to resent and hate him. One of the main reasons: having been forced to serve him as a steed or a step-ladder, according to need. Admittedly, of course, there were other motives. For example, having to obey me blindly. Knowing that even the Dictator obeys me. As for the wretch's behavior toward other people, what could you expect? In spite of appearances to the contrary, they're always fighting like cats and dogs over their victims. As for myself, I'll tolerate patiently whatever the Amautas order. Am I not at their mercy? His cavilings were interrupted by the loudspeaker. There was another message like the one before. This time it was Piggy Rigoletto, no less, who was requesting an interview. His proposition, it turned out, was remarkably like Wiley Warhorse's. Curiously, just such an interview was also requested and obtained by the Secretary of Aviation. And, later on, by the Secretary of the Navy. And after that, by still other high officials in the Government. Of course each one boasted about the many benefits that he, from his particular position, could offer. But there were still more. In a short time, similar interviews with a good number of prominent bigwigs in Babelandia had taken place. Soon after the last one, Gleam assembled all the interviewees. He ordered the blindfolds removed their eyes. None seemed suspicious, disillusioned, or ill at ease. Although each disbelieved the motives of the rest in approaching the Amautas, they all outdid one another in mutual compliments:

—Just like being in agreement, right?

—We all really had the same idea.

—To see if we could work something out.

—I wasn't able to contact the rest of you.

—Neither was I.

—Nor I.

—Nor I.

—In the end, here we are anyway.

—Right. And that's the important thing.

—Now, among us all, we can reach a solution.

Gleam watched them slyly.

—That's enough.

Only at that instant did they notice him.

—You!

He smiled scornfully.

—Right. It's me.

—I might have imagined, muttered Warhorse.

Gleam spoke:

—I've prepared a surprise for you.

He led them to the edge of the cage where Pithecanthropus was. He seemed peaceful. At that moment, in spite of everything, he displayed an imposing dignity. Squinted at the recent arrivals with his half-closed eyes. He was absolutely still. But they misinterpreted his attitude. Sounded a chorus of gelatinous, sugared flattery.

—At last!

—At last we've found you.

—We were getting desperate.

—All Bab is desperate.

—We're doing everything possible to get you out.

—To save you.

—That's why we're here.

—Luckily, there's still time.

Soon the caged one was frothing green at the mouth.

—Sons of bitches!

Those insulted were distraught. Lost in conjectures. As far as Pithecanthropus could assume or tell, their conduct was unquestionable. It was correct and honest. Enthusiastic in loyalty to and solidarity with him. Why this aversion? Why this excessive and unjust treatment? Wiley Warhorse, for his part, reasoned: Could this moron have discovered what we were up to? How could he know? Neither our present attitude nor our past actions reveal anything. And besides, it's risky to imagine what motive the Amautas would have coming to him with this gossip. Even if they had, would he have believed them? Ridiculous! And so? Well. There were other, bigger problems. For example, not knowing what the future held for them. More exactly, what the Amautas' whim was. For the time being, all they could do was to carry on their policy of mutual understanding with the Hostage. He put on a perfectly innocent expression.

—What's the trouble, General?

The others felt obligated to follow suit, and echo the Secretary of Defense's sentiments.

—Claustrophobia, maybe?

—Easy does it.

—We'll soon have you out of here.

—In a matter of minutes.

Jonas in his fury climbed to the top of his cage until touching its ceiling. Gripping the bars with both hands and feet, he rapidly swung around the cage three times. From above them, he roared:

—Sons of whores, sons of whores, sons of whores . . .

Those referred to consulted one another visually. Although they had a remote suspicion of what had occurred, they were unable to explain it fully. Pithecanthropus went on:

—Hypocrites!

Some tried to humor him. Making an effort, they preserved an innocent air.

—How can you say that?

—Calm down now.

—We can explain.

—Maybe you've been tricked.

The Simian shot a colossal gob of spittle. All found themselves enmeshed in its thick and sticky web. They were paralyzed by shock and revulsion. He continued:

—I heard you . . . over the loudspeaker.

The exposed culprits again looked at one another. This time, anxiously. Trying to estimate how much each one had revealed. Then they looked at Pithecanthropus. Stopped looking at him and shifted to Gleam. Wiley Warhorse asked in his anxiety:

—Is it true?

—Yes.

Jonas threw himself on the cage floor. It teetered a little. Was seized by an impulse and rushed against the bars. Extended his arms through them, trying vainly to reach the group. Realizing his impotence in attacking them, he made every evil gesture he could think of. The others stepped back instinctively. With a voice like a whip, he lashed out at his human ex-steed.

—Wiley Warhorse, you wretch: So you want to hand me over to the guerillas? Are you going to withdraw all the troops from Babelandia, leaving the capital unprotected, completely at the mercy of the Amautas? Are you going to betray the Dictator, the top Generals, and the leading members of Babelandian society? Will you set free the political prisoners they asked for? Will you give them still more cadavers than they demanded? And all that for what? To save your own hides, and your riches!

To a man, the prisoner's infamous accomplices leaped to liquidate him. But the accusing voice immobilized them.

—Stop! Haven't you all come for the same reason? If I had to pick out the worst bastard and double-crosser among you . . . I couldn't decide! Each one of you's worse than the rest!

Just moments before, several Amautas attacked the National Television Center. Fully armed, they got into the news broadcasting booth. They menaced the peerless Golden Ace. First he ignored them. Laughed in their beards. They set the muzzle of a submachine gun against his ear. He bellowed with laughter. Whoever was threatening him was momentarily confused. Another of the announcers come up to him. He explained the traditional metallic contribution required by his colleague in order to function. At the same time he implored him not to judge the others by this strange model. For many were idealistic, noble, generous. Devoted to their profession for its own sake. And because it was a fabulous medium for education and good works. The Amautas assented. He was persuaded that such as the case. Thanked them. Took out some coins. Deposited them in the slot in Golden Ace's head. Right away the latter began functioning according to the programmed instructions. His deep-throated voice, as on other memorable occasions, assumed a pompous tone:

—Attention! Attention! Babelandians! Now that certain technical (ahem) problems have been taken care of, we'll be transmitting to you "live" one of the most crucial events in our history. Somewhere in the nation, right at this moment, a conference is underway between the Secretary of Defense and the guerillas! Yes. Just what you heard, a meeting between Wiley Warhorse and the Amautas! Attention, attention! The meeting has begun.

The clear, bright, precise voice of Captain Gleam was heard. "Speak up." A brief silence. The same voice added, in a more severe tone: "We're waiting." Next came the familiar accents—they had heard so many times—of an ambitious politican: "First, could I ask a few questions?" From the instant of Golden Ace's first words, radios and TV sets were turned on throughout the Capital. This was, in any event, quite unnecessary. Loudspeakers installed in the Main Plaza and other principal public places were also broadcasting the event. Their invisible fingers were drawing in people from all corners of the city. Probing their ears. Poking into them, as if cleaning them so that they'd hear better. At times even infiltrating their eyes with a visual suggestion of who was speaking. Thus, not only did they hear Warhorse's nauseating propositions, but he was also visually present. He looked like an insect trampled by a rhinocerous. Meanwhile the crowd grew in the Main Plaza. At first the faces showed astonishment, then a kind of joy. Cautious guesses were made. No doubt it was one more "show" staged by those guerillas, whose fame had grown almost overnight. Like good practical jokers they were probably amusing themselves while waiting for their ransom. But little by little the audience's expression changed. The smiles, the easy gestures, the peaceful conversations faded away. No. It was no joke or game. As they heard the details of the complicated treachery, they began to feel angry and a bit sorry. How could anyone be capable of such infamy? Of course, most of the citizens that wretch promised to hand over did deserve the worst possible punishment. Despite their high positions they were among the lowest species in all Babelandia. Everyone stood to benefit by their elimination. But that wasn't the worst and most repulsive part of it. The revolting thing was their closeness to Wiley Warhorse; he had shared their food and drink as well as their interests and enthusiasms. But the whole story had to be heard before a fair judgment could be made.

The congregation continued growing. As usual in such cases, rational animals were thrown together with others who disputed their rationality. Suppose they weren't truly rational. Or not completely? Wasn't it just a question of degree on a zoological scale? Who could know? Even the ten thousand asps had fearfully mixed in the crowd. Could they also have been denounced? Would they also be included in the ransom? They began to wriggle up the trees near the loudspeakers. There, the vibrations absorbed by their bodies would penetrate deeper. The oxen, for their part, had stopped chewing their cuds. Several monkeys were hanging by their tails from whatever projection they could find. A herd of pigs pressed their way down the lower Palace hall, straining to hear better. In general, there was little movement. Those who arrived late walked on tiptoe. The silence grew thicker. As if all were sinking, second by second, into a concave mirror of echoes. As the successive interviews ended, nausea gripped the listeners by the thorax and burned them in the pits of their stomachs. No one looked at anyone else. All eyes were fixed on the loudspeakers, as if from them were coming, in addition to their voices, their figures—statues of garbage—of the abominable. They were tense, clenched, furious. No one had imagined anything like this. And these were the ones who ran things in Babelandia? If by some chance the Amautas were to set them free, they'd have to be drawn and quartered, pulverized, buried in the ground, in order to return them to the anonymous region from which they never should have emerged. Something had to be done for the Country. To set it going in reverse. Or, rather, straight ahead. Because reverse was what it was in now. Transformation. To create a new language for everyone, one that all could not only speak but also understand. A new language that would call things, facts, and beings by their true names. A language to express the speaker's intended meaning and not (like this one) something else or even the opposite meaning. Yes. Babelandia had to be transformed. Circumstances and values had to be changed—except for a very few acceptable ones—for the benefit of its inhabitants. The crowd's indignation had reached its peak when General Pithecanthropus' voice began to be heard. They said that the words of anathema with which he lashed out at the Secretary of Defense seemed to be engraved in the air: Wiley Warhorse, you wretch: So are you planning to hand me over to the guerillas? Are you withdrawing all the troops from Babelandia . . . ? And when it got to the end of the first paragraph, after a momentary pause in which the multitude murmured in expectation, the same voice thundered on:

—Stop! Haven't you all come for the same reason? If I had to pick out the worst bastard and double-crosser among you . . . I couldn't decide! Each one of you's worse than the rest!

It was as if the entrails of the earth had begun to show their fire. The Plaza broiled. People, animals, trees, the Cathedral, the Palace, the ground, all were tinged with red. Everything trembled, as in the shock wave of a quake. Hundreds of thousands of rocks, leaves, and eyes crossed little swords of anxiety. Seven lightning flashes lashed the landscape. Seven awesome thunderclaps rocked the sky. No one said a word. What would be the point? They knew that now there was a battlecry: Action. Already they could see the course to follow. One thing was sure: never again would they tolerate people like those making up this regime and their cronies, the *crème de la crème,* the elitiest elite of Babelandia.

Twenty-Six

SHORTLY before, Holofernes Verbophile had returned to the Palace and was chatting with the foreign deligates. Once again he explained the painful circumstances faced by the Babelandians these last two days. Naturally, he asked them to have patience. It was only a matter of minutes. When least expected, General Pithecanthropus would appear in martial splendor. There was no doubt that he'd join the party. The delegates didn't think much of that. Remembering their previous experiences, they were sure the hostage would be long delayed in presenting himself. Still they agreed with a diplomatic gesture. The Dictator, in turn, reiterated that if for any reason Pithy should not be on time, the party would move on to the Boll Weevil Club. Everyone knew that elaborate hom-age would be paid there to the illustrious commander of the army. And if for some unforseen circumstances he could not appear, the festivities would proceed just the same. When all was said and done, present or absent, Jonas was the centerpiece . . .

Suddenly and unexpectedly, Bacchus the Groveler crawled in. This time he didn't knock, or announce himself in any other way. He just slithered under the door. With tear-filled eyes, he stammered:

—Excellency! Excellency!

The latter looked down from his calcareous Olympus.

—Disappear. *Ipso facto!*

Groveler bent low until he kissed the dust. Then he licked the Rigid One's instep, or calciferous foot. Despite the order, he remained prostrate.

—I can't, your Excellency.

His empty eyesockets fulminated—well, tried to fulminate.

—How dare you . . . ?

—Something unprecedented is happening, your Excellency.

Without waiting for the Dictator's approval, he connected one of the loudspeakers in the salon. At that moment, Golden Ace's voice was announcing: " . . . Somewhere in the nation, right at this moment, a conference is underway between the Secretary of Defense and the guerillas . . . " Holofernes turned to his distinguished visitors. Proudly, as if to say: "Now you're hearing it. Didn't I tell you? Wiley Warhorse must have reached an agreement with the Amautas. Surely by now he's negotiating the final details of the ransom." Nevertheless, he was distraught. What could this good-for-nothing be up to? Acting out his first and last names—wily horse. Treacherous mount? Why didn't he consult me on what he was doing? And planning? In every way, it's an obvious outrage. While he meditated, more details of Jonas' several interviews and statements were transmitted. The relentless, disturbing facts were affecting Verbophile more and more. First his skeleton turned blue. Then it began to flutter, as if it were being tossed about in a blender. Next, its movement gravitated toward a single point. He began to rotate around his coccyx, changing into an ivory-like sunflower. Suddenly he was still, rigid, hieratic. A few seconds passed. Then he dispersed into countless pieces, which fell to the floor. A minimal plink-plunk of vertebrae, femora, tibiae, et cetera. As if possessed, Bacchus the Groveler crouched beside him. Examined him. Smelled him. Touched him. Whined:

—Excellency!

Some now pounced on the osseous remains with a single thought: to make a pair of dice from them. But they didn't get the chance. Harpitune had arrived and was upon them like a whirlwind. Violently she snatched away the hands that were trying to defile the beloved bones.

—First, you have to kill me.

Holofernes' assistant—now bathed in tears—repeated:

—Excellency!

He could not convince himself that the number-one orator of Bab had suffered the worst punishment: he'd be mute forever.

The Volcano raised a luminous hymn, warm and ancestral. It opened out its musical fans. Its notes soared, as if they were wings rising over the mountains. It was Eneas Pioneer, the Organ-Man. But he wasn't using his fingers, nor did he require the usual soft-throated metallic pipes. He himself was the instrument. Light and sound, shadows and silence. Melodies and harmonies emanated from his soul, like flowers of the spirit spiraling upward, higher and higher in myriad petals. It was a kind of requiem for things and events of the past that had simultaneously merged in a hymn to faith, hope, and triumph. But it wasn't just Eneas Pioneer. His voice was everyone's. Through him the people expressed their ideal of brotherhood, and their will to persevere in their struggle for a world worth living in.

Inside the Volcano changes had taken place. From the great cage occupied by General Pithecanthropus the Amautas had strung a whole series of smaller cages. Each one of these contained a cabinet member or other prominent Babelandian. So, when the Simian moved from one side to the other, the whole assemblage swayed and his steps echoed above the captives, giving them the sensation of repeated knocks on their heads. Their fright was wetting their pants. Each one silently cursed the moment he'd thought of betraying the others. But it was late for repentance. All they could do now was try to escape. How idiotic! The thought of it was preposterous. Who could ever escape from a cage suspended in a volcano's crater? Maybe the Amautas could be persuaded to set them free. Free? Fat chance. These guerillas seemed to be made of asbestos and steel. Nothing would pierce the armor that covered them, or the fortress of their ideas and sentiments. Besides, after the way we acted today, antipathy and scorn is all we deserve. Just the same, Warhorse was going to give it one more try. Telling himself "Nothing ventured, nothing gained," He shouted:

—Captain Gleam!

The latter approached the strings of cages.

—What?

—We can offer a large amount of money if . . .

Gleam glared at him coldly. But as if he hadn't noticed it, the other went on:

—. . . if you set us free.

—Impossible.

Wiley's lip quivered. Suddenly he realized he'd been walking on all fours. He tried to straighten up, but couldn't. Despite the odds, he persisted:

—You've no idea how much it would be.

—It makes no difference how much.

—You could arm yourselves with the latest weapons.

—Don't go on. It's useless.

—And carry out thousands of public works.

—I told you it's impossible.

—You don't want to know how much?

—What for?

—You don't realize what you're missing.

—Yes I do. And we need plenty of money for the reconstruction period. But even if I wanted to accept, I couldn't. For now, financing isn't our biggest problem.

The Secretary of Defense wilted.

—I didn't think you were all so resentful.

—You're judging us from your own bias. You're mistaken. It isn't resentment. Pity is all we feel for you. After all—even if you don't deserve to be—you're also human. Now you've defeated yourselves in full view of the people. That's why we're not setting you free. If we did, you might not survive for a second.

—No? But why?

—Your propositions to us and Pithecanthropus' foul language have been broadcast nationwide. All Babelandia is outraged. Now they'd lynch you as soon as look at you. Furthermore, when the Dictator heard the broadcast—he died of a heart attack.

All of them—those who had heard the dialog in silence—now whispered from cage to cage.

—Is that true?

—It is.

—Absolutely sure?

—Absolutely.

One after another stammered:
—What a disaster!
—What a horror!
—What a disgrace!
—What a pity!
And Gleam:
—Do you still want your freedom?
They responded, in anguish:
—No!
—No!
—No!

A little later Harpitune approached the bones—already accommodated to a coffin—of Holofernes Verbophile. Shed not a tear. Spoke not a word of sorrow nor showed a gesture of sadness. With a soft piece of felt, she began delicately to polish them, one by one. She wanted to see them shine, as if she were preparing an exhibition of fossils. Her witnesses—bordered by the black drapes—looked on in astonishment. But no one dared interrupt her in this task. Bacchus the Groveler had been following her everywhere like a famished dog. Suddenly, the First Lady of Babelandia stopped. Gazed with pride on the finished work.

—It's done.

She turned to her Jack-of-all-Trades.

—He looks great. Doesn't he?

—Yes, Excellency.

—He never looked better.

—That's right.

—Right now he's preparing to join Sinbad.

—Will he really see him?

—Didn't you know?

—No, your Excellency.

—Sinbad promised me: When my Father begins his infinite voyage, I'll set out to meet him.

—Ah!

Harpitune searched everywhere for the manuscripts of his verses. Stapled them together. Made a kind of rustic cloak. Wrapped it around herself. Went up on the Palace roof. Embraced Melopea. And scrutinized the horizon. Did she actually believe she'd be watching—if only from a distance—Holofernes' rendevous with Sinbad?

Intiyacuna—the setting sun—aimed its final lances at the hunchbacked peaks. The cages with their shadowed prisoners blended into the darkness. Tranquillity grew like a deep purple beard in the crater's depths. A jungle voice cut through the darkness.

—And my wife? And my daughters?

Gleam soothed him:

—They'll live normally. In civilization. They won't lack anything. The children will study. They'll have our guidance and protection. Right, Maria?

—Yes, Gleam. And love. They'll also have love.

There was a pause. The jungle voice sounded again, hoarser.

—And me?

—What?

—Am I going to be killed?

—No.

—Where will I end up?

—What's your name?

—Jonas.

—So you can't guess where?

—No.

—Where did Jonas live for three days?

—In a whale's belly.

—Well, good, you too will live in a whale's belly. But for more days. Many more days. To the end of your days.

—Uuuuaaaa! Uuuuuaaaa!

—That way you won't hurt anybody, ever again.

He tried to keep the muscles in his face from twitching. So that no one would discover the terrible anxiety he felt, especially while he was thinking about his wife and daughters. Also about himself: a creature of the forest imprisoned in the belly of a cetacean, a living prison in the ocean depths. Death was preferable. Should he ask to be executed? That would be useless. Well. He'd have to think for a while. Couldn't he smash his head against the bars? Or rip open the veins on his arms with his teeth, and there take his blood and life? He'd have to think for a while. Meanwhile, he continued looking, looking. Many questions were burning on his tongue. Should he ask them? Or shouldn't he? He would:

—And the others?

—They'll be tried by the people. We'll hand them over when emotions are calmer. If we can intervene in their sentencing, I can assure you it won't be death. Death is no punishment. Or it isn't punishment enough. We will make them live, to witness the transformation of Babelandia. And, if it's possible, to work with their hands and live like any other Babelandian. Moreover, we condenm useless killing. No violence appeals to us, in any form.

—Then why, since you boast about that and about being so pure, scrupulous, and proper, do you use guerilla warfare and kidnapping as your method of struggle?

—Out of desperation. Is any other way left to us? Those who want to hold the world back, don't they have, both here and abroad, every means at their disposal? Of course we'd prefer to fight using reason, at a debating table; or on an open, sunlit battlefield, facing an enemy with the same kind of weapons. That's the day we're waiting for. Meanwhile . . .

Jonas doubted he could continue with his questioning. But curiosity triumphed.

—What I can't understand is the ransom they demanded. Especially, what was to be gained from two-hundred first-class burials? And what good was a pound of Holofernes' bones?

—We were almost certain that they would not comply with those two conditions. The only thing we really wanted—and now we're achieving it—was to stimulate a kind of collective catharsis. So that the leaders of Babelandia would be exposed to the public. Of course if there aren't basic changes, we'll do whatever's necessary! This . . .

—What?

Gleam was looking over the horizon, toward the future. He seemed to be addressing an audience that was constantly multiplying. Beyond the volcano, as far as the eye could see.

—This is just part of a process. Our definitive encounter is not with men. Men come and go, like gusts of wind. We confront systems and stoneage structures and stasis. We're not concerned simply with the changing of one government for another, possibly worse. We await the day of regimes that will allow the creation—or that will create—a new, livable society. For the world belongs to everyone. Not just to a few.

Translator's Afterword

Translator's Afterword

"WHEN will we have our own system of political thought?" a well-known poet and essayist from Latin America recently asked.* He wrote in the context of legendary instability of over a century-and-a-half (since the wars of independence against Spain), of capricious caudillos, Machiavellian intrigue, and sadistic military dictatorships. He wrote also in the context of a dependent economy and a dependent culture; in many senses Latin Americans are still waging a war of independence.

The complexity of the problems and obstacles they have encountered is illuminated in the contemporary political novel, a form that has

*Octavio Paz, *El ogro filantrópico* (Barcelona: Seix-Barral, 1979), p. 225.

thrived more because of the 20th century development of political manipulation as an art form in itself than because of any literary fashion or theory. Indeed, the imaginative use and abuse of power has a lot in common with the literary imagination. Both exceed the limits of historical tradition and consecrated social norms; both are creative; both attribute great importance to technique. The Latin American political novel has entered its golden age. Augusto Roa Bastos (*I, The Supreme One*), Gabriel Garciá Márquez (*The Autumn of the Patriarch*), Mario Vargas Llosa (*Pantaleón and the Service Girls*) and the author of the present work, Demetrio Aguilera-Malta, are major contributors to this vigorous genre of the grotesque within contemporary fiction. Nothing that happens in these novels is too preposterous to have some basis in reality. Aguilera-Malta's sharp satire and free-wheeling magic never distort life; rather, they light it up and magnify it to reveal its absurdities.

Does ultimate power belong to those who twist the meaning of words (the Dictator Verbophile and his servile collaborators) and to those who multilate people (General Pithecanthropus and his homicidal henchmen)? Or will the meek, uniting behind their valiant Captain Gleam, inherit the earth? Demetrio Aguilera-Malta wrote *Babelandia* in mock-epic style. His polarization of Good and Evil is quickly recognized as deliberate. The name-symbolism is obvious: Pithecanthropus is primitive in method and manner; Maria is as pure and virtuous, almost, as her biblical namesake; Bacchus the Groveler is the Dictator's most obsequious cabinet member, etc. When I first spoke with the author about translating this work he stressed the importance of its comic-book format. To a large extent people continue to think in comic-strip terms. One likes to believe there are still heroes who can straighten things out: King Arthur, Robin Hood, Buck Rogers, Superman. As in their cases, Captain Gleam is an ideal that persists through the most adverse circumstances. He can fly under his own power; he can defeat an enemy in hand-to-hand combat. When he appears in Chapter One of *Babelandia* he is young and strong, but he's been reborn many times over the centuries, starting long before the Spanish conquest of the New World. The basic change he has noticed over all that time is an expansion of the ancient rule "an eye for an eye and a tooth for a tooth" to "armies for armies and nations for nations."

Arrayed against Gleam, of course, are the Forces of Evil. Three of the characters in this category deserve special mention:

General Jonas Pithecanthropus. The negligent father of five sets of triplet daughters who live with their mother on a remote tropical island. He quickly changes, when excited or angry, into a gorilla. He'll do anything at all for a banana; the aroma of one leads him, on a dark night, into a trap set by his rebel abductors (the title of the novel in the original is *El secuestro del general*). In the spirit of his name, he is sentenced in the last chapter to serve out his days in the belly of a whale.

Holofernes Verbophile, Dictator of Babelandia. An animated skeleton with two passions: giving recorded speeches with the aid of casettes that he inserts in his thorax, and dancing wildly to classical music whenever he happens to hear it. Verbophile can disperse (and reassemble) his bones in the air at will. When Pithecanthropus is kidnapped and locked in a cage in the crater of a volcano, the rebels demand as part of his ransom one pound of the Dictator's bones.

Father Polygamo (the Devil incarnate?) practices little of what he preaches; his lecherous desires contradict his sermons. He has many nocturnal adventures and an unmentionable part of his anatomy reaches the length of several meters. Ludivina, one of his young victims, gives birth to a sulfurous green offspring in a bizarre, two-pronged Caesarian section. Shortly afterwards, Polygamo is attacked and beaten to death by a mob in the streets; he is buried in one casket; his vital organ, in another.

And so forth. Many other vivid figures and episodes highlight this nightmarish novel, published forty years after Aguilera-Malta's first success, *Don Goyo* (1933).* In the works of this imaginative writer one finds the highest virtues of 20th-century Latin American narrative works: polit-

*Demetrio Aguilera-Malta, *Don Goyo,* translated by John and Carolyn Brushwood, illustrated by George Bartko (Clifton, New Jersey: Humana, 1980).

ical conscience and political consciousness, an intuition for magic in popular culture, a clear perception of the comic. An Ecuadorian, Demetrio Aguilera-Malta lived for many years in Mexico, where he was named his country's ambassador in 1978. He died in an accident at home in December, 1981.

P.G.E.